# International Human Resource Management

# INTERNATIONAL HUMAN RESOURCE MANAGEMENT

## A Multinational Company Perspective

Monir H. Tayeb

OXFORD
UNIVERSITY PRESS

# OXFORD

UNIVERSITY PRESS

Great Clarendon Street, Oxford OX2 6DP

Oxford University Press is a department of the University of Oxford.
It furthers the University's objective of excellence in research, scholarship,
and education by publishing worldwide in

Oxford  New York

Auckland  Bangkok  Buenos Aires  Cape Town  Chennai
Dar es Salaam  Delhi  Hong Kong  Istanbul  Karachi  Kolkata
Kuala Lumpur  Madrid  Melbourne  Mexico City  Mumbai  Nairobi
São Paulo  Shanghai  Taipei  Tokyo  Toronto

Oxford is a registered trade mark of Oxford University Press
in the UK and in certain other countries

Published in the United States
by Oxford University Press Inc., New York

British Library Cataloguing in Publication Data

Data available

Library of Congress Cataloging in Publication Data

Data available

ISBN 0-19-927727-3
ISBN 0-19-925809-0 (pbk.)

1 3 5 7 9 10 8 6 4 2

Typeset by Newgen Imaging Systems (P) Ltd., Chennai, India
Printed in Great Britain
on acid-free paper by
Antony Rowe Ltd, Chippenham, Wiltshire

# ■ FOREWORD

For academics researching and teaching international human resource management this is a good time. For many years, the small numbers of academics in the field—amongst whom Monir Tayeb was one of the more prominent figures—were seen as working in a somewhat arcane and idiosyncratic specialism. This is changing rapidly. More and more people are getting involved in the subject: either entirely new researchers, or longer-established authors in HRM, who have decided to internationalise their work. Since 2003 there has been a plethora of articles and a number of substantial texts published on the topic. The reason is not hard to find: the increasing globalisation of markets, the extending role of the multinational companies, and an ever-growing awareness of the importance of international human resource management amongst those companies. As ever, developments in the world of practitioners have been mirrored in and structured by developments in the academic world.

What has been lacking so far is a comprehensive text that synthesises thinking from a range of relevant disciplines and develops clear and accessible understandings of international HRM from the point of view of the multination company. That is the text Monir Tayeb has produced here. Amongst a number of other features to be welcomed in this text is the direct connection to the issues and problems of international companies. Thus the text has a wide focus: taking a broader view of HRM; including smaller-scale operations; indicating the place of regional and global conventions; and addressing topics typically less covered, such as the role of knowledge management and transfer, the range of international joint ventures and self-initiated expatriation. Of particular value is the attention to the perspective of the subsidiary.

One of the major lessons that Monir Tayeb draws is that international companies need to balance their need to impose common practices across borders with their ability to be responsive to and to learn from the specific circumstances of each country. In line with such a thesis, she presents a series of relevant case studies, one at the end of each chapter, to enable the reader to learn from existing practice as they grapple with the theoretical issues she discusses. It is surely through such a process that we will come to understand better the complexity of international human resource management.

Chris Brewster
**Professor of International Human Resource Management**
**Henley Management College**
**July 2004**

# ■ ACKNOWLEDGEMENTS

I am grateful to Professor Michael Poole, Editor-in-Chief of the *International Journal of Human Resource Management*, for permission to reproduce the following copyright materials:

Extracts of text and Figure 3 from:
Tayeb, M. H. (1998). 'Transfer of HRM policies and practices across cultures: an American company in Scotland', *International Journal of Human Resource Management*, vol. 9, no. 2, pp. 332–58 (Figure 10.2, page 209).

Extracts of text and Figure 4 from:
Tayeb, M. H. (1999). 'Foreign remedies for local difficulties: the case of Scottish manufacturing firms', *International Journal of Human Resource Management*, vol. 10, no. 5, pp. 842–57 (Figure 4.2, page 87).

Figure on page 505 from:
Budhwar, P. S. and Debrah, Y. (2001). 'Rethinking comparative and cross-national human resource management', *International Journal of Human Resource Management*, vol. 12, no. 3, pp. 497–515 (Figure 2.2, page 22).

I would also like to thank Heriot-Watt University for awarding me a grant from the Regeneration Fund which financed one of my International HRM projects in Scotland and enabled me to recruit a research associate, Kathryn Thory, to assist me with data collection.

**Monir Tayeb**
**Heriot-Watt University**
**July 2004**

# ■ CONTENTS

# ■ LIST OF FIGURES

# ◼ LIST OF TABLES

# Part I
# Setting the Scene

# 1 Introduction: Why Study International HRM?

## Learning outcomes

When you finish reading this chapter you should:
- be able to differentiate between personnel management and HRM
- know about the origins of HRM
- realise the important role that IHRM plays in the management of multinational companies
- have a preview of the major challenges that MNCs face which you will learn about in the rest of the book
- be familiar, through a real-life case study, with some of the HRM issues faced by staff in a foreign subsidiary of a major multinational company.

## Introduction

The chapter sets the scene for the rest of the book by discussing general issues of concern to multinational companies and then homes in on the main purpose of the book, management of human resources across diverse national boundaries. The chapter will also draw a distinction between large-scale multinational operations such as those undertaken by IBM, Toyota, Philips, and Microsoft, and small-scale operations which might involve only a handful of neighbouring nations or specialised niche international markets. The implications of the size of multinational operations for HRM will be emphasised throughout the book as and where appropriate.

The concept of HRM, its components and its various models have been extensively defined and discussed in non-international oriented books on HRM. This chapter gives a summary of these discussions and models and, given the international nature of the book, points out the American origins of the HRM.

The chapter also distinguishes between a narrow interpretation of HRM (bread and butter issues such as selection, training, compensation, etc.) and a broader view in which other aspects of people management such as leadership style/behaviour, management–employee relationships and power and authority structure are included. The book intends to subscribe to the latter view.

You will then be given a 'guided tour' of the rest of the book in which international HRM and its various regional and national models are discussed, together with the challenges that such a variety poses.

## Multinational companies in our time

Throughout the history of the human race, trade between different tribes, societies and, later, nation states have always been a feature of our economic lives through the ages, albeit at a different pace and intensity. The Industrial Revolution, which began in the mid 18th century in England and grew rapidly first through Europe and then spread to the Americas, Asia and the rest of the world, gave international trade an unprecedented boost. In our time, the advances in telecommunication and information technology have rightly been considered by many scholars and practitioners as a second industrial revolution, which has in turn increased the volume of trade between nations. The increasing trend in lowering, and in many cases the breakdown, of trade barriers has also helped the process along.

Multinational companies (MNCs) have played a powerful and dominant role in this process because they are *the* main vehicle by which most goods and services move around the world. As Ferner (1994) points out, they have been the principal agents of the internationalisation of the world.

Major MNCs, such as Microsoft, Hewlett Packard, Toyota, IBM, Sony, and Intel, are in the forefront of cutting-edge technology and innovation; they spend huge amounts of money on research, development and design of their products, and in the process spawn similar activities down the hierarchy of firms.

MNCs have a great deal in common with single-nation firms, but at the same time they are unique because their operation sites, distribution networks, suppliers, and their customers are spread across nations beyond their familiar home ground. In order to operate internationally or globally, they need to negotiate entry into other countries, adjust their operations to comply with the host country legal requirements, modify their products and services to reflect the religious and other cultural preferences of their foreign customers, and deal with a variety of accounting and taxation systems and trade policies. They also employ people from different parts of the world. The multicultural nature of MNCs' workforces makes their human resource management strategies, policies and practices perhaps one of the most delicate and complicated of all managerial tasks.

It should be noted however that the size and geographical reach of these companies are an important factor here. The larger the company in terms of market and number of employees, the more complicated its business affairs and the more complex its management. A small MNC with a few hundred employees and a customer-base in a handful of neighbouring countries has a lot less to worry about compared to an MNC which has subsidiaries in, say, over 50 countries, serves a global customer base, and recruits tens of thousands of employees from many parts of the world.

The main focus and objective of this book is to examine how multinational companies go about managing their multicultural workforce, what complications they may encounter in doing so and how they might deal with these complications.

## MNCs and people management

There is nothing new under the sun, as a British saying goes. The process of organising a group of people and managing them in order to get certain tasks down and certain goals achieved, has probably been with us since the days of our hunter-gatherer ancestors. The techniques and styles have obviously changed and evolved over the millennia, but the notion of achieving goals through managing people has remained the same.

In modern times, personnel management can be safely regarded as the immediate ancestor of HRM. The two concepts and their respective characteristics have been exhaustively dealt with in many books (see also further recommended reading at the end of the chapter) and there is no point in repeating the debates and arguments concerned in any detail here. It is however useful to remind ourselves of some of the core issues.

The traditional personnel management involves a set of functions, usually performed by the personnel department in companies, dealing with such issues as selection and recruitment, training, compensation (pay and benefits), performance appraisal, promotion, motivation policies, pension and so forth. The personnel manager is usually a middle- or senior-rank manager who does not have a say in his or her company's strategic decisions.

HRM is essentially an American invention. It was first entered into university courses as part of MBA programmes by the 'Harvard group' and 'Michigan/Columbia group' in the United States in the early 1980s (Beer et al., 1984; Fomburn et al., 1984). It was in the most part a response to US companies' requirements and the country's labour market conditions. It was mainly practised by, and gained popularity among, non-unionised American companies. After its perceived positive track record in the US it was adopted, with varying degrees of success, first in some western European countries, notably the UK, and then in some other countries further afield—more discussion on HRM's 'travels' abroad later in the book.

The concept of HRM is based on the notion that people management can be a key source of sustained competitive advantage and research evidence shows that effective HRM can lead to lower employee turnover and greater productivity and corporate financial performance (see for instance Maybe et al., 1998).

HRM, as mentioned above, deals with personnel functions, but these are planned and implemented with regard to the overall strategies of the company and the ways in which human resources (HR) can contribute to those strategies. The person in charge of HR and its development correspondingly occupies a very senior position in the company, such as a director, sits on the board of directors and participates in strategic decision making.

Porter (1985) distinguishes between a company's primary and support activities and places HRM among the latter which have a pivotal role in ensuring the effective and efficient operation of the former. See Figure 1.1 drawn on the basis of Porter's argument.

The Figure clearly suggests an important strategic role for HRM. Further, as Legge (1989, 1995) argues, human resource management is distinctive from personnel management in at least three ways. First, personnel focuses on the management and control of subordinates, HRM concentrates on the management team. Second, line managers play a key role in HRM

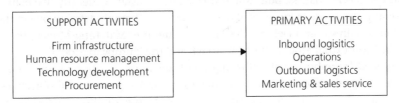

**Figure 1.1** The position of HRM within the structure of organisation

*Source*: drawn on the basis of Porter's arguments (1985).

in coordinating resources towards achieving profit, which is not the case under personnel management. Finally, the management of organisational culture is an important aspect of HRM, but plays no role in personnel management.

HRM has generally been viewed from two different perspectives: hard and soft (Storey, 1992). According to the hard model, reflecting utilitarian instrumentalism, HRM is used to drive the strategic objectives of the company; human resource, the object of formal manpower planning, is a 'resource', like other factors of production, and an expense of doing business, rather than the only resource capable of turning inanimate factors of production into wealth.

It could be argued that this is a degrading view of humans and in any case ignores fundamental differences between people and other resources. Production factors other than humans are comparatively less anchored and therefore can be moved around, shuffled, reduced, increased, transformed and discarded relatively freely to suit the managers' requirements. Their value is subject to market forces in most cases in a straightforward manner. But humans are different. They have needs, emotions, interests, and attachments, and perform their tasks best if these are reasonably catered for. They cannot be easily discarded and shuffled around against their wish without causing individual and/or social upset. A woman manager, with young children and a working husband and located in London, is far less mobile compared to a sum of £200,000 which can be electronically transferred from the City of London to Hong Kong within seconds (Tayeb, 1996).

Concerns such as these are encapsulated in what is called a soft, developmental humanist view of HRM. This model, while still emphasising the importance of integrating human resource policies with business objectives, sees this as involving treating employees as valued assets, a source of competitive advantage through their commitment, adaptability and high quality. According to this view, employees are proactive inputs in production processes and are capable of development, worthy of trust and collaboration, to be achieved through participation and informed choice. The stress is therefore on generating commitment via communication, motivation and leadership. If employees' commitment yields better economic performance, it is also sought as a route to greater human development.

As some scholars argue, many companies employ both soft and hard models either at different times or for different groups of employees. For instance managers, core employees and skilled workers may be treated according to the soft model, and casual or unskilled workers according to the hard model. Also, at times of economic downturns and high unemployment, managers are in a position to drive a hard bargain and disregard many niceties involved in the softer model of HRM. Conversely at times of full employment, employees may have the upper hand and are probably treated more according to the soft model.

There are of course many more theoretical models of HRM than discussed above, known sometimes by specific names. Budhwar and Debrah for instance identify five main models, encompassing also those mentioned above, and analyse them in detail in one of their joint publications (Budhwar and Debrah, 2001). These are: the 'Matching Model', the 'Harvard Model', the 'Contextual Model', the '5-P Model' and the 'European Model'.

*Matching Model* (Fomburn et al., 1984) highlights the resource aspect of HRM and emphasises the efficient utilisation of human resources to meet organisational objectives. It also emphasises a 'right fit' between organisational strategy, organisational structure and HRM systems.

*Harvard Model* (Beer et al., 1984) stresses the 'human', soft, aspect of HRM and is more concerned with the employer–employee relationship. It highlights the interests of different stakeholders in the organisation (such as shareholders, management, employee groups, government, community, unions) and how their interests are related to the objectives of management.

*Contextual Model* (Hendry et al., 1988; Hendry and Pettigrew, 1992) is based on the premise that organisations may follow a number of different pathways in order to achieve the same results. This is so mainly because of the existence of a number of linkages between external environmental context (socio-economic, technological, political-legal and competitive) and internal organisational context (culture, structure, leadership, task technology and business output). These linkages contribute directly to forming the content of an organisation's HRM.

*5-P Model* (Schuler, 1992) melds five human resource activities (philosophies, policies, programmes, practices and processes) with strategic needs. The model shows the inter-relatedness of these activities and explains their significance in achieving the organisation's needs.

*European Model* (Brewster, 1993, 1995) is based on the argument that European organisations are constrained at both international (European Union) and national level by national culture and legislation. They are also constrained at the organisational level by patterns of ownership and at the HRM level by trade union involvement and consultative arrangements. These constraints need to be accommodated while forming a model of HRM.

Chapters 2 and 3 will build on the contextual model in particular to explain the implications of national culture and other institutions for HRM policies and practices.

An important point to consider is the scope of HRM—the functions involved. As was discussed above, for many researchers HRM functions are the same as those of traditional personnel management with a strategic slant. But some might argue that management of human resources goes beyond this narrow definition and could also include management–employee relationship, leadership style, power and authority, and organisational structure and so forth. All these are part of people management and make up the whole approach of a company to its employees. This is especially significant for multinational companies because these aspects of people management as well as those involved in the narrow definition of HRM are very much susceptible to cultural influences. This book subscribes to this broader view of HRM.

But what is international HRM? How do MNCs go about managing their human resources and what challenges do they face in the process? Why is understanding IHRM important anyway? Let's try to answer the last question first.

## International HRM

An understanding of international HRM, as Scullion (1995, pp. 352–353) points out, is of growing importance for a number of reasons, the most significant of which are:

1. Recent years have seen a rapid increase in global activity and global competition. As the MNCs increase in number and influence, so the role of international HRM in those companies grows in significance.

2. The effective management of human resources internationally is increasingly being recognised as a major determinant of success or failure in international business.
3. Research evidence shows that (i) shortage of international managers is becoming an increasing problem for international firms, (ii) to a large extent the successful implementation of global strategies depends on the existence of an adequate supply of internationally experienced managers, (iii) business failures in the international arena may often be linked to poor management of human resources, and (iv) expatriate failures continue to be a significant problem for many international firms.

In this connection, Schuler et al. (1993) argue that:

1. HRM at any level is important to strategy implementation;
2. Major strategic components of MNCs have a significant bearing on international management issues, functions, policies and practices;
3. Many of these characteristics of strategic international human resource management can help or hinder the MNCs in their attempt to achieve their goals and objectives; and
4. There are various factors that make the relationship between MNCs and strategic IHRM complex, thereby making the study of IHRM important.

To the above must also be added the issues which are important from the employees' point of view and the effect that MNCs' HRM policies and practices might have on their morale and future career prospects. This is especially crucial because the bulk of employees of major MNCs come not from the companies' home country but from many other nations with sometimes totally different ways of doing things. Employees in the host countries for instance might have different expectations from their job and their workplace than do the home country employees. In addition, host countries' labour laws and regulations and industrial relations are very likely to be different from those of the MNC's home country. These must be understood and acted upon. Understanding how MNCs manage overseas employees is therefore an important aspect of learning about companies, how they function and what makes them succeed or fail.

Many students of IHRM have traditionally focused on expatriate management and, as Harris and Brewster (1999) observe, for many IHRM and expatriate management are virtually synonymous.

A useful definition of international HRM, which takes on board both strategic and international dimensions of MNCs' human resource management, and also moves away from the narrow function of expatriation, has been offered by Schuler and colleagues. For them strategic IHRM is 'human resource management issues, functions and policies and practices that result from the strategic activities of multinational enterprises and that impact on the international concerns and goals of those enterprises' (Schuler et al., 1993, p. 720).

Human resources, however defined and viewed, must function and be managed in such a manner as to support the rapid pace of internationalisation of companies and enhance and maintain their competitiveness in the marketplace. As Pucik (1998) points out, many companies competing globally are facing a multitude of new demands on their organisational structures and personnel. Often they are pushed simultaneously in several contradictory strategic directions. In order to survive and prosper in the global competitive environment, companies are embracing closer regional and global integration and coordination. At the same time, they face demands for local responsiveness, flexibility and speed. Human resources are very much part and parcel of all this.

A challenging aspect of HRM in most firms with multinational operations is the multicultural nature of their workforce, which is further compounded by its geographical dispersion. In addition, HRM, like so many other managerial functions, takes place not in a vacuum but within the overall internal organisational environment and the external national and international context in which the company operates. Examples of internal organisational factors are management philosophy and preferences, overall business strategies and policies, technologies and machinery employed and the skills required to operate them, employees' and management's attitudes to work and to one another, and organisational culture. Examples of major factors outside the organisation, both nationally and internationally, are government economic and trade policies, labour market conditions, trade unions and their power, rules and regulations concerning employee relations and health and safety at work, various bilateral and multilateral international conventions and obligations covering employee-related issues, and so forth. All these internal and external factors exert tremendous influences, sometimes contradictory, on a company's HRM strategies, policies and practices.

As we shall see in later chapters of the book, the business imperatives associated with the form of MNCs' internationalisation, and their overall business and market strategies can also influence the ways in which they manage their employees located in their subsidiaries scattered around the world.

For instance, a company which 'goes international' through joint ventures with foreign companies will face different HRM issues and concerns than those who set up wholly-owned foreign subsidiaries in green-field sites. To give another example, a global company with global strategies will manage its employees differently compared to a multi-domestic company. In the former, all strategies, including HRM, are integrated across subsidiaries and affiliates. In the latter, each subsidiary or affiliate looks after the market which it is set up to serve almost independently of the other subsidiaries, and its activities are loosely integrated with those of the others in the sense that it does not deviate from the overall objectives of the parent company, such as making profits.

This book points out the major challenges that MNCs face in managing their employees and discusses the ways in which they might deal with them. Throughout the book both theoretical augments and practical solutions and possibilities will be discussed in detail with real-life examples and case studies.

## Plan of the book

As you will see in Figure 1.2, the book is divided into three main parts. Part one consists of four chapters, including the present one, and focuses on various theoretical and practical HRM issues. Part two consists of five chapters and examines those same issues more closely from a multinational company's perspective. The final chapter, together with its long case study, forms Part three. Here is how the book's discussions and arguments will unfold:

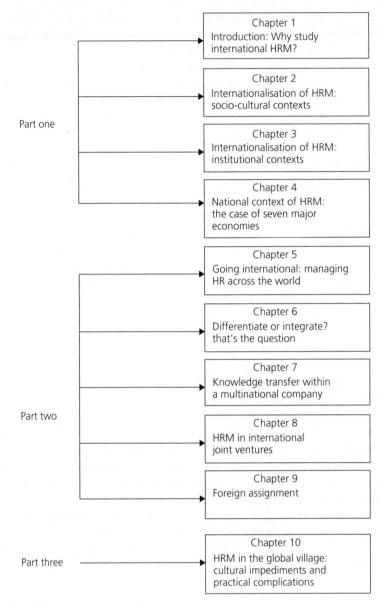

**Figure 1.2** Plan of the book

## Part one

Chapters 2 and 3 will deal with the debate concerning internationalisation of HRM, and attempt to answer the question: Is there such a thing as a uniform set of best HRM policies and practices applicable across nations irrespective of their diverse cultural and institutional features?

The two chapters aim at making the readers aware of the complex web of causal relationships which make HRM, like many other social constructs, a largely nation-specific concept. But at the same time, these relationships, given the right circumstances, could allow for lessons to be learned from outsiders and therefore make a degree of internationalisation of best practices possible.

Chapter 2 concentrates on national culture and its influences on management practices in general and HRM in particular. Business imperatives and other non-cultural influences will also be discussed in the chapter.

Chapter 3 focuses on major national, regional and global institutions within which HRM is performed. At the macro level, it deals with political-economic context, such as government economic and trade policies, which set the national tone, so to speak, and could directly and indirectly help or hinder development and cross-fertilisation of ideas and practices. National laws and regulations, especially those which deal with employment, trade union activities and industrial relations as a whole, will also be covered.

In the increasingly interdependent modern world, there are a large number of regional and global conventions and agreements to which many nations subscribe. Some of these, notably, European Union and International Labour Organisation, directly relate to the welfare of employees and by implications to HRM policies and practices. The chapter will cover these institutions and their aims and discuss their implications for the convergence and internationalisation of HRM.

Chapter 4 builds on the previous two and examines further the question of influence of culture and other institutions on workplace behaviour with special reference to a selection of major economies. The six countries and one region covered in the chapter represent a cross-section sample of the world at large. The chapter intends to demonstrate major socio-cultural roots of the HRM policies and practices currently prevalent in those economies.

## Part two

Chapter 5 begins by discussing briefly the main reason for which some firms engage in international business and the forms that their internationalisation might take. Here there will be a discussion concerning the forms of internationalisation which would require companies to set out their IHRM strategies and take necessary actions to have them implemented throughout the organisation. For example, exporting and importing companies do not need such strategies, but companies with fully-staffed subsidiaries do. The chapter then moves to the issues related to parent–subsidiary relationships and discusses them from two angles:

Parent perspective—which involves issues such as multinational companies' strategies in general, and HRM strategies in particular; global/international business imperatives which force the MNCs to adopt a more or less uniform set of HRM strategies for all their subsidiaries and affiliates.

Subsidiary perspective—which discusses issues such as subsidiary mandate and autonomy and local issues and their implications for HR.

In other words, the chapter highlights the factors that push for divergence and differentiation, and those that push for convergence and integration. This theme will be picked up and built upon in Chapter 6.

The differentiation–integration dilemma has been debated by scholars within the international business discipline for many years. Building on the previous chapter, Chapter 6 argues that similar debates are relevant to our understanding of MNCs' HRM strategies, policies and practices and the dilemma that they face when deciding how much power to give to their subsidiaries regarding their employee management.

The chapter addresses questions such as: How do multinationals maintain integration while allowing differentiation? How are HRM issues dealt with locally and centrally? What tensions might arise and how are they resolved? The discussion will then revolve around the various mechanisms that MNCs might employ to maintain integration while enabling them to introduce a workable and necessary measure of differentiation.

Chapters 2 to 6 demonstrate the widely different and complex contexts within which multinational companies operate. Chapter 7 discusses the implications of this state of affairs for the transfer of HRM policies and practices across borders in general and within MNCs in particular. Building on arguments advanced by scholars within the knowledge management and transfer discipline, it applies their major relevant findings to the question of HRM transfer within MNCs.

The chapter further argues that the direction of such transfers is not only from the parent to subsidiaries, but also from the subsidiaries to the parent and between various subsidiaries. Various knowledge transfer strategies and the complications involved will also be discussed in the chapter.

International joint ventures (IJVs) have been increasing in numbers in the past two decades or so along with the burgeoning of international trade. Joint ventures between two or more companies from different national backgrounds are in many ways mini-MNCs located in the same country, but because of their multi-parentage status their management is much more complicated and prone to frequent bouts of tension. The management of human resources in such companies brings to a head, among other things, different national and organisational cultures of the parents and their leadership style preferences. The institutional and other characteristics of the IJVs' host nation also have a major role to play. Issues such as the choice of company language can also become a source of tension and complication. Chapter 8 deals with the above and other relevant issues, but starts with a discussion of why some companies engage in international joint ventures and the advantages and disadvantages of this mode of internationalisation.

The theme of foreign assignment and expatriation touched upon in Chapter 6 will be expanded in Chapter 9 since expatriates are still a major part of MNCs' day-to-day running of their subsidiaries, especially if they are located in less developed countries.

The chapter starts off by discussing the reasons why MNCs might send some of their staff on foreign assignment. The discussion will then move on to major advantages and disadvantages of expatriation from both the parent company and the subsidiaries' perspectives. The chapter will discuss topics such as the preparation of expatriates and their families for foreign assignments, culture shock, and the problems associated with return to their home country, such as career planning and 'reverse' culture shock.

The chapter includes a section on freelance expatriates, who do not work for any single MNC as a permanent or long-term member of staff. The nature of freelance expatriation and its attraction to the individuals concerned and the employers will be discussed.

## Part three

Chapter 10 pulls together the common threads running through all the chapters. It places the preceding discussions within the ongoing globalisation debate and examines two inter-related issues: internationalisation of HRM and international HRM as practised in MNCs. The chapter highlights the factors which mitigate against convergence and internationalisation of HRM policies and practices and their unmodified transfer across nations and within MNCs. The chapter will however point out the ability of people around the world to learn best practices from others and to modify them to suit their specific circumstances and requirements. Two dynamic models of internationalisation of HRM and international HRM within MNCs are also proposed.

Each chapter of the book, including the present one, ends with a case study based on the author's own extensive qualitative research in a large number of foreign multinational companies operating in the UK. The case studies are an integral part of their respective chapter and put in sharp focus the practical implications of the theoretical issues discussed in the chapter.

### ■ CHAPTER SUMMARY

The chapter briefly discussed the origins of HRM in the US and how it came into being as a response to the American companies' requirements and their socio-economic context. Comparisons were also made between traditional personnel management and HRM especially with regard to the strategic character of the latter. The chapter then outlined the characteristics of major HRM models proposed by various scholars. The discussion then focused on international HRM as practised in multinational companies and the challenges that the multicultural nature of their workforce poses with this regard.

The chapter also presented a preview of the rest of the book; it ends with a case study which highlights the practical implications of some of the main theoretical issues discussed in the chapter.

### ■ REVISION QUESTIONS

1. What are the main HRM models?
2. In your home country, do companies have an HRM department? If yes, which HRM model do they usually follow?
3. What makes multinational companies distinctive from single-nation firms?
4. What is the most challenging aspect of the management of an MNC? Why?

## Case study: NCR in Scotland[1]

NCR (Manufacturing) Ltd Dundee is a subsidiary of NCR, an American multinational company, whose headquarters is situated in Dayton, Ohio.

---

[1] Source: Tayeb, M. H., 1998, 'Transfer of HRM policies and practices across cultures: an American company in Scotland', *International Journal of Human Resource Management*, vol. 9, no. 2, pp. 332–58. Reproduced with permission.

NCR set up its subsidiary in Dundee in 1946 as part of a wave of inward investment in Europe by major American multinational companies. The incentives had come from various European governments, coupled with the Marshall Aid Plan, a brain child of General George Marshall, who aimed to revive Europe's economy after the ravages of the World War II.

NCR as a whole has about 38,000 employees worldwide. The Dundee subsidiary employs around 1,500 people of whom about 100 are on temporary contracts. The company is involved in 126 countries, but it does not have subsidiaries in all of them. In some countries they deal with local parties such as distributors or are engaged in joint ventures with local partners. NCR was taken over by another American multinational company, AT&T, in September 1991, and the name of the company was changed to reflect the new ownership. The union, however, did not work out quite as expected. The two companies officially parted ways early in 1997.

Dundee NCR's products are all called self-service systems and they split into two categories. ATMs (automated teller machines) which provide cash, amongst other things, and other financial automated machines which provide a variety of services other than cash, such as bank statements, and marketing machines.

Dundee NCR exports 90% of its products and competes with major players in the field, such as IBM, Olivetti, Siemens, Fujitsu, Hitachi, and Toshiba, worldwide.

The company's overall market share is very high and they are probably number 3 or 4 in the global financial machines market. But in some products they clearly hold first place. In the self-service business, for instance, they hold a third of the market. Their nearest competitor in this business is IBM which has about 14 to 15 per cent of the market share.

At the apex of the company there is a Managing Director, who is also a Vice President of the parent company. Eight directors and senior managers report to him directly. He also represents the subsidiary at Dayton. The Managing Director, a Scotsman, was appointed in the 1980s by the HQ giving him only 6 months to either turn the company around, or shut it down—it had been losing a great deal of money for some time. He did turn it around and made it into a world class company, and his HRM strategies, policies and practices played a crucial role in the process.

## HRM in NCR

In Dundee HRM is very much part of the company's overall strategic plans, and its significance is reflected in the fact that a senior director heads the HRM department. The HRM Director has been in fact the MD's right-hand man since the early stages when they turned around the company's fortune in the 1980s. They used to, and still do, set their human resources strategy as part of the company's overall strategies.

'I think for us here in Dundee, we would distinguish between, on the one hand, what the HQ calls human resources and personnel management, which is all the basic things that personnel people have always done, hiring people, training, many different things. On the other hand in the UK side HRM or HRM programmes which are about using rather more advanced HR techniques, or bringing together a number of different approaches, bringing them together to the same action to create a significant improvement in company performance. And this is were HR can make a big difference to the bottom line, a big difference to financial performance, fairly directly.'

The Managing Director confirms this and gives an example of how HRM is incorporated in the company's business strategies.

'The HRM Director was my right-hand man from day one, he had to be. In fact he and I used to set our strategies, our HR strategies on what we would try and achieve and how we would do it. The speed in which we moved was dictated by how well we thought we could bring on the management team with us and the workforce with us because we had to appeal to 3 or 4 different levels. . . . One of the most exciting things we developed was the education for all programme. We were looking out towards the year 2000 and we said, what sort of workforce will we have, what will the company look like, what will the people look like? How can we make sure that this business will go on to re-create itself and be a permanent entity and continue to grow and prosper? As we were looking at the skills of the people and the nature of the people, an odd thing struck me. At least half of the people who were here now would be in that business in the year 2000. If that's the case we'd better not just look at bringing in new people, we better look at these, this core of our being. When we looked at that we found that there were a lot of people who had, or would have the wrong skill sets, and wouldn't have the right education for where the business was moving to. And we 'looked into the future' and found over the period of 16 years that the skills were moving up, the un-skilled had disappeared completely, the semi-skilled were still there but were fast diminishing, to the point where the vast majority of our people would be degreed in one form or another. So we said if that's the case how do we take the population we've got now and make them fit that new model? So we said, well, we've got to get them back on to the education wheel.

These people have learnt an awful lot in the ten or twelve years that they've been working on this production line and in manufacturing, there's a lot of skills there. So we set about preparing what we called accredited prior-learning. We worked with some of the local professors. We created a series of tests that would allow us to grade people and accredit their skills level. We started with a plan to get people into learning and my thought was let's create a system that says to everybody: I'm issuing you a challenge, I want you to raise your academic qualification level one notch. We will provide the time and money to do it. Two provisos, one, that whatever you're learning it has to be relevant to the business, and secondly no pass no fee. Now you can take a degree in Japanese or French or German but you can't take a degree in knitting because it isn't relevant to the business. So apart from that if you go and find something you'd like to do we'll help you do it and we'll help you in the stages and the steps that you do it. We even created an NCR tailored degree. We got three of the local universities to accept modules from here that people had taken their test in here to pass, and given creditation for various vocational qualifications.

So we have unlocked enormous potential from people, and given some people a fresh start. A number of people who were in here who were secretaries, who have moved into marketing, people who were on the gate as a guard, now have moved into development, we've given people a second shot, what an opportunity! Somebody leaving school at 15 or 16 who thought that they had reached the end of education and suddenly they're in their 40's go and take a degree (I didn't set any age limit on this). Why not? So right now I think we've got something like 140 people who are on degree courses. About a third of our people right now are on some form of further education, improving themselves. And I think that's really exciting.'

In addition to enhancement of the employees knowledge and skills, the education for all programme was helpful in building employee trust and loyalty.

'I was trying to unlock doors. What I said was: if you want to get the best out of your people what you have to do is you have to take away the barriers that they find to realising their potential and if some of these barriers are that they don't have the right bits of paper or their skills or that they need new skills, then help to create that. And there will be a degree of loyalty built up from that that will be very hard to beat. Right now if I walked down to the people here and said we're shutting the doors on that and we're going to build a whole new product, I bet you ninety percent of the people would say yes, we're with you.

It didn't happen overnight. That took a long time to create, you have to overcome suspicions by *doing*. You can talk to your hearts content, but you've got to be seen to *do*.'

The Managing Director is accessible to the employees; they can come and see him whenever they wish and he goes to the shopfloor frequently to see them too.

'I guess I was able to talk to people in their own language on the things that were important to them and I made no bones about it. I said we've got six months and we're not going to survive, but I'm not here to close the place, I'm here to have a go and save it. They feel they can talk to me and that they can at any time come to see me. I walk through the place as well. They used to see me morning, noon and night down on the shop floor, walking, lifting pieces of material, having a look, pushing people, patting people on the back, smacking them on their backside when they've not been doing things right and very much the father figure round the place.'

## HRM and company performance

The turn around of the company from a total failure on the brink of closure to an international star was due to a number of reasons some of which were described by the Managing Director thus:

'I think there are a few main reasons for our success. One was that we made it our business to know the customer's business better than he did. So we went out and really understood what it was that we were trying to do. Secondly, we spent a lot of money on the research and development of the product that the customer wanted. So from the customer knowledge, we created the right product and we were fortunate in having universities around; we were able to get some of the best graduates. So it was the people who were able to develop these products, and we developed skills and core competence in this arena, and said these are the things that are going to separate us in the business. The next thing that we were really fortunate in is that we had all the skills in the house for assembly and test and manufacture and so that was there and available. And I guess we just created a niche around that so it was people in the first instance, having a good core of universities and being able to tap graduates, spending more than the competition, and understanding the market. We spent a phenomenal amount of time out in the market place.'

### ■ CASE STUDY QUESTIONS

**1.** In what ways is NCR's HRM different from traditional personnel management?

**2.** How did the HRM strategies and policies of the company contribute to its success?

**3.** How did the Managing Director earn the trust and loyalty of his employees?

**4.** Why did he think their trust and loyalty were important to the company?

### ■ RECOMMENDED FURTHER READING

Budhwar, P. S. and Debrah, Y. (2001). 'Rethinking comparative and cross-national human resource management', *International Journal of Human Resource Management*, vol. 12, no. 3, pp. 497–515.

Kamoche, K. N. (2001). *Understanding Human Resource Management*. Buckingham: Open University Press.

Legge, K. (1995). *Human Resource Management: Rhetorics and Realities*. Basingstoke: Macmillan.

Maybe, C., Salaman, G., and Storey, J. (1998). *Strategic Human Resource Management: A Reader*. London: Sage Publications, in association with the Open University.

## ■ REFERENCES

Beer, M., Spector, B., Lawrence, P. R., Quin Mills, D., and Walton, R. E. (1984). *Managing Human Assets*. New York: Macmillan.

Brewster, C. (1993). 'Developing a "European" model of human resource management', *International Journal of Human resource Management*, vol. 4, pp. 765–84.

—— (1995). 'Towards a European model of human resource management', *Journal of International Business*, vol. 26, pp. 1–22.

Budhwar, P. S. and Debrah, Y. (2001). 'Rethinking comparative and cross-national human resource management', *International Journal of Human Resource Management*, vol. 12, no. 3, pp. 497–515.

Ferner, A. (1994). 'Multinational companies and human resource management: an overview of research issues', *Human Resource Management Journal*, vol. 4, no. 3, pp. 79–102.

Fomburn, C., Tichy, N. M., and Devanna, M. A. (1984). *Strategic Human Resource Management*. Canada: Wiley.

Harris, H. and Brewster, C. (ed.), (1999). *International HRM: Contemporary Issues in Europe*. London: Routledge.

Hendry, C. and Pettigrew, A. M. (1992). 'Patterns of strategic change in the development of human resource management', *British Journal of Management*, vol. 3, pp. 137–56.

—— and Sparrow, P. R. (1988). 'Changing patterns of human resource management', *Personnel Management*, vol. 20, pp. 37–47.

Legge, K. (1989). 'Human resource management: a critical analysis', in J. Storey (ed.) *New Perspectives on Human Resource Management*. London: Routledge. pp. 19–40.

—— (1995). *Human Resource Management: Rhetorics and Realities*. Basingstoke: Macmillan.

Maybe, C., Salaman, G., and Storey, J. (1998). *Strategic Human Resource Management: A Reader*. London: Sage Publications, in association with the Open University.

Porter, M. E. (1985). *Competitive Advantage: Creating and Sustaining Superior Performance*. The Free Press.

Pucik, V. (1998). 'Creating leaders that are world-class', *Financial Times*, February, survey page 4.

Schuler, R. S. (1992). 'Linking the people with the strategic needs of the business', *Organizational Dynamics*, Summer, pp. 18–32.

—— Dowling, P. J. and De Cieri, H. (1993). 'An integrative framework of strategic international human resource management', *Journal of Management*, vol. 9, pp. 419–59. Reprinted also in the *International Journal of Human Resource Management*, vol. 4, pp. 717–64.

Scullion H. (1995). 'International human resource management', in J. Storey (ed.), *Human Resource Management*. London: International Thompson Business Press.

Storey, J. (1992). *Developments in the Management of Human Resources*. Oxford: Blackwell.

Tayeb, M. H. (1996). *The Management of a Multicultural Workforce*. Chichester: Wiley.

# 2 | Internationalisation of HRM: Socio-Cultural Contexts

## Learning outcomes

When you finish reading this chapter you should:
- know about the culture-specific nature of the HRM as a concept
- understand the ways in which employee management in general might be influenced by national culture
- know how HRM functions might be performed in various cultures
- understand that non-cultural factors can also have a significant influence on employee management in general and HRM in particular
- get an idea from a real-life case study at the end of the chapter as to how some HRM functions are carried out in a UK subsidiary of a Japanese company.

## Introduction

Chapter 1 briefly touched upon the significance for HRM of the broad context within which a company operates. This chapter and the next will elaborate on that point. The present chapter concentrates on national culture and its influences on management practices in general and HRM in particular. It will address the question: Can there be universal best HRM policies and practices applicable across nations irrespective of their diverse cultural characteristics? The chapter will also explore the significant role that non-cultural factors sometimes play in shaping a company's HRM policies and practices.

## National culture and HRM

Chapter 1 argued that the management of human resources of a company does not take place in a vacuum and various factors inside and outside the company influence its shape and content. One of the major external factors is the socio-cultural environment within which the company operates. For a multinational company with business interests and activities in different parts of the world, this environment is all the more complex because of the sheer variety of it.

A review of the history of evolution of management thoughts and theories shows that this argument has not always been advocated by scholars and practitioners. In the early parts of the 20th century, when the history of modern management began, management and organisation theorists tended to ignore the environment in which organisations operated and argued for a universalistic 'one best way' of organising work organisations and prescribed bureaucracy as the rational and efficient model of organisations (Taylor, 1911; Urwick, 1943; Brown, 1945; Mooney, 1947; Fayol, 1949; Brech, 1953). Henry Ford's method of car assembly production and employee management epitomises this so-called classical approach.

It was only in the 1950s and 1960s that many students of management started to challenge this universalistic view, at first on human relations grounds (Roethlisberger, 1944; Mayo, 1945; McGregor, 1960), but still implied that there was a 'one best way' of organising activities with an emphasis on human beings' needs and abilities which, according to this new school, had been overlooked by the classical theorists.

There were also challenges on the grounds that different technologies (Woodward, 1958; Harvey, 1968; Hickson et al., 1969) require different styles of management. This view was later developed into the contingency theory where the main criticism of the earlier theories concerned the alleged inability of bureaucracies to adapt to the changes in the environment. The premises of this theory are based on the argument that the survival of an organisation depends upon its efficient and effective (optimum) performance. This optimum performance, in turn, can be achieved if the organisation responds and adapts to its environmental demands 'appropriately'. The appropriate response is crystallised in a 'match' or 'fit' between the structural characteristics of organisation on the one hand and contextual and other environmental variables on the other (Lawrence and Lorsh, 1967; Pugh et al., 1968; Hickson et al., 1974, Hickson et al., 1981). For example, an increase in environmental change and complexity should be 'matched' by an increase in decentralisation, in order to ensure a prompt and appropriate response, if the organisation is to achieve a 'high' level of performance.

This line of argument was then advanced further by researchers who advocated the moderating influences of national culture on organisations (Crozier, 1964; Haire et al., 1966; Hofstede, 1980; Child and Tayeb, 1983; Tayeb, 1988).

From time to time the question of best practices and their implications for company performances surfaces again, especially whenever certain practices such as teamwork and just-in-time come to the forefront of discussions put forward by theorists and practitioners. But each time empirical research evidence shows that the influence of national culture is still significant and cannot be ignored without detrimental effects on company performance (see for example Wright and Brewster, 2003).

## HRM and its broad context

The above brief discussion on the evolution of management thoughts and theories demonstrates that the broad context within which organisations operate is of utmost relevance to the ways in which their human resources are managed. Figure 2.1 and Figure 2.2 show the main components of this broad context. The present chapter and the next one will discuss those components that are most relevant to this book.

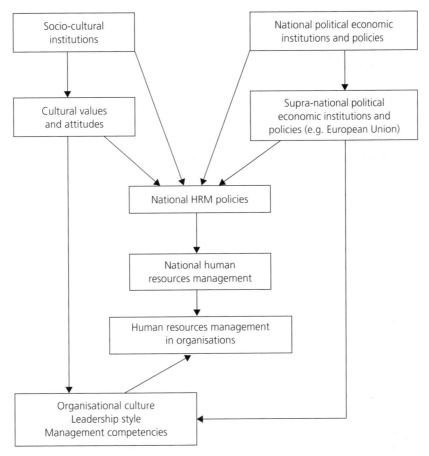

**Figure 2.1** Broad context of HRM

Adapted from: Tayeb (1995).

## National culture

What is national culture and how does it affect employee management in general and HRM in particular?

Culture is a 'woolly' concept which has aroused controversy and confusion among scholars as to its precise meaning and definition. For instance, Kroeber and Kluckhohn (1952) cited 164 different definitions of culture. Moreover, culture has at least two broad meanings, depending on the context in which it is discussed. In anthropological and sociological terms culture refers to values and attitudes that people belonging to a given society hold. Outside the academic world and in day-to-day life, culture is usually identified with the arts and literature, for example poetry, theatre, music, opera, painting, ballet, and so forth.

The present chapter focuses on culture in its anthropological and sociological sense. Within this broad scope, management scholars have offered their own definition of national culture. Hofstede (1980), for instance, defined it as the collective programming of the mind based on a broad tendency to prefer certain states of affairs over others. Tayeb (1988) defined culture as historically evolved values, attitudes and meanings which are learned

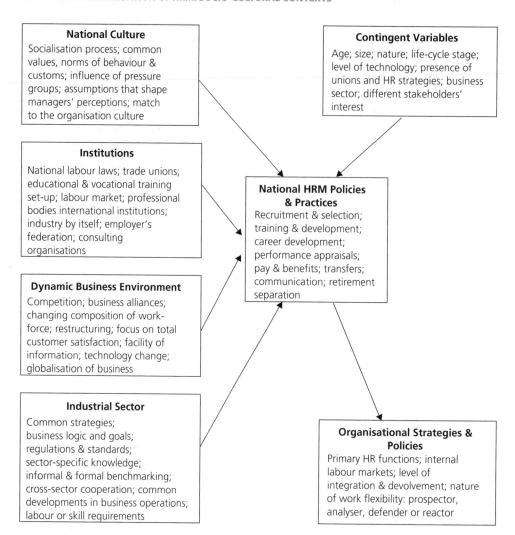

**Figure 2.2** Contextual factors determining HRM policies and practices

*Source*: Budhwar and Debrah (2001, p. 505), reproduced with permission.

and shared by the members of a given community, and which influence their material and non-material way of life. For Hickson and Pugh (1995) culture is the shared values that typify a society and lie beneath its characteristic arts and architecture, clothes, food, ways of greeting and meeting, ways of working together, ways of communicating and so on.

Despite these controversies and varied definitions, as Denny (2003, p. 68) points out, 'it is clear that culture is different between nations. A nation's culture or national character is shaped by historical, geographical and philosophical factors. As each country has a different (view of) history, geography and philosophy, so they have different cultures.'

In management studies, as indeed in studies of any other aspects of human relations, the recognition of cultural differences between different peoples is essential and helps us understand the motives and behaviours of those with whom we interact. Many scholars have written in great detail about various culturally-influenced work-related attitudes and values and explored how they might affect different aspects of organisations and their interaction with their cultural context (see for instance Hofstede, 1980; Tayeb, 1988; Trompenaars, 1993; Gatley et al., 1996; Adler, 1997; Schwartz, 1999).

In addition, it has been argued that certain people-related issues, or the so-called 'soft' aspects of organisations, such as HRM, are more readily influenced by culture compared with the 'hard' aspects, such as financial and technical matters (Tayeb, 1988). For example, the power relationship between a shopfloor worker and his or her line manager is likely to reflect the general pattern of power and authority between any junior–senior relationship as present and accepted in their national culture.

But what about the concept of HRM itself? Is that also influenced by national culture?

## Concept of HRM and national culture

Before exploring the ways in which culture might influence HRM and other employee management issues it is worth bearing in mind that the concept of HRM, like many other social constructs, is not totally independent from the cultural values of people who 'invented' it. As we saw in Chapter 1, HRM is a product of Anglo-American scholarly culture rooted in its wider political economic and societal context. HRM, as we now know it, came to being within the United States' business system and as a response to major American companies' need to face up to the challenges posed by foreign competitors mainly from Japan, which had entered the American market with high quality but low-priced products and/or invested there. In addition, it bears all the hallmarks of that country's managerial priorities and a business community which is opposed to trade unions and collective bargaining. HRM would allow, in theory at least, decentralisation and employee empowerment and participation in one form or another, and would eliminate the need for unions to act as the employees' agents in collective bargaining and negotiation with the management.

HRM 'travelled' first across the Atlantic Ocean into Europe and then to many other countries. However it has not quite taken root in Europe (Clark and Pugh, 2000), let alone in countries further afield, especially the developing nations with widely-diverse political systems, social structures, and business priorities and preferences.

Clark and Pugh (2000), building on the vast literature on the implications of national culture for management techniques and models, conducted a 'polycentric' study into the conceptions of HRM in a sample of European countries, namely Germany, UK, Denmark, Spain, France, Sweden and the Netherlands. The authors found that the concept of HRM has not been accepted or established as an academic discipline evenly among the sampled nations. For instance, there has been little discussion of HRM in Spain, due to a period of shake-out of labour, with rising redundancies and unemployment, which the country has been undergoing for some time until recently. This has meant that appreciation of the competitive value of human resources, which is at the basis of HRM, has not been much in evidence. The authors further argued that Sweden's strong collectivist culture counters the development of a more individualistic orientation to employment relationships, and the Dutch 'feminine' culture encourages the antipathy of Dutch employees to 'hard' HRM. Similarly, the institutional factors in Germany of the strong role of the unions and the formal consultative structures between employers and employees attenuate the rise of the managerial prerogative. In France the power of the *patronat* hinders decentralisation.

Even in the United Kingdom, a country second only to the US in its enthusiasm to embrace HRM, and where the present author has conducted a number of empirical studies, many companies have simply renamed their personnel department to HR department, not because the function has any strategic role but because the title is considered as 'cool'.

In sum, there needs to be a 'fit' between what is imported from abroad and the local environment for the adoption of HRM, or any other imported practices, to be complete and successful. And this can occur only when the local environment is identical or very close in character to that of the 'exporting' country—or at the very least duplicates or simulates the original context. To give an example, for HRM to be successfully implemented in Bangladesh, this country must have a similar business system and political-economic structure to that of the United States.

The above argument does not of course mean that various companies around the world have not tried to import and implement HRM. Throughout history nations and organisations have learnt foreign ways of doing things and, with some adaptation and modifications, have achieved a degree of success with at least some of them. And this learning and adaptation process, as we shall see in later chapters, applies to HRM and indeed many other management practices as well.

A proposition, advanced by Brannen (2002), about the 'recontextualisation' of imported practices is of relevance to this point. Although her arguments are about exporting company strategies and other 'offerings' (e.g. products) to other countries, it can be applied to the transfer of such concepts and practices as HRM.

Company offerings are transferred into a new environment that is already familiar with the company's home country and often has pre-existing knowledge of the offerings. As a result, the transferred offerings go through recipient cultural sense-making filters that attach pre-existing meanings onto them as they enter the new environment—this is, if you like, the first phase of the recontextualisation of the offerings. As they are implemented and inter-mixed within the new host environment they continue to undergo recontextualisation, and receive unexpected positive or negative meaning in their new cultural contexts.

An excellent example that Brannen (2002) gives is Walt Disney's Mickey Mouse: it goes from being the 'All American' Disney mascot in the United States to 'safe and reliable' in Japan where he has a high profile at Tokyo Disneyland and sells money market accounts on the side, to 'cunning and adventuresome' in France where he has a relatively low profile both at Disneyland Paris and in the cultural environment at large. As Brannen argues, while Walt Disney's characters have travelled far and wide, basic assumptions about Mickey Mouse's personality and how people perceive, enact and experience theme parks have not.

So although Mickey Mouse is still called by that name and looks exactly identical in the above three countries, it means and symbolises different things in these three different places. The same recontextualisation and transformation of character and function can be argued to be the case with HRM, even though many companies in many countries might genuinely, and sometimes not so genuinely, believe that they have imported and successfully implemented HRM. Here is an example of a developing country with very distinctive social, cultural and political-economic characteristics where many domestic companies are said to have HRM departments.

In a study of HRM in a sample of international joint ventures in Iran, Namazie (2000) found that Iran's perception and role of HRM is very different from that seen in developed countries. Whereas, as was discussed above, some western and other developed countries view HRM as a strategic function seeking to achieve competitive advantage by making full use of human resources, in Iran the role of HRM is more basic and has been dependent on its particular internal and external politics. The redundancy of female staff in top managerial and industrial sectors following the Islamic revolution and the recruitment of large numbers of war veterans following the Iran–Iraq eight-year war in the 1980s are telling examples here. As Tayeb (2000) points out, HRM in this country is really the 'old' personnel management with a heavy local colour especially in recruitment and training areas.

The remainder of this chapter focuses largely on the extent to which national culture shapes the nature and character of HRM, and by implications the different forms that it might take in various countries.

It would be useful at this stage to explore what aspects of people management and HRM are more susceptible to influences of national culture and then examine the process by which this influence manifests itself. Table 2.1 lists a number of major soft aspects of organisations and Table 2.2 shows major cultural work-related attitudes and values which are likely to shape them.

**Table 2.1** Soft aspects of organisation which are susceptible to cultural influences

| Broad employee management issues | Specific HRM issues |
| --- | --- |
| Management style: | |
|   Participative | Staffing policies |
|   Consultative | Recruitment and selection process |
|   Paternalistic | Remuneration |
|   Autocratic | Motivation |
| Authority structure: | Job expectation |
|   Decentralised | Training and development |
|   Centralised | Performance appraisal |
| Organisational structure: | Promotion |
|   Hierarchical | Retirement |
|   Network | Redundancy and lay-off |
| Leadership style: | Industrial relations |
|   Task-oriented | Foreign assignment |
|   Employee-oriented | |
| Employee Relationship with the company: | |
|   Emotional | |
|   Contractual | |

**Table 2.2** Major cultural attitudes and values which influence the soft aspects of organisation

Attitude to power and authority
Tolerance for ambiguity and uncertainty
Attitude to risk and risk taking
Individualism, self-orientation
Collectivism, group orientation
Acceptance of responsibility
Interpersonal trust
Attitude to other people's opinion
Attitude to sharing information and knowledge with others
Recognition of the rights of others to be consulted with
Preference for certain leadership behaviour
Preference for independence and autonomy
Self confidence, self-reliance
Achievement orientation, ambition
Attitudes to conflict and harmony
Work ethic, honesty
Attitude to the nature of human beings

Later in the present chapter the non-cultural influences on the items listed in both tables will be discussed, but for the moment let us focus only on culture.

# National culture and broad employee management issues

## Attitude to power and authority and its implication for employee management

In every culture, it is safe to argue, there is inequality of power between people, based on many factors such as wealth, education, political and social positions. At the macro-level, this inequality manifests itself in hierarchical stratification, for example class, caste and feudal systems. At the micro-level it can be seen in the extent to which individuals might be willing, or able, or reluctant or even scared to challenge the authority of people in senior positions, be it their parents, religious leaders, teachers or their rulers.

What does, however, differentiate between cultures is the degree to which the inequality between members exists or is accepted in a society (Hofstede, 1980). To paraphrase British writer George Orwell (1945), all humans are unequal but some are more unequal than others. In other words, one could place various nations on a continuum at one end of which are located high-inequality cultures and at the other low-inequality ones, with others somewhere between these two extreme poles.

At the organisational level, the inequality of power can be observed in formal and informal hierarchical structure and relationships between organisational members. The degree of the inequality between holders of various positions, could be influenced by the national cultural setting within which the organisation is situated.

In high-inequality cultures where people are afraid of those in positions of power, or are too respectful of them to disagree with their views and actions, it is less likely that employees would challenge their superiors in the workplace, and their superiors may also be reluctant to give them the opportunity to do so. The management style is more likely to be paternalistic or autocratic, decisions tend to be taken by a few senior managers and carried out by subordinates, and organisations are highly centralised with a rigid hierarchical chain of command—instructions flow from the top and obedience is expected from those in the lower levels.

In low-inequality cultures, all these characteristics tend to be reversed: employees respect their managers but feel able to point out to them when they do not agree with their views or actions. Junior employees expect to be consulted with when major decisions affecting their jobs and careers are taken and their seniors are also willing to oblige. The management style is therefore likely to be participative or consultative, authority hierarchy is flat and flexible or even replaced by networks and leaderless workteams.

## Tolerance for ambiguity and attitude to risk and their implications for employee management

These characteristics can directly influence the degree to which people are willing or able to make decisions on their own and accept responsibility for the outcome (Hofstede, 1980).

This is likely to be the case in cultures where people are encouraged from childhood to cope with uncertainty and take risk, through for example family-rearing traditions and practices at home and experiment-based teaching at school (Tayeb, 1988).

In organisations, employees who have less tolerance for uncertainty and are unwilling to face ambiguity and risk are more likely to avoid making decisions on their own and without direction from above, in the form of procedures, regulations and/or direct supervision, or without at least sharing responsibilities with others. Consequently, senior managers who are ultimately responsible for the smooth running of the companies will take all the major decisions, with or without consultation with their subordinates, depending on their attitude to sharing power and authority as discussed above.

In cultures with high tolerance for uncertainty and willingness to take risk, people tend to be entrepreneurial, able to handle uncertain situations and are prepared to take risky decisions on their own. Their managers also tend to be comfortable to let them do it, while ready to come to their aid if needed. Organisations as a result generally have a decentralised structure and the 'man or woman on the spot' is empowered to do the job as he or she sees fit.

## Interpersonal trust and its implications for employee management

One of the major factors which could influence the extent to which managers are willing to share their power and authority with their subordinates is whether they can trust their ability and intentions or not (Tayeb, 1988). Are they capable of making decisions on their own? Do they have sufficient knowledge about the task at hand? Will they put the company's interests before theirs? This is sometimes not only related to the specific individual employee or a group of employees but also to national cultures. For example, in some cultures the level of trust in other people's good intentions is very low and in others relatively high. This sort of attitude may have its roots in such factors as the extent of corruption prevalent in a society especially in public bureaucracies and sometimes in private companies as well. If people are in general honest, with high levels of work ethic as well as of course required skills and capabilities, in the workplace their managers tend to trust them to make important decisions on their own and just report back on the outcome. In cultures characterised by rampant corruption and generally low levels of skills and competence, managers are likely to delegate decision-making authority only to a few trusted employees, preferably their own relatives and friends.

## Individualism and collectivism and their implications for employee management

These concepts do not easily lend themselves to clear-cut interpretations. Individualism, for instance, can be thought of as self-interest and selfishness, and collectivism as self-sacrifice (Tayeb, 1988). One can argue that an individualistic culture is generally characterised by a high value placed on one's independence, autonomy, and privacy, a belief in one's own worth, confidence in one's own ideas and opinion. To borrow an idea from Macfarlane (1978), an individualist person is at the centre of his or her own world. By contrast, in a collectivist culture the group(s) to which a person belongs, such as family, community, or even work organisation, is the centre of his or her world. Here people put their group's interests before theirs, even if this entails serious personal sacrifices.

The relationship between employees and their work organisation could reflect their individualism or collectivism (Hofstede, 1980; Triandis, 1995). In individualistic cultures the relationship is contractual; that is, employees offer their labour for a commensurate pay during their working hours. A vast majority of employees, especially those who work on the shopfloor and at lower clerical levels, do not work beyond the daily official hours without being paid overtime. In addition, the employee–company relationship does not spill over to their private lives. The two are completely separate spheres of their lives. In collectivist cultures, by contrast, the employee–workplace relationship is emotional as well as contractual. The boundary between private and professional spheres of life in many instances are blurred. The superior is not just a manager, he or she could also be a father or mother figure to seek advice from on private issues, such as a need of loan to buy a house or get married. Employees at lower levels of the hierarchy as well as senior managers and directors are prepared to work well beyond the official working hours if required, without expecting overtime pay. In other words, the workplace looks after the employees' well being and in return expects loyalty and commitment; this is in addition to the pay in exchange for labour as stated in formal employment contracts.

It is important at this point to draw a distinction between in-group and out-group (Triandis, 1980, 1981). In all cultures there are various groups that an individual belongs to: family, sports team, a regular class attended at the university with the same students, local community, country and so forth. Some of these groups, called in-groups, are closer emotionally and in other ways to a person than others and for which one is willing to offer a great deal of loyalty and personal sacrifices if called upon.

The size of the in-group (numbers involved) and the kind of people who are in it, vary from culture to culture. In general, in individualistic cultures the in-group is very small, in collectivist culture relatively large. For instance in an individualistic culture a family unit as an in-group consists of parents and children and sometimes grandparents. In some collectivist cultures this in-group consists of not only the immediate family members but also aunts, uncles, cousins, and their children.

The distinction between in-group and out-group has also implications for employees' relationship with their workplace. In some cultures, like Japan for instance, the workplace is part of an individual's in-group, for which one is prepared to make personal sacrifices. In individualistic cultures and some collectivist ones like India and Iran, the workplace is part of the out-group, and receives a lot less loyalty and commitment from employees than its Japanese counterparts (Tayeb, 1994a).

## Preference for certain leadership behaviours and its implications for employee management

People living in different parts of the world have different expectations from those who are in leadership positions, be it a country ruler, a local community leader or a senior member of the family like a grand old uncle or a grandfather. These leaders also, following the prevalent custom in the culture, discharge their duties in a manner as to be compatible with those expectations; if they do not, they will lose respect and affection of their followers and, in case of political figures, be thrown out of office one way or another.

There are four broad categories of leadership/management styles which are generally observed in various cultures and at different levels of society (Likert, 1961). They range from 'democratic participative' to 'democratic consultative', 'benevolent autocratic' and 'coercive autocratic'. Each of these is characterised by a distinctive decision-making pattern.

When for instance there is an important decision to be made on an issue, say building a hospital in the community, a participative leader puts the issue before the members of the community or their representatives and invites discussion. At the end the decision accepted by the majority is the final decision, and everybody abides by it.

The consultative leader seeks the views and advice of the community members but makes the final decision himself or herself having listened to all the arguments. The final decision is accepted by all.

A benevolent autocrat may not necessarily consult people but he or she has the interests of the community at heart and makes a decision which he or she genuinely thinks is right. He or she then persuades people to accept the merit of the decision and 'sells' it to them.

A coercive leader has a total disregard for what people think and after having made the decision will force everybody to abide by it, whether they like it or not.

There are differences between nations in the extent to which each of these styles and their variations are practised and accepted, and these differences reflect various aspects of their cultures. For instance people who have low tolerance for ambiguity and risk taking, might prefer major decisions affecting the community to be taken by their leaders provided that their interests are not sacrificed (benevolent autocratic model). In cultures characterised by higher tolerance for ambiguity people would prefer to participate in decision making or at least their leaders to take their views into account when making decisions on their behalf (participative consultative model). It is fair to say that in many parts of the world the prevalent leadership styles are broadly close to these two models.

The preference for leadership models are more or less mirrored at the organisational levels. For instance, in cultures with preference for benevolent autocratic leaders, managers are looked up to like father figures who know best. In cultures with preference for a participative consultative model, the manager is viewed by his or her subordinates as just another team member who contributes to the discussions the same as anyone else, but also makes the final decision having regard to other views expressed.

In addition to the above four models, some researchers (see for instance Fleishman, 1953; Fiedler, 1967, 1987) have identified two specific leadership styles at organisational levels: task-oriented and employee-oriented. The first gives the priority to how a task is performed and the second to the employees well being. These two are not necessarily incompatible and both could well be pursued by the same manager, but the emphasis on one or the other model might be different from one manager to another. It can also be argued that the extent of emphasis on the two approaches could be different from one culture to another. In some cultures managers are generally more employee-oriented than their counterparts in other cultures.

A related argument advanced by many researchers emphasises the employees' perception of their manager's style (Smith and Peterson, 1988; Smith et al., 1989), i.e. what really matters is what employees perceive as being their manager's style. In some cultures, for example, people might like to have employee-oriented managers but may believe that their own manager does not really care about them, even though the manager does his best and thinks he cares for his employees. In addition, what is perceived as employee-orientation or task-orientation varies from culture to culture.

Misumi, a scholar from Japan, where managers are considered to be more employee-oriented than in some western countries, has proposed a theory which adds a new dimension to the understanding of leadership styles in different cultures. His theory (Misumi, 1985) is based on the argument that leaders' behaviour must be understood in terms of genotypes, i.e. the core intention of an action, and phenotypes, that is the manner in which that intention is expressed in a particular cultural context. In other words, there may well be certain underlying universal structures in the behaviour of managers which are 'genotypic' or inherent in the nature of superior–subordinate relationships. But these genotypic structures are usually expressed in a manner which is influenced by the managers' culture.

A comparison between Japanese and British leadership styles conducted as part of a four-country project (see Tayeb, 1994b for details) shows that there are some behaviours which are associated with a high employee-oriented (M) behaviour by respondents in one country but not by those in the other.

The Japanese see as an M behaviour if/when the supervisor:

- spends more time at work compared to official work hours;
- learns that a member is experiencing personal difficulties, the supervisor discusses the matter in the member's absence with other members;
- talks with the subordinates frequently about progress in relation to a work schedule;
- spends some time with the subordinates socially;
- spends time with subordinates discussing their career plans;
- evaluates performance on the work of the group as a whole;
- meets the group frequently for social or recreational purposes;
- consults the subordinates when substantially new work procedures are being discussed; and
- meets with the group as a whole frequently.

The British employees see a supervisor as an M leader if/when he or she:

- frequently uses or demonstrates how to use any of the equipment used by the group;
- makes it possible for the subordinates to make many suggestions for work improvement;
- discusses with the group if he or she believes that there is a substantial problem in the group's work procedures; and
- may be addressed by first name.

In sharp contrast to the Japanese employees, the one behaviour which is definitely not perceived by the British respondents as an M behaviour is the supervisor trying to discuss the subordinates' personal difficulties behind their back with other group members. Judging by the comments that many of the British respondents wrote on the survey questionnaires, they considered this as an invasion of their privacy and unacceptable behaviour.

The findings of the study also reveals that British supervisors who are high on M are seen as more task-oriented and more consultative than those from Japan. This, along with the British subordinates' negative views about a supervisor who talks about their personal difficulties to other people behind their back, reflects some of the cultural characteristics of the respondents. British culture is characterised, among other things, by a willingness to take account of other people's opinions, consultation and participation, and a love of privacy and keeping themselves to themselves, and individualism. The Japanese respondents, in contrast, do not seem to mind their superiors discussing their personal affairs in their absence with others. This is highly consistent with a collectivist culture.

# National culture and specific HRM issues

## Selection and recruitment

The procedures that are followed by companies in various nations, be it a domestic single nation firm or a multinational multicultural one, are different due to different societal and internal organisational factors. In advanced industrialised countries, such as the US, perhaps because of managers' high level of professionalism, formal procedures such as assessment centres, interviews and written tests are employed to select the appropriate person. In many traditional and industrialising societies, such as some Middle East and African nations, recruitment especially to higher ranks is largely done through informal networks of relatives, friends and acquaintances. This should not be confused with nepotism, which of course exists in many societies industrially advanced or not. Rather, this is a time-honoured way of doing things, and is also in response to the limited scope and development of mass communications media and their use for advertising job vacancies. Moreover, many companies in some of these nations do not have highly specialised departments or functions regarding, for instance, selection and training of new recruits. Some of the western-style selection techniques have not crossed their borders yet, perhaps by design and for better or worse.

There are also variations within industrialised and industrialising nations as well as between them. For example, in Japan companies aim at selecting someone with broad educational qualifications who will then be put through months if not years of formal training and on the job cross-functional experience. The aim is to create a flexible and skilled internal workforce which would then be able to perform nearly any job if called upon.

In the US, the selection criteria are primarily based on specialism which would allow the new recruit to fit the already determined position, with or without further training as may seem necessary at a later stage. In response to such policies American educational establishments such as business schools, which have close relationships with major companies, are also geared up to provide specialist managers and employees. They do in fact, arguably, provide training rather than education for future managers.

In Britain, where such close relationships between industry and academia do not exist to any great extent, new recruits are selected on a broadly fit-the-job basis, and are then trained to perform that job properly.

## Training

In most companies, new recruits are usually subject to some sort of induction and a period of initial on-the-job training, especially for skilled jobs. Later as the need for learning new skills and competencies arises, employees undergo further training. Training in some countries takes the form of informal apprenticeship, in others is more formalised and takes the form of either in-house tuition or externally-provided services, or a combination of the two. In the UK for instance until a few decades ago apprenticeship was a widely-used form of employee training, it has now been replaced by more formal courses. In many developing nations apprenticeship is still the main channel through which new recruits learn the skills needed to perform their jobs. The relationship between the young recruit and the supervisor is very much like that between teacher and pupil, even parent and child.

Training policies and practices in many countries are recognised as management prerogative, and therefore are not prescribed by the law. However, in some nations such as France, medium-sized and large companies are required by law to spend a certain percentage of their annual turnover on employee training. Traditionally, Japanese, German and US companies spend a large amount of their time and finances on training their employees upon recruitment and also later throughout their career with them. By comparison, some nations like the UK do not rank as high on this aspect of HRM.

## Job expectations and motivation policies

Many theories on motivation were developed, mainly in the United States, in the 1950s and 1960s. Of these the most significant were related to achievement motive (McClelland, 1961), hierarchy of needs (Maslow, 1954), and hygiene and motivating theory (Herzberg, 1966), all of which by implication could explain people's expectations from their job.

The debate about motivation concerns the need for achievement or achievement motive. In all societies the majority of people want to do well and have certain goals that they strive to achieve. The implication is that if you are ambitious and wish to succeed at work and indeed in life, you put in more energy and efforts and work harder in your workplace and elsewhere in order to achieve what you want. McClelland who was a proponent of this kind of argument further suggested that in economically-advanced societies people's need for achievement tends to be higher compared to those in less-developed nations. And that is why ambitious people as a nation are successful. He also implied that individualistic nations have a higher need for achievement compared to the collectivist ones, and that is why they are more economically advanced.

Arguments of this kind have since been regarded as simplistic and are now dated (Tayeb, 1988; Kanuango and Mendonca, 1994). For example, when one looks at many collectivist countries, such as Japan and China, which have achieved phenomenal economic success in the decades since McClelland wrote his book, one does not find their achievement motive wanting.

The apparent difference between various societies with regard to achievement motive and ambition may lie behind the way in which people view these issues. In individualistic cultures, an individual strives for his or her own achievement in life. By contrast, in collectivist nations, the achievement of the group is what matters. For instance, in the collectivist India some people spend their life's savings on their children's education so that they get good qualifications, find a good job, and marry a person from a respectable background, etc. If necessary, all the members of the extended family, from grandparents to uncles and cousins and second cousins, may collectively support the education of the younger generation. The children's achievement is the achievement of the family as a whole, and their failure brings shame to the whole family. Children in turn try to do well not only for themselves but also for the sake of their family, who will thereby be elevated to a higher status.

As far as companies are concerned, employees need for achievement and success at work could manifest themselves in an individualist or collectivist manner, depending on where the company is located and which culture the employees come from. This could have implications for teamwork versus individual assignment and corresponding reward and inducement policies—more on this in the next section.

Maslow (1954) introduced the notion of a needs hierarchy, consisting of, in ascending order, physiological, safety, social, esteem, and self-actualisation needs. Further, he argued that what motivates people depends upon their individual circumstances and where their unsatisfied needs are located on the need hierarchy. Each set of needs comes into effect as and when the one lower down has been satisfied. For instance as long as a person is hungry and has no shelter, food and a safe home are the only rewards that can motivate him to do a job assignment. Once those needs are satisfied, a promise of more food and shelter will cease to act on him as a motivator, because now the next level up, e.g. social standing, becomes active as motivator, and so on it goes. Maslow's model implied universality of the hierarchy of needs, that is it applies to all nations and all cultures.

A somewhat related theory, put forward by Herzberg (1966), distinguishes between *Hygiene* factors, or features of the job which are external to it, such as pay and benefits, working conditions, job security and holiday entitlement, and *Motivating* factors, features which are intrinsic to the job, such as intellectual or physical challenge, variety, autonomy, power, and so forth. Herzberg further argued that the hygiene factors are not motivators, but they do decrease employees' motivation if they are not provided at acceptable levels. The intrinsic motivating factors, as their label implies, actively motivate people by providing them with a sense of achievement, recognition, responsibility and opportunities for personal growth. Herzberg's theory too implies that it is universal and similarly applicable across nations, regardless of their cultural differences.

If you put Maslow's and Herzberg's theories side by side, you will notice that the hygiene factors are located on the lower levels of Maslow's needs hierarchy, and the motivating factors on the higher levels. On the basis of this juxtaposition, one can argue that some people are motivated by extrinsic hygiene features of the job, and others by the intrinsic motivating ones. This can also be linked to the conditions under which people assign significance or importance to either intrinsic or extrinsic factors: a poor person is more likely to want to have more pay than decision making power, a rich person would prefer the opposite.

Extrapolating this argument to national cultures, one could argue that in some cultures people might prefer extrinsic rewards, in others intrinsic rewards are sought. This is of course a simplistic argument. People are very complex and their expectations from their job depend on a whole host of factors. It is therefore unwise to make any generalisation about them on the basis of the culture they belong to. The above theories have indeed been challenged and proved unsubstantiated when cultural and other differences are taken into consideration.

Here is an example. As part of an extensive multi-staged investigation into the implications of national culture for organisations Tayeb (1988) conducted an employee attitude survey questionnaire in a sample of English and Indian organisations. The questionnaire included, amongst others, a number of items derived from various motivation theories. She found that the two features which were of utmost importance to English employees were 'being creative and imaginative at work' and 'having an opportunity to learn new things'. These were closely followed by 'good pay' and 'job security'. 'Having freedom and independence' ranked fourth. The least important feature of the job was 'belonging to a group'.

To the Indian respondents the most important feature of a job was 'having an opportunity to learn new things'. It was followed by 'being creative and imaginative at work', 'having freedom and independence', and 'status and prestige'. 'Belonging to a group' was of least importance to the Indian employees, but they gave it significantly greater importance than did their English counterparts. In addition, 'freedom and independence' were more important to Indian employees than to the English employees. Good pay and fringe benefits were more important to the English employees than to the Indian employees.

As one can see, contrary to the assumptions behind Anglo-Saxon theories, to Indian employees the so-called intrinsic aspects of a job—learning new things, having freedom and independence, and status and prestige—were more important than the extrinsic ones; to the English employees a mixture of both—learning new things, being creative, good pay, job security, and having freedom and independence—was important.

## Performance appraisal, reward and promotion policies

Different nations have developed and hold different views on these aspects of HRM. In many traditional societies such as some of those in the Middle East, loyalty to a superior takes preference over effective performance of subordinates as measured by the western notion of quality and quantity of output (Mellahi, 2003). Moreover, sometimes coherence and harmony in a company are more vital to its smooth running and survival in uncertain economic and political circumstances than setting out performance measures which would encourage competition and perhaps discord among employees and departments.

Going back to the individualism/collectivism debate, in collectivist cultures performance appraisal could be team based. Teams and not individuals are also subsequently rewarded for higher productivity. In individualistic cultures, by contrast, the individual-based performance appraisal and reward systems are usually the norm.

The assessment of employees' performance and the kind of rewards that they might be given are further influenced by the class system inherent in capitalist societies. For instance, the performance of managers and other higher-level white-collar employees are usually assessed by setting targets and objectives to be met within a certain time, and through employee-generated periodical reports. But for blue-collar workers performance is measured by setting daily targets by their supervisors, for example number of units produced. And in many cases quality inspectors rather than the employees themselves judge whether or not a job has been properly done.

Segalla's (1998) study of 100 European managers is a good example of differences in a number of countries with regard to promotion, remuneration and redundancy decisions.

The German sample stood nearly alone in its concern for promoting managers on the basis of objective performance criteria. French managers were at the other extreme in basing promotion on seniority or group loyalty criteria. The German sample again stood alone with its concern that remuneration should be based on measurable individual performance factors. Again the French sample held the extreme opposite belief that remuneration should be based on group, not individual, performance. English managers most often based staff-reduction decisions on the performance-to-salary ratio. More than 70 per cent of the English respondents would have made redundant a middle-aged, high-salary manager with average performance. In contrast, less than 10 per cent of the German respondents would have discharged the same manager. They favoured discharging young managers who could find jobs more easily, thereby preserving social stability. French respondents were not as concerned with the ratio of performance to salary as the Italians or Spanish. They usually made average-quality employees redundant but were more likely to choose a younger average-quality manager than an older one.

# Business imperatives and other non-cultural influences on HRM

In Chapter 3 we shall see how national institutions such as trade unions and legal systems can influence the ways in which organisations manage their employees, and indeed some of their other internal functions. Here we look at major non-cultural factors at both organisational and individual levels and their implications for HRM and other employee management issues. The main argument here is that certain individual and organisational characteristics may either cancel out the influence of national culture completely or moderate its effects to some extent.

## Influence of non-cultural factors at individual level

In one of her research projects Tayeb (1988) examined the implication of a number of personal and professional attributes such as education and position for employee management style.

She found that the level of employees' education, expertise and skills has a major influence on how they perceive their job, their power, and what they expect to get from it. The more educated and skilled a person is, the more he or she would like to have independence and authority to carry out his or her job and would expect to be trusted with his or her judgement as to whether or not the job is done properly. The supervisor or senior manager of such an employee is also more likely to respond accordingly by loosening his or her grip over how that person does their job. A surgeon's job is a good example here. A competent surgeon will have absolute control over his or her task in the operating theatre, and barring any financial and administrative constraints, he or she can decide whether the operation is needed and how, when and where it should be done.

The implication here is that in many countries even where managers would generally prefer a centralised and authoritarian management style, educated and highly skilled employees are likely to have more decision making power delegated to them and be trusted with their professional judgement than their less educated and non-skilled colleagues.

The position that an employee holds in a company can also have a similar effect. The higher up the hierarchy the position is, the more power and authority the position-holder will have. For instance, a middle manager has more control over what he or she does compared with an office clerk or a shop floor manual worker. A senior director will have different expectations from his or her job (e.g. challenge and autonomy) than a factory supervisor (e.g. high wages and reasonable lunch breaks).

## Influence of non-cultural factors at organisational level

Following Hickson et al. (1974) and Hickson et al. (1981), the same study by Tayeb mentioned above examined and found major organisational characteristics such as technology and immediate task environment (Tayeb, 1987, 1988) had a strong influence on employee management.

### Market conditions

If a company operates in volatile or fiercely competitive markets, the employees who are responsible for the design, production and the marketing of the products and services need to be able to respond quickly to events and changes in the customers' taste and preferences. As a result they will have to be constantly trained to learn the required skills. They also need to have autonomy and discretion to act as and when required without having to go through layers of hierarchy to get permission for every single move. Appropriate motivation policies and compensation schemes are also very important. By contrast, companies operating in non-competitive or more or less stable markets (e.g. monopolies) or in protected sectors do not always need to respond to their customers' demands quickly. And employees in lower levels of hierarchy, when faced with difficult or novel issues, can afford to refer the matter to their superiors and wait for a decision to be made by them and get filtered down.

### Production technology and industry

These factors have similar effects to competition on the ways in which a company is managed. For instance, companies operating in electronics and biotechnology sectors not only need to catch up with their competitors but also come up with new ideas and products in order to get ahead of them. This may mean constant employee training and delegation of decision making power to well-motivated employees for prompt and timely action.

### Size

The magnitude of complexity that large companies, including multinationals with wide-spread geographical and production sites, face in managing their employees and other internal organisational matters, such as coordination, integration and control, brings with it its own imperatives, irrespective of the national cultures within which they operate. For instance, the management style needed to coordinate the activities of 120,000 employees is totally different from that needed for a company with 50 employees.

Large organisations usually have well-established personnel or HRM departments, with extensive procedures and policies to deal with employee-related issues. The size of a large organisation by implication prevents them from being centralised, but decision-making power may be delegated hand-in-hand with standard procedures and manuals to ensure that employees at all levels carry out their duties properly. The relationship between management and employee is indirect and highly formalised.

In small organisations, the management of employees is far more personal and direct than is the case in their larger counterparts. Almost everybody knows everybody else and their relationships are informal rather than codified in the form of policy manuals and standard procedures. Many small companies do not even have personnel or any other large departments as such. Major functions are normally carried out by individuals rather than departments. In some cases an individual may be in charge of more than one major function. For instance marketing, sales and customer relations may be handled by just one person.

Marlow and Patten's (1993) study makes a similar point with regard to informality of management in small companies. The authors conducted the study in a sample of small enterprises in the UK and found few owners 'indulged' in forward planning in terms of employment. The researchers' tentative conclusion was that although there is some evidence that HRM strategies and techniques are accessible to small firms and some elements are being incorporated into the management of the employment relationship, it is doubtful if this is HRM; it could instead be a new variant of informal unskilled management.

## Organisational culture

A company's own culture and philosophy is also an important factor influencing its management style and HRM strategies and policies. The founding fathers' vision and style set the tone and culture of the company. Hewlett-Packard is a good example here. Amazon.com, founded in 1995, is another. Here are some extracts from a letter by the company's CEO, Jeff Bezos, written in 1998 and addressed to shareholders, customers, and employees, in which the philosophy behind the HRM strategy is set out (source: present author's email communication with Amazon's contact person in January 2001):

*Work Hard, Have Fun, Make History*
It would be impossible to produce results in an environment as dynamic as the Internet without extraordinary people. Working to create a little bit of history isn't supposed to be easy, and, well, we're finding that things are as they're supposed to be! We now have a team of 2,100 smart, hard-working, passionate folks who put customers first. Setting the bar high in our approach to hiring has been, and will continue to be, the single most important element of Amazon.com's success.

During our hiring meetings, we ask people to consider three questions before making a decision:

*Will you admire this person?*
If you think about the people you've admired in your life, they are probably people you've been able to learn from or take an example from. For myself, I've always tried hard to work only with people I admire, and I encourage folks here to be just as demanding. Life is definitely too short to do otherwise.

*Will this person raise the average level of effectiveness of the group they're entering?*
We want to fight entropy. The bar has to continuously go up. I ask people to visualise the company 5 years from now. At that point, each of us should look around and say, 'The standards are so high now—boy, I'm glad I got in when I did!'

*Along what dimension might this person be a superstar?*
Many people have unique skills, interests, and perspectives that enrich the work environment for all of us. It's often something that's not even related to their jobs. One person here is a National Spelling Bee champion (1978, I believe). I suspect it doesn't help her in her

everyday work, but it does make working here more fun if you can occasionally snag her in the hall with a quick challenge: 'onomatopoeia!'

## ■ CHAPTER SUMMARY

This chapter examined the universality of concept of HRM and explored the impact of contextual factors on a company's HRM policies and practices. The chapter then focused on the national culture as one of the major factors which influence and shape such policies and practices. Certain relevant cultural values and attitudes were identified and were conceptually and practically linked to certain aspects of employee management in general and HRM functions in particular. The chapter also drew attention to non-cultural factors at both individual and organisational levels and their implications for HRM policies and practices. The next chapter will focus on national and supra-national institutions and their influences on HRM.

## ■ REVISION QUESTIONS

1. Why does the broader context within which an organisation operates matter with regard to its human resource management?

2. What is national culture and why is it important for us to learn about people's cultural background?

3. Has HRM as a concept been accepted and adopted successfully in various parts of the world? Why?

4. What major non-cultural factors might moderate or even eliminate the influence of culture on policies and practices implied in questions 2 and 3 above?

# Case study: Oki UK Ltd

Oki was founded in 1881 and is engaged in a variety of businesses with sites in Asia, US and Europe.

Oki (UK) Ltd at Cumbernauld is part of Oki Data Communications and was set up in 1987. It is the oldest Oki printer factory in the UK. It manufactures and supplies dot matrix printers, page printers and fax machines. It is recognised as one of the most cost-effective manufacturing plants of its kind, achieving some of the highest quality levels within the international electronics industry.

Oki Data Communications is an independent company, on the board are British, American and Japanese nationalities. The three main geographical areas (i.e. Japan, US and Europe) have distinct HRM policies and have little to do with each other. In the UK there is a senior director who is responsible for HR and corporate affairs. For the first few years they had a Japanese MD on site who referred most things back to Japan.

## Management practices

The company's policy can be summed up thus: Management manages the process and the individual employee manages his or her own job.

Supervisors have very different roles in Oki Japan compared to Oki UK. In Japan team leaders are expected to maintain continuity throughout the whole process—they develop part of the process, and are involved in it and keep adding knowledge elements to it. In the UK, as one manager puts it,

'we are taught a more status approach, when you come in to industry as a graduate engineer you have a certain status; when you become a proper engineer after 18 months or so your status changes and you don't have to do things you did as a graduate engineer. When you become a senior engineer and a team leader you get your own office and you definitely don't do the things you did when you were a graduate. In the early days the UK site lost a number of engineers because they [Japanese managers] didn't give them the status they expected, they adopted a more Japanese approach. People on the shopfloor in Japan call out engineers when they have a problem. In the UK companies the engineers have a status—they tell employees when and how things are made, when they will arrive.'

For many years, in management meetings in the UK company a Japanese manager would always stand up and describe a problem, for example an engineering problem. He would be queried and if he did not know the answer he would call up the actual operator to the meeting who had been working on the machine which was having problems. It took the site a long time to get the message the Japanese were trying to pass on:

'A manager is not just a reporter of the problem, he has got to be part of the solution and if he stands up and only becomes a reporter that's all he'll ever be. So he's got to go down there and touch that machine and feel what the problem is. Unless he touches cold metal he shouldn't be standing there explaining the issue—they would rather have the operator there who found the problem.'

There is emphasis on empowerment: employees are encouraged to get involved in decisions and are given power to do so. The company has MAD (Make a Difference) suggestion schemes—with rewards for best suggestions. Everyone gets a personal and individually written response to their suggestion, e.g. 'thanks, but we have thought of that', or 'thanks, yes it's a great idea', etc.

## Some HRM functions

### Recruitment

A lot of direct recruitment is done through Manpower, a recruitment agency. They advertise in the local press, agencies and sometimes assessment centre type organisations for more senior positions. The tools they use are interviewing and testing (verbal, numerical and personality). Nearly all operators come in as temporary staff, through Manpower agency.

Aside from the actual job requirements, personality is important—to make sure they fit into the company, for example sense of humour, enthusiasm, contribution, flexibility.

HR department normally involves relevant line managers in the assessment process and in the formulation of assessment criteria mainly because they look for technical and personal skills as well as intellectual ability even from an early assessment stage.

### Training and Development

In 1994, 4,500 man days were spent in 'off the job' training. Up to 30% of staff are now currently engaged in higher education, in most cases helped and supported by the company. There are a lot of training and development opportunities. Technical training includes apprentices in line with the Government's Modern Apprenticeship Scheme. The company have so far put 10 technicians through Train the Trainer courses to pass on their skills effectively to the apprentices. The company is considering developing vocational qualification frameworks for operators too. Someone from manufacturing is studying Information Systems because they have skills in this area and a post may arise in the future, some are reading for Higher National Certificates in Electronics. The company pays for training and education outside as well as those organised in-house. Those who enrol for external courses will pay back the cost if they fail the end of course examinations.

A lot of operators receive on the job training as well. There are also career development opportunities, and the culture and philosophy promote shared learning.

The company has strong links with a local college. They have lecturers who come on site to run the courses in the evenings. It costs a little more but it means that employees can finish the course a little earlier than if they ended their shift, drove to the college then travelled back home afterwards. The courses can also be more tailored to Oki. There is a good take-up of courses every year. Generally the local external environment has been very supportive towards Oki's training and development—as illustrated by the adaptation of some standard courses to Oki's needs.

Training needs assessment is conducted through appraisals and discussions with department managers every 6–12 months. When individuals apply to go on training, objectives are formulated and then improvements are identified against targets after training is completed. This is then compiled into reports on general improvements for each individual, and is fed back to the managers.

## Pay and Benefits

Here there seems to be a great deal of influence of Japanese ways of doing things on the company located in the UK. For example, in the early days when they talked about giving bonuses, HR Director submitted a proposal to give staff a bonus of approximately £250 because they had met all their targets in the first period.

'It was agreed that we would give bonuses and I said I would arrange for payroll to pay these and the Japanese MD was horrified. He said "What do you mean? You've talked to me about how these people should be congratulated and looked after. If you put it in their pay packet who is going to shake their hands and say thank you. Why don't we give them cash?" I automatically thought it was nonsense because no one uses cash in the UK, certainly not pound notes, or £5 as the case may be. What he was really getting at was that the real point of contact was to thank personally rather than just shove something in the payroll. My conditioning for many, many years had been you reward someone by throwing cash in their pay packet.'

Here is another example, the case of an employee who had worked really hard and whom the HR Director said he wanted to reward:

'A manager had worked really long hours and I said I wanted to give him a bonus and we talked about it and how he was missing his family and I was going to give him £500. The Japanese manager said "why do you do these things?" and I thought he was arguing about the amount of money. "You said he was missing his family so how does this bonus impact on his family? Why don't you give him a holiday; a holiday means that he will spend more time with his family that he has neglected for the last few months." This idea of connecting the problem with a solution instead of having a universal solution for every problem has been quite revealing in the way we should go about things.'

## Performance management

The company has an appraisal process in place. Everyone gets an appraisal once a year. Managers involve the individual in all stages of the process, such as setting objectives and the steps to be taken to achieve them. Appraisal is usually conducted by the team leader, off line and on a one-to-one basis. The format is explained to them and it is a two-way process. Employees can ask for more than one appraisal per annum. Assessment criteria are based on the company targets and personal targets. There is no team assessment in this process. The assessment outcome affects employees' salary and promotion.

The company has a list of competencies to assess individuals on for promotion. Unlike the Japanese parent company, length of service has little influence on promotion. In Japan, there would be little opportunity for employees to jump ahead of their older colleagues in the promotional ladder. In the UK there are real opportunities to do just that—career progression is based on performance and not on seniority.

### ■ CASE STUDY QUESTIONS

**1.** What is the main difference between a British supervisor and a Japanese team leader?

**2.** How does a Japanese manager's approach to dealing with problems differ from that of a British manager's?

**3.** How does the company assess employees training needs and in what forms do they receive their training?

**4.** How does Japanese management style influence the company's pay and benefits practices?

**5.** To what extent does this case study confirm or reject the discussions in the main text of the chapter? In what way?

### ■ RECOMMENDED FURTHER READING

Cray, D. and Mallory, G. R. (1998). *Making Sense of Managing Culture*. London: International Thompson Business Press.

Gately, S., Lessem, R. and Altman, Y. (1996). *Comparative Management: A Transcultural Odyssey*. London: McGraw-Hill.

Jackson, T. (2002). *International HRM: A Cross-Cultural Approach*. Sage Publications.

### ■ REFERENCES

Adler, N. J. (1997). *International Dimensions of Organizational Behavior*. Ohio: International Thomson Publishing. Third edition.

Brannen, M. Y. (2002). 'When Mickey loses face: recontextualization and the semiotics of internationalizing Walt Disney', paper presented at the Identifying Culture Conference, Stockholm, 13–15 June, 2002.

Brech, E. F. L. (1953). *The Principle and Practice of Management*. London: Longman.

Brown, A. (1945). *Organization*. New York: Hibbert.

Budhwar, P. S. and Debrah, Y. (2001). 'Rethinking comparative and cross-national human resource management', *International Journal of Human Resource Management*, vol. 12, no. 3, pp. 497–515.

Child, J. and Tayeb, M. H. (1983). 'Theoretical perspectives in cross-national organizational research', *International Studies of Management and Organization*, vol. XII, pp. 23–70.

Clark, T. and Pugh, D. S. (2000). 'Convergence and divergence in European HRM: an exploratory polycentric study', *International Studies of Management and Organization*, vol. 29, no. 4, pp. 83–99.

Crozier, M. (1964). *The Bureaucratic Phenomenon*. London: Tavistock Publications.

Denny, S. (2003). 'Culture and its influence on management: A critique and an empirical test', in M. Tayeb, *International Management: Theories and Practices*. London: Pearson Education.

Fayol, H. (1949). *General Industrial Management*. Bath: Pitman.

Fiedler, F. E. (1967). *A Theory of Leadership Effectiveness*. New York: McGraw-Hill Book Company.

—— (1987). *New Approaches to Effective Leadership*. New York: John Wiley & Sons, Inc.

Fleishman, E A, 1953, 'The description of supervisory behavior', *Personnel Psychology*, vol. 37, pp. 1–6.

Gatley, S., Leesem, R., and Altman, Y. (eds.), (1996). *Comparative Management: A Transcultural Odyssey*. London: McGraw-Hill Book Company.

Haire, M., Ghiselli, E. E., and Porter, R. W. (1966). *Managerial Thinking: An International Study*. New York: John Wiley & Sons.

Harvey, E. (1968). 'Technology and structure of organizations', *American Sociological Review*, vol. 33, pp. 247–59.

Herzberg, F. (1966). *Work and the Nature of Man*. Ty Crowell Co. Reissue edition.

Hickson, D. J. and Pugh, D. S. (1995). *Management Worldwide*. Harmondsworth, Penguin.

—— —— and Pheysey, D. C. (1969). 'Operation technology and organization structure: an empirical reappraisal', *Administrative Science Quarterly*, vol. 14, pp. 378–97.

—— Hinings, C. R., McMillan, C. J., and Schwitter, J. P. (1974). 'The culture-free context of organization structure; a tri-national comparison', *Sociology*, vol. 8, pp. 59–80.

—— —— (1981). *Organization and Nation: The Aston Programme IV*. Farnborough: Gower.

Hofstede, G. (1980). *Culture's Consequences*. California: Sage Publications.

Kanuango, R. N. and Mendonca, M. (1994). *Work Motivation: Models for Developing Countries*. New Delhi: Sage.

Kroeber, A. L. and Kluckhohn, C. (1952). 'Culture—a critical review of concepts and definitions', papers of Peabody Museum of American Archaeology and Ethnology, Harvard University, vol. XIVII, no. 1.

Lawrence, P. R. and Lorsch, J. W. (1967). *Organization and Environment: Managing Differentiation and Integration*. Boston: Harvard University Press.

Likert, R. (1961). *New Patterns of Management*. New York: McGraw-Hill Book Company.

Macfarlane, A. (1978). *The Origins of English Individualism*. Oxford: Basil Blackwell.

Marlow, S. and Patten, D. (1993). 'Managing the employment relationship in the smaller firm; possibilities for human resource management', *International Small Business Journal*, vol. 11, pp. 57–64.

Maslow, A. (1954). *Motivation and Personality*. Harper & Row.

Mayo, E. (1945). *The Social Problems of an Industrial Civilization*. Boston: Harvard University Press.

McClelland, D. (1961). *The Achieving Society: Characteristics of Entrepreneurs*. Wiley & Sons.

McGregor, D. (1960). *The Human Side of Enterprise*. New York: McGraw-Hill.

Mellahi, K. (2003). National culture and management practices: the case of Gulf Cooperation Council countries', in M. H. Tayeb, *International Management: Theories and Practices*. Harlow: Pearson Education. Chapter 5.

Misumi, J. (1985). *The Behavioral Science of Leadership*. Ann Arbor: University of Michigan Press.

Mooney, J. (1947). *Principles of Organization*. New York: Harper.

Namazie, P. (2000). 'A preliminary review of factors affecting international joint ventures in Iran', paper presented at the 27th Annual Conference of Academy of International Business (UK Chapter), Strathclyde University, April.

Orwell, G. (1945). *Animal Farm: A Fairy Story*. London: Secker & Warburg.

Pugh, D. S., Hickson, D. J., Hinings, C. R., and Turner, C. (1968). 'Dimensions of organization structure', *Administrative Science Quarterly*, vol. 13, pp. 65–105.

Roethlisberger, F. G. (1944). *Management and Morale*. Cambridge, Mass.: Harvard University Press.

Schwartz, S. H. (1999). 'A theory of cultural values and some implications for work', *Applied Psychology: An International Review*, 48(1), pp. 23–47.

Segalla, M. (1998). 'National cultures, international business', *Financial Times*, 7 March, survey page 8.

Smith, P. B. and Peterson, M. F. (1988). *Leadership, Organizations and Culture: An Event Management Perspective*. London: Sage Publications.

Smith, P. B., Tayeb, M. H., and Peterson, M. F. (1989). 'The cultural context of leadership action: a cross-cultural analysis' in J. Davies, M. Easterby-Smith, S. Mann and M. Tantonÿ (eds.), *The Challenge to Western Management Development: International Alternative*. London: Routledge. Chapter 7.

Tayeb, M. H. (1987). 'Contingency theory and culture: a study of matched English and Indian manufacturing firms', *Organization Studies*, vol. 8, pp. 241–62.

—— (1988). *Organizations and National Culture: A Comparative Analysis*. London: Sage Publications.

—— (1994a). 'National culture and organizations: methodology considered', *Organization Studies*, vol. 15, no. 2, pp. 429–46.

—— (1994b). 'Japanese managers and British culture: a comparative case study', *International Journal of Human Resource Management*, vol. 5, no. 1, pp. 145–66.

—— (2000). *The Management of International Enterprises: A Socio-Political View*. Basingstoke: Macmillan.

Taylor, F. W. (1911). *The Principles of Scientific Management*. New York: Harper Bros.

Triandis, H. C. (1980). 'Value, attitudes and interpersonal behavior', in M. M. Page (ed.), *Nebraska symposium on motivation, beliefs, attitudes and values*. Volume 27. Lincoln: University of Nebraska.

—— (1981). 'Dimensions of cultural variations as parameters of organizational theories', paper presented at the International Symposium on Cross-cultural Management, Montreal, Canada. October.

—— (1995). *Individualism and Collectivism*. Boulder, CO: Westview Press.

Trompenaars, F. (1993). *Riding the Wave of Culture*. London: Economist Books.

Urwick, L. F. (1943). *The Elements of Administration*. New York: Harper.

Woodward, J. (1958). *Management and Technology*. London: HMSO.

Wright, P. and Brewster, C. (2003). 'Editorial: learning from diversity: HRM is not Lycra', *International Journal of Human Resource Management*, vol. 14, no. 8, pp. 1299–307.

# 3 | Internationalisation of HRM: Institutional Contexts

## Learning outcomes

When you finish reading this chapter you should:
- know about some of the major national institutions and the ways in which they might influence organisations and their HRM policies and practices
- get an in-depth knowledge about a major regional institution and an important international institution
- know the implications of the above institutions' directives and rulings for HRM policies and practices employed in the companies which operate in their member states
- be able to explore how these influences translate into practice in the case study which closes the chapter.

## Introduction

The previous chapter discussed some of the ways in which cultural norms, values and attitudes influence HRM and other aspects of employee–management relationships. The present chapter focuses largely on the impact of various institutions on such matters.

It is worth pointing out at this stage that some researchers distinguish between cultural and institutional make up of a nation (see for instance Child and Tayeb, 1983) and some scholars, usually referred to as institutionalists, consider institutions as including culture (e.g. DiMaggio and Powell, 1991). For instance, North (1990, p. 3) defines institutions as 'the rules of the game in a society or . . . the humanly devised constraints that shape human interaction'. For Davis and North (1971, p. 6) an 'institutional framework is the set of fundamental political, social and legal ground rules that establishes the basis for production, exchange and distribution'. From what we learned in the previous chapter, this definition is wide enough to include culture as well as other societal institutions.

This debate is obviously beyond the scope of the present chapter, but for clarity of argument, the present book distinguishes between culture as defined and discussed in Chapter 2 and various national and supra-national institutions as discussed in the present chapter. It is further argued that the way in which culture and institutions influence management is fundamentally different from one another. Culture exerts its influence and constraints *informally*, that is through internalised socially accepted norms of behaviour (e.g. it is wrong to be discourteous to people). Institutions' influence, by contrast, is *formal* and in most cases backed up by enforceable sanctions (e.g. imprisonment for stealing).

So what are these institutions and why should we learn about them?

# National and international institutions

These institutions have their roots either in individual nations, evolved over time or created by design, or are creations of two or more nations with common interests in a given type of activities. In either case they exist in order to achieve certain collective goals and objectives and have rules and regulations which govern their structure, activities and code of conduct. Some of these institutions, depending on their goals and scope, can have significant bearing on the ways in which organisations operating within their jurisdiction manage their employees and some of their other internal and external affairs.

## National institutions

These are the so-called secondary institutions which normally have a two-way relationship with a nation's cultural values and attitudes. In the sense that they are created by these values and attitudes and at the same time they reinforce them. For example a culture which emphasises an egalitarian power relationship between people is more likely to have a democratic and egalitarian political system and people in position of power are elected to their office in free and fair elections. The system in turn enforces and encourages people to challenge their elected representatives and hold them to account, and drive them out of office at elections if they are not satisfied with their performance.

## International institutions

The 20th century saw a proliferation of political, military, legal, economic and trade regional and global institutions, conventions and agreements to which many countries belong or aspire to belong, e.g. United Nations, World Trade Organisation, North Atlantic Treaty Organisation, European Union and North American Free Trade Agreement. All these institutions have more or less enforceable rules and regulations which govern the relationship between member states and prescribe codes of conduct which all members should abide by.

International laws can emerge from global, regional or bilateral sources and cover all the countries which are signatories to them. They cannot be violated without serious consequences, such as economic and political sanctions, for those countries which ignore them. In practice however such sanctions are imposed selectively on nations and companies operating within them, mainly for political reasons.

Some of these various bodies have rules and regulations which are related to organisations operating within the member states and their jurisdiction ranges from trade and investment to environmental issues, business ethics, and internal organisational matters. The rules and regulations governing internal matters are usually either related to employees' individual rights, such as equal opportunity, job security, wage levels, work schedules, work injuries and post-employment economic security. Or they are concerned with employees' collective rights, such as unionisation, bargaining, the resolution of contract disputes, and participative decision making.

As we shall see later in the chapter, international laws substantially alter the domestic laws that historically structure employment relationships (Florkowski and Nath, 1993).

This generally occurs when a country accepts a new international standard which covers an aspect of work that was previously unregulated or less rigorously regulated by that country. Indigenous employees inevitably become covered when their own government expands employment protections. There are however some who argue that national development policy has priority over international requirements. The importance of foreign investment for national development results in demands for 'competitive' labour market structures, where wage levels, labour conditions and labour institutions have to adapt to the level of economic 'realities' (for a detailed discussion of the arguments see Tsogas, 1999).

# National institutions and HRM

In this section we learn about some major institutions and the ways in which they might, directly or indirectly, influence a company's policies and practices with regard to human resource management and other related matters. See also Figure 3.1.

## Political economic system and HRM

The political economic system has a profound impact on how a nation as a whole and its people as individuals organise their public and private lives. In a sense, it sets the tone and provides the framework within which all other activities take place. The nation's overall broad strategies are then determined at micro-levels within the parameters set by this framework. Some of these strategies and ensuing policies are relevant to business organisations' external and internal affairs, including HRM.

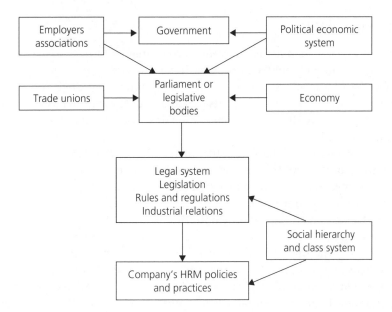

**Figure 3.1** Institutional influences on human resource management

In many of the former communist/socialist countries workers participation in management decision making was legitimised and accepted as the norm, in theory at least. In practice the situation was of course different from one country to another, as witnessed in the former Soviet Union and present China. The former Yugoslavia's self-management with provisions for worker directors was perhaps the most extensive form of workers participation practised in a socialist country. The model disappeared when most of the country's constituent republics gained independence after a bloody civil war in the 1990s.

In capitalist economies, especially those with 'right of centre' policies, market conditions determine to a large extent what rights employees will have. At times of economic boom and low unemployment, workers are sought after and have a great deal of power and influence over their choice of working conditions, pay and other employment rights. At times of recession and high unemployment managers have more power to impose working conditions and other employment contracts, such as no-strike deals, on their employees. Some governments may also take sides with managers, and through various legislation, increase management prerogatives and erode workers' power and influence.

In some capitalist countries, such as Germany, where there is a great emphasis on social market ideology, workers' rights are enshrined in law. Co-determination and workers councils are examples of the ways in which the participation of employees in the management of their workplace is ensured (Lane, 1995).

In most developing countries protection of workers is part and parcel of a larger design based on the principle of social welfare through industrial policies (Tayeb, 1988). Almost all these countries lack an extensive and well-developed national welfare state. People largely depend on their families and other relatives for help when they get old, or are sick or are without a job. Social issues such as poverty, unemployment and even ethnic problems are usually tackled through economic plans via business organisations.

## Government and HRM

The degree to which governments intervene in companies' internal and external activities varies of course from one country to another. Some like communist regimes and capitalist dictatorships have more or less total control over everything in their territory, from the content of literary outputs and performing arts to political ideology, from business transactions to the religion people are allowed to practise, from dress code to what students are taught at schools and universities.

Capitalist democracies generally keep the intervention to a minimum necessary for the smooth running of the country, e.g. law and order, broad economic policies and defence. They sometimes regard the government at best as an enabler and at worst as a nuisance as far as business activities are concerned.

However, there are many capitalist democracies in which the government plays a more active role in the business sector, not only through rules and regulations as we shall see below, but also through ownership and management of business companies, especially in energy, arms and other strategic sectors. Companies which are owned and managed by government appointees are ultimately accountable to the parliament for their internal and external activities and are normally run in a centralised and bureaucratic manner. Their HRM policies and practices are also as a result subject to bureaucratic rules. Government's engagement and intervention in macro- and micro-level business activities are particularly extensive in many capitalist developing countries, especially those which have a less developed private sector.

Some governments believe that the running of strategic and operative activities of companies is the prerogative of their management teams. When there are disputes between management and the workforce, the government either takes a hands-off approach or sides with the management. The siding with the management sometimes goes beyond individual cases and is extended to initiating laws and acts of parliament to reduce or circumvent the employees' ability to challenge the management (cf. some of the industrial relations laws passed by the British Conservative government in the 1980s).

Government intervention in trade policies can have a more indirect impact on companies' HRM policies and practices as well. One of the major consequences of growing internationalisation and globalisation of business is the increase in foreign direct investment and international joint ventures. One consequence of this, as we shall see in later chapters, is the exposure of host-country companies to foreign HRM policies and practices. Foreign subsidiaries of Japanese, US and European multinational companies have been role models for local firms in many parts of the world. Teamwork, quality circles, cell manufacturing and just-in-time are examples of practices which have spread this way (Strier, 1984; Turnbull, 1986; Tayeb, 1999*a*).

However, one of the preconditions for local firms having the opportunity to learn from foreign companies is that they are allowed to enter and invest in their country in the first place. This takes us back to government intervention in economy, trade and business activities.

Here too there are differences between nations. At both national and company levels, decisions to engage in foreign direct investment are influenced by political and cultural factors as well as economic and commercial ones—at the entry stage and, once operational, within the host country.

Foreign direct investment among the industrialised nations of western Europe and north America and other OECD member states are relatively unproblematic. There is virtually no political control over the process. British companies can just as easily set up plants in the US and American firms in the UK as they can in their respective home countries. They are more or less subject to the same laws and regulations in their host country as are their local counterparts.

However, in spite of the remarkable increase in the openness to trade and investment flows in a large part of the world since the 1990s, for various historical and political reasons (e.g. colonisation), many third world countries are still reluctant to open their doors fully and without restriction to foreign investors, especially in strategic industries. Governments in these countries are most reluctant to let go of the control and ownership of such industries, and pass them on even to their own private sector domestic firms, let alone foreign multinationals (Tayeb, 1999*b*). As a result there are not very many opportunities for the business firms in these countries to learn from their foreign counterparts.

## Economy and HRM

In economically advanced and fully industrialised societies, the vast majority of people live in urban areas; they are educated, sophisticated and aware of their political and civil rights, including those related to their workplace. They can articulate their wish to have good working conditions, to be consulted with on major decisions affecting their jobs and their career and so forth. The higher their level of expertise and skill the more they are likely to expect and be given what they ask for.

In less economically developed nations, where the economy is predominantly based on agriculture and the vast majority of people live in rural areas, the industrialised sector is relatively small and the level of education and professional expertise is low. As a result, fewer people compared to their counterparts in the advanced nations are either aware of their workplace-related rights or have the power to enforce them.

Even in economically advanced nations the power of employees can vary from time to time depending on the state of the economy. For instance when the economy is booming, unemployment is low and skilled employees are in demand, employees and would-be employees with the desirable skills can and do exert a degree of power and influence over their pay and working conditions and even over some strategic decisions related to their specific job or department. At times of economic downturns, some if not all of these prerogatives are lost. As companies lose money and shed jobs, unemployment rises and many people may be willing to accept less than ideal conditions in order to hold on to their current job or to get one if unemployed.

## Trade unions and HRM

In some countries, usually where the right of citizens to be heard and consulted with is recognised, trade unions can and do flourish. There you will find many shopfloor workers and office staff are by choice members of one trade union or another and participate through their union representatives in collective negotiations with the management over issues of mutual interest, such as pay, working practices and sometimes even strategic decisions such as closure of a plant or joint ventures with other companies.

In some countries, like Japan, unions are company based; in others like the UK they are craft based. Negotiations can also be conducted at different levels: company, region and country. Trades unions' power and influence over various policies, including those related to employee management and HRM, vary from country to country, depending on where they are situated and under what economic and political conditions they function at any given point in time. French unions, for instance, are more powerful than their US and UK counterparts. It is also important to note that there are quite a few countries in which trade unions are not allowed to exist or if they do, they do not have any real power and clout as a collective. In practice employees in these countries do not have any formal representation and cannot engage in collective bargaining and negotiations with the management.

## Employers' associations and HRM

In many countries various companies, large and small, formally or informally organise themselves into an employers' body whose main objective it is to promote their professional interests, just as trade unions in many countries aim at protecting the employees' interests. And just like trade unions, the employers' associations' power and influence vary from country to country and under different governments. In the United Kingdom, for instance, the major employers' association is called the Confederation of British Industry (CBI) and its influence has considerably increased since the 1980s, especially in comparison with that of trade unions.

Employers' associations normally use various formal and informal means, such as lobbying members of the parliament, cabinet ministers and the media in order to express their views and preferences on various issues. They can thereby influence laws and regulations related to business activities, ranging from interest rates and foreign trade policies to industrial relations, workplace practices and other internal employee–management issues. For instance the provision of minimum wage regulations was for many years opposed by the CBI in the United Kingdom. When it did eventually become a statutory obligation for the employers to pay not less than a certain minimum wage to their manual workers, the level was nearer to what the employers had lobbied for than the employees' representatives would have wished. The European Unions' Social Chapter, which sets out directives governing workplace issues, such as parental leave, maximum weekly working hours and overtime, was another case in which the employers' associations in the member states were able to exert some influence.

## Legal system, industrial relations laws and HRM

One of the ways in which a country's legal system can influence such internal organisational activities as HRM and industrial relations is of course through the laws and regulations passed on to it by the legislative bodies and government decrees, such as the UK minimum wage regulations mentioned above. All nations regulate business activities to some degree and companies like individuals are subject to the laws of the country in which they operate. However, some nations have relatively hands-off policies as far as business laws are concerned. There, usually the limits beyond which domestic and foreign companies cannot venture are specified and within those limits they are free to pursue their legitimate commercial interests. By contrast, there are other countries where detailed rules and laws cover everything from permission and license to operate, choice of location, and social responsibility to specific internal organisation activities. In general, health and safety, maternity and paternity leave, statutory minimum wage, physical working conditions, protection of the employees against dust and noise pollution, pension and medical provisions, childcare facilities are examples of workplace activities which are governed by laws and regulations in many countries.

Legal systems can also have indirect bearing on organisations. For instance in some countries, the resolution of a dispute between an employee and his or her employers in the court can set precedence for similar cases in the future. If a Muslim woman, for example, wins her case in the court to wear Islamic head dress at workplace against the company's own preferred practices, all women in that company and indeed in that country may be able to do the same if they so wish.

Industrial relations legislation exerts perhaps the most powerful external influence on the internal affairs of companies, and for this reason various interest groups such as trade unions and employers' associations tend to focus their efforts on it before it gets passed through the parliament.

Industrial relations and the laws governing it, like so many other societal institutions, vary from country to country. In some countries like Germany certain employee rights such as union membership and representation on various levels of decision making and co-determination, are enshrined in the law. In the UK, by contrast, the unions' right to be recognised was until the late 1990s left to the management's goodwill and even since 1998, when a minimum wage law came into effect, the vote of a majority of employees is required before the management consents to recognise trade unions in the company. In France, as was mentioned in Chapter 2, companies larger than a certain size are obliged by law to spend a certain percentage of their annual turnover on employee training. In many countries, by contrast, employee training policies are considered as a matter for the management and there are no legal provisions for them.

In some countries, such as India, which has traditionally had socialist-oriented policies, the organised sector is relatively very small compared to the total workforce, but industrial relations laws are 'pro' workers and the unions have more power compared to their counterparts elsewhere. One reason for such pro-workers laws, is the extensive poverty in the country. In India and in fact in many other developing counties, as was mentioned earlier, social issues such as poverty, unemployment and even ethnic problems are tackled through industrial relations and other business-related laws. There are, however, sometimes political motives behind pro-workers legislation. In the pre-1979 revolution Iran, the Shah's regime would attempt to secure workers' loyalty by measures such as compulsory employee profit sharing schemes and share ownership of medium- and large-sized firms (Tayeb, 1999b).

The laws regulating human resource management practices are sometimes tied in with other government policies and programmes, especially in some developing countries. Here HRM and indeed other business activities must be in line with the national development plans that have been prepared by central planning authorities. For instance if a country has planned to achieve certain targets regarding the expansion of its manufacturing sectors and reduction of its dependence on cash crops and agricultural produce, manufacturing companies are required to plan their workforce requirements (numbers and skills needed) in step with the government's overall plans.

Business and employment laws cover of course both domestic and foreign firms, and can sometimes create confusion and difficulties particularly for multinational firms. For instance, some Japanese companies' practice of forcing older managers into 'voluntary' retirement by withholding their work assignments would violate the Age Discrimination in Employment Act if done in the US.

As Florkowski and Nath (1993) point out, failure to adapt to the prevailing laws can have serious financial and operational repercussions for companies. For example, Japanese subsidiaries in the US would have the right to staff their facilities with managers during a strike to continue operations, thereby putting pressure on the unions to settle the bargaining dispute. In contrast, a Japanese subsidiary in Italy that attempted to do so was ordered to abandon this strategy because it was considered illegal and an anti-union activity in that country (Negandhi et al., 1985). The company not only faces financial sanctions in the latter instance, but also may be confronted with costly 'down-time' if alternative responses have not been formulated. Conversely, while the parent company in Japan could base employment decisions on personality with impunity, US Equal Employment Opportunity laws would prohibit its American subsidiary from utilising this factor in the absence of documentation of job-relatedness.

It should be pointed out that international laws may alter the domestic laws of nation-states over time, prompting their inclusion as a moderator variable. This amalgamation of laws in turn defines the range of appropriate labour market choices, terms and conditions of work and government–company relations for the company as a whole. In the case of subsidiaries of multinational companies existing restrictions may sometimes be bypassed if alternative arrangements are secured from the host countries through negotiations and proactive strategic initiatives, such as lobbying government ministers and officials and parliament to repeal laws, and to get exemptions. Otherwise the companies are expected to change their human resource management policies and programmes to achieve compliance throughout the organisation (Florkowski and Nath, 1993).

## Social hierarchy and class systems and HRM

Different nations organise their society differently. The degree of rigidity of social structure and the relationships between the various social strata are to a large extent reflected in work organisations as well.

In industrialised societies and those in which industrialisation is well under way, social structure is based on class differentiation. In some countries like India there is also a parallel hierarchy based on the caste system. In predominantly agricultural societies a feudal system divides people into masters and serfs. Tribal primitive communities also have their own simple but hierarchical orders.

The extent to which social differentiation is entrenched in a society varies among nations too. In some societies there is a marked rigid hierarchy in terms of power, wealth and opportunities. In others this is less the case. For example, in Sweden, and indeed other Scandinavian countries, class differentiation is not as visible as one can observe in, say, the United kingdom. People certainly do not think of themselves as members of one class or other. Although there are income, occupational and educational differences among people, the gap between the various layers of the society, thanks to the country's taxation policies and welfare system, is much smaller than that in many other advanced countries. Their workplace management also reflects this. Management–employee relationship, for example, is based on non-discrimination and equality of opportunity.

Another example of the reflection of social structure in the workplace can be seen in a comparative study of English and Indian national cultures and organisations conducted by Tayeb (1988). In England managers consider themselves as members of the middle class, which shares in the ownership and participates in the control of the means of production, and manual workers see themselves as members of the working class exploited by the former. In most cases, the relationship between management and workers is characterised to a large extent by mistrust and hostility, emanating from a conflict of interests between the two classes. In India, in addition to the industrial class conflict, the caste membership further exacerbates the generally hostile relationship between managers and workers. The former mainly belong to higher castes, and the latter are largely recruited from among lower-caste villagers and slum dwellers of the urban areas.

In some countries, certain employees are discriminated against, quite legally and in accordance with their domestic laws, on other grounds as well: local vs foreign, women vs men, non-white vs white, gay vs straight, minority religion vs dominant religion, young vs old. Such discriminations are in many cases considered unacceptable, even abhorrent, by people in other countries. For instance, in South Africa before the abolition of the apartheid regime black people were discriminated against in recruitment and promotion even if they were more qualified than their white counterparts. In Israel Arab Israelis are not allowed to serve in the army, at the same time having served in the army is a prerequisite for getting many jobs in that country. By implication potential Arab employees are discriminated against in comparison with their non-Arab counterparts. In Saudi Arabia women are barred from public office and many jobs are the preserve of male applicants; women are allowed to become teachers or run their own women-only shops and enterprises.

In many Arab countries in the Persian Gulf region, foreign employees are treated differently from one another depending on their country of origin. For instance, western expatriates generally receive higher pay than the local nationals, who in turn receive more than the Indians and so on, with Nepalese at the bottom of the pay levels—even when they all perform the same work as other nationalities. Management takes the view that market forces in the worker's home country should determine rates of pay not the market rate for a job within the host country. Therefore the job being done is not the basis for pay (Harry, 2003).

These cases are of course all against international labour laws and standards, as we shall see below.

# International institutions

In this section we focus mainly on two major institutions, one global and the other regional, in order to illustrate the ways in which international institutions influence the management of employees of various companies, including the multinationals.

## International Labour Organisations (ILO) and HRM

The ILO, with over 170 members, is one of the most significant international institutions whose directives and rulings have direct bearing on HRM and other workplace regulations in member states. It was set up in 1919 after the Russian revolution to show workers elsewhere that capitalism cared. Its core standards are freedom to form trade unions and bargain collectively, a ban on forced labour and child labour, and non-discrimination in the workplace. These are the subject of ILO conventions and are implicitly accepted by countries when they join the organisation.

The ILO facilitates the growth of 'universal' labour law through the passage of conventions and recommendations. Conventions articulate legal principles that should be present in the indigenous law of member nations, and must be separately ratified by each affiliated sovereignty. Recommendations act as guidelines for government action on issues that are not ripe for a convention or as supplements to existing conventions. Both instruments are designed to furnish minimum standards that do not supplant any law, custom or agreement which already is more favourable to workers.

As Tsogas (2000) points out, ILO Conventions and Recommendations (the 'International Labour Code') are a steadfast point of reference for international standardisation of conditions of employment. All discussions on labour standards in trade refer to ILO Conventions and Recommendations and all definitions of labour standards are based on this Code. That is to say national trade legislation and bilateral and multilateral trade agreements between two or more nations contain labour standard clauses which are based on ILO's conventions and have a common reference point to them.

The most generally accepted labour standards in current trade-related schemes include the following, and all have a common reference point in relevant ILO Conventions:

- Freedom of association (Convention No. 87)
- Right to organise and collective bargaining (No. 98)
- Minimum age for employment of children (Nos. 5 and 138)
- Right to occupational safety and health (various Conventions)
- Prohibition of forced labour (Nos. 29 and 105)
- Prohibition of discrimination in employment and occupation on the grounds of race, sex, religion, political opinion, etc. (No. 111)

These labour standards form a core of fundamental rights that men and women of all races and nationalities are equally entitled to and should be equally guaranteed to, regardless of their level of economic development. Other labour standards, such as wages, hours of employment, length of holiday entitlement and other benefits reflect a country's level of development. As we saw earlier, these labour standards—unlike the basic labour/human rights—are and could remain different from country to country (Tsogas, 2000), and violations of these laws by many countries and companies continue to take place. However, many multinational companies are becoming increasingly concerned about the damages that such violations might inflict on their reputation as socially responsible businesses. See for instance Bies and Greenberg (2002) for a case involving Nike.

## European Union and HRM

Chapter 1 briefly noted that European organisations are constrained at both international (European Union) and national level by national culture and legislation (Brewster 1993, 1995). The European Union is the most prominent example of influence of regional rules and regulations on human resource management policies, through both institutional and non-institutional channels. This section discusses various relevant rules and regulations which are originated at the European Union level and cover most organisations operating within member states.

The first moves towards European integration were made as long ago as 1952 with the establishment of the European Coal and Steel Community. This was followed by the signing of the Treaty of Rome by six countries on 25 March 1957, which led to the establishment of the European Economic Community in 1958. The idea behind the Treaty was to strengthen the economic power of the member states and to increase their influence in the world. This was followed by two further founding treaties, as shown in Table 3.1.

The main objectives of the European Economic Community, as set out in Article 3 of the Treaty, were (a) the elimination of customs and restrictions on imports and exports between member states; (b) the establishment of a common customs tariff and a common commercial policy towards third countries; (c) the abolition of the obstacles to the free movement of persons, services and capital between member states; and (d) the setting up of a common agricultural policy.

**Table 3.1** European integration founding treaties

- The Treaty establishing the European Coal and Steel Community (ECSC), which was signed on 18 April 1951 in Paris, entered into force on 23 July 1952 and expired on 23 July 2002;
- The Treaty establishing the European Economic Community (EEC);
- The Treaty establishing the European Atomic Energy Community (Euratom), which was signed (along with the EEC Treaty) in Rome on 25 March 1957, and entered into force on 1 January 1958. These Treaties are often referred to as the 'Treaties of Rome'. When the term 'Treaty of Rome' is used, only the EEC Treaty is meant;
- The Treaty on European Union, which was signed in Maastricht on 7 February 1992, entered into force on 1 November 1993. The Maastricht Treaty changed the name of the European Economic Community to simply 'the European Community'. It also introduced new forms of cooperation between the member state governments—for example on defence, and in the area of 'justice and home affairs'. By adding this inter- governmental cooperation to the existing 'Community' system, the Maastricht Treaty created a new structure with three 'pillars' which is political as well as economic. This is the European Union (EU).

*Source*: Based on various sets of information on European Union website http://europa.eu.int/abc/treaties_en.htm

From the start, the Community intended to be much more than a customs union and it was designed to bring about the adoption of common economic and social policies by the participating states. The subtle change of the name from European Economic Community (EEC) to European Community (EC) and then European Union (EU) over time reflects the fact that the Community is about more than just an economic grouping.

In 1985 a major step was taken to materialise some of the hitherto unaccomplished objectives of the Community. The Commission was instructed by the member countries to investigate and report on various ways in which this could be done. A White Paper containing legislative proposals was submitted at the end of 1988 by the Commission in order to remove barriers within the Community. The report resulted in the Single European Market Act, which came into effect on 1 January 1993.

The Act specifically calls for the removal of physical, technical, financial and legal barriers to trade between the member states, leading to the establishment of a single internal market within which people, goods, services and capital can move freely. It is intended to cover and harmonise the following areas within the member states and between them and the outside countries: external relations; industrial relations and industrial affairs; competition; agriculture; transport; science, research and development; telecommunications, information technology and innovation; financial institutions and company law; energy; and customs levies and indirect taxation.

Since 1993, in response to the Single Market Act, there has been a rapid expansion in the number of mergers and acquisitions within the European Union. This means that increasingly companies with operation sites in more than one member state have to face up and respond to the new challenges that the Single Market is posing, with regard to among others, their human resource strategies. They have to, for instance, develop a greater European approach to employee relations, in part because according to the Single Market Act, employees, as well as capital and goods are free to move between member states and live and work wherever they wish without any legal barriers. As Teague (1993) argues, many of the better graduates will only join a company which gives them the prospect of working and living in another European country. As a result, it becomes increasingly difficult for enterprises to operate significantly different personnel policies, particularly when they involve large disparities in wages and conditions.

In order to take these developments into account the Commission proposed a Social Policy Agenda in 2000 which set out the employment areas in which further legislation was needed. The subsequent report entitled Industrial Relations in Europe, published in 2002, highlighted the principal advances made in this regard.

The Social Policy Agenda, which was adopted by the European Council meeting in Nice in December 2000, builds on the decisions made at Maastricht, in the Netherlands. The Maastricht Treaty placed the social partners and industrial relations at the heart of the European venture. The consultation process established by Article 138 of the Treaty and the social partners' ability to open negotiations on any topic coming within their responsibilities gives tangible recognition to their contribution. Europe has clearly opted for a system of labour relations based on the social partners' bargaining capacity. More than in other areas, this option distinguishes and gives a strong identity to the EU, which is not found in the other similarly developed regions.

The salient feature of labour relations in the EU member states is the role played by the social partners who represent the interests of employees and businesses. Recognition has been given to their rights, which are based on their ability to regulate, by means of agreements, numerous aspects of labour relations; at the same time, they have become partners of the public authorities in many economic and social fields. Today this partnership takes shape in different ways, in particular in the negotiation of national pacts and when the social partners are consulted on government initiatives and policies.

In addition, since the Luxembourg Summit in November 1997, the social partners have been closely associated in the European employment strategy. The 2001 employment guidelines further reinforced their involvement by confirming their participation in national action plans for employment and their role in monitoring and assessment, inviting them to establish their own process in accordance with their national traditions and practices.

The European employment strategy covers such areas as fundamental rights and equal opportunities, social protection, health and safety and industrial relations. Various initiatives within the European employment strategy framework are now in place at both sectoral and cross-industry levels.

For instance, a code of conduct concerning fundamental rights and equal opportunities was signed by the leather/tanning industry on 10 July 2000. This innovative code covers the guiding principles of health and safety at work, maximum working times, rest periods, overtime and minimum wages. It enforces respect for workers' dignity and strictly prohibits any physical abuse, threats and sexual harassment. The code also covers activities that are contracted out—even at international level—and establishes a number of control, verification and appeal mechanisms.

Health and safety issues, which are of paramount importance to workers, received similar attention. For example, in farming and the cleaning and sugar industries, information packs have been produced for workers and disseminated widely. The construction industry took part in the preparation and monitoring of Community law on health and safety. The code of conduct in the leather/tanning industry, mentioned earlier, includes also guidelines on health and safety.

Another prominent industrial relations area where EU-wide directives are in place concerns the establishment of a European works council to ensure consultation with employees on issues which affect them. Adopted in 1994, the directives build on the Community Charter of Fundamental Social Rights of Workers, which provides, *inter alia*, that information, consultation and participation for workers must be developed along appropriate lines, taking account of the practices in force in different member states. The Charter states that 'this shall apply especially in companies or group of companies having establishments or companies in two or more Member States'.

The directives specify that in order to guarantee that the employees of companies operating in two or more member states are properly informed and consulted it is necessary to set up European Works Councils or to create other suitable procedures for the transnational information and consultation of employees. In accordance with the principle of autonomy of the parties, it is for the representatives of employees and the management of the company to determine by agreement the nature, composition, the function, mode of operation, procedures and financial resources of European Works Council or other information and consultation procedures so as to suit their own particular circumstances.

As Burmester (2000) points out, with the evolution of European integration from a customs union to a political union, the EU's influence over all business between its member states begins to rival, even overtake, that of the members within their territories. EU law applies directly within the member states, and is enforced by the national courts of those states. In future, business enterprises expanding into or within the Union will give as much consideration to the EU institutions as to particular host states when engaged in political risk assessment.

■ **CHAPTER SUMMARY**

Companies have to interact with their external environment constantly and this interaction has implications for their HRM and other internal organisational operations as well as their overall business strategies. Salient among the constituent factors of this external environment are various social, political and economic institutions, such as political regime, government, legal systems, trade unions, employers' associations and so forth. It is important to note that the huge differences among various nations with regard to these institutions are major factors pushing for divergence in HRM policies and practices adopted by companies operating within them.

Global and regional conventions and agreements such as the International Labour Organisation and the European Union also form a part of external environment. Directives and policies laid out by these institutions are ultimately translated into practices in the workplaces within the countries which are signatories to them. The Social Policy Agenda of the European Union was cited as an example of a supranational factor which requires managers in member states to incorporate certain employee rights into their HRM policies and practices.

By setting out common directives and requirements, global and regional institutions such as those discussed in the chapter act as a 'push factor' for convergence of certain HRM policies and practices in member states.

■ **REVISION QUESTIONS**

1. Why is it important to know about national institutions within the context of a multinational company's HRM?

2. What are the most significant national institutions in this respect?

3. Choose any two of these and explain how they might influence a company's HRM.

4. Give two examples of national institutions in your own country and describe how they might have impacts on the HRM policies and practices of domestic and foreign companies.

**5.** Is your country a member of national and regional institutions similar to those discussed in this chapter? What directives and rulings have they got that might be relevant to the companies operating in your country?

# Case study: Elementis and Michelin

The companies some of whose HRM policies form the basis of this case are subsidiaries of two multinational companies located in Scotland.

## Health and safety in Elementis

Elementis is a subsidiary of an American multinational chemicals manufacturing company and is located in the industrial central belt of Scotland. It has 60 employees and makes additives that alter the flow of substances. It has an excellent safety management performance and its care for environment record has won various national and regional awards.

The company works to corporate standards tailored to US culture and environment but modified to comply with UK regulations. They also comply with health and safety regulations specific to Scotland. For instance, in the US window glass must be tinted in order to protect computer operators from the reflection of sunshine on their screens, but in the UK this is not acceptable and office windows must have adjustable blinds or curtains instead of tinted glass. As a result, the office windows have both tinted glass and curtains.

'Our subsidiary's rules contents reflect all the health and safety aspects of the corporation, all the way from Houston down to Erskine [in Scotland]. There are 43 standard operational procedures from the US, added to that are EU and UK and Scotland, even local council regulations. The parent company involvement is limited to us having to comply to the 43 items which come from the US. If there are conflicts between these and the UK ones, the latter take precedence.'

Compliance to local rules is part of the company's strategy, and indeed its legal obligation. In the US each state has a different set of regulations, as a result each subsidiary has to be compliant to its respective local regulations.

The decentralisation of health and safety matters goes beyond the obligation to comply with local rules and regulations. The subsidiaries have specific health and safety initiatives which are sharper than is the norm in many companies because they are at the near end of the industry. They have short term initiatives as they need to respond to accidents and problems immediately. They must be able to change things within weeks. The Head Office takes a more long-term approach to health and safety (2–3 years time scales).

## Industrial relations in Michelin

Michelin, the well-known manufacturer of tyres, is a French company with subsidiaries in 80 locations and 125,000 employees around the world, including Germany, Spain, Poland, USA, Asia, Mexico, Brazil and Columbia. It was established in 1889, and has its headquarters in Claremont, France. The majority of the factories are in France and the company has a huge segment of the French market. The Dundee site (in Scotland) is 27 years old and has just under 1,100 employees.

The company is unionised and around 750 of its employees are represented by two unions: Transport and General Workers Union (TGWU) and Amalgamated Engineering Workers Union (AEWU).

The union recognition agreement that the company employs states the employees' rights in terms of bargaining with their employer and covers all wages and conditions of the 750 members.

'We develop our policies, or wish list if you like, through consultation with our members, an awareness of economic situation within the company and external to the company and we are provided with a whole host of support resources from the union research department and at the end of the day we determine the employment policy issues we wish to develop. So its not AEWU or TGWU dictating what issues we should peruse. It's up to us to arrive at what we believe is in the best interests of our members with an awareness of the policies of the union. Within that we have a lot of flexibility. We would then submit our proposals to the personnel department who would then circulate to the other three UK sites. They will then be discussed at the annual meeting of the union convenors and lay delegates of the four sites.'

The union officials also seek advice from their international affiliates and academics to inform themselves on such matters as current rates of pay, allowances and benefits, and get a feel of the overall health of the industry in general and the direction it is going in, the kind of technology that is employed, and the effect of globalisation on the tyre industry.

'We also meet on an international basis through tyre organisations [i.e. trade unions] and the Transnational Information Exchange, a Dutch based organisation for the labour movement. And through that we sometimes get European funds. We would pull on people from Brazil, America, Europe and Japan and we would exchange information. So we are a very well organised industry at the trade union level.

We believe it's in our interest to ensure that minimum standards are applied within the UK and the best way for us to understand what is happening in the industry and to achieve those minimal standards across the board so we are not played off against one another, is to have this sort of meetings where we exchange information. It is also a good vehicle for us to see new trends coming in and to point us in the right direction that Michelin may not have raised with us yet but that we know is getting raised in other multinationals and it's coming to our door soon; it allows us to educate ourselves and make ourselves aware of relevant issues.'

Under the legislation regarding the European Works Councils, the unions have negotiated with Michelin to set up a works council in the Scottish subsidiary and work out employee representation through the council.

In the last two decades or so there has been a sea change in UK industrial relations, especially in those companies where employers have recognised trade unions and see them as a valuable asset. In order to succeed, the relationship had to change from one of adversarial, confrontational, and industrial muscle vs capital to one based on mutual respect and co-operation. 'These were recipes which were ruining British industry in the manufacturing base in the past', says one of the union officials in Michelin, which is located in Dundee, a city known for its strong working class traditions and entrenched support for trade unions (see also Tayeb, 1998).

In the current atmosphere of cooperation, 'we believe that with a strong trade union organisation and open management style and new HRM policies being deployed in a way that isn't selfish but respect people and benefits the community that it represents in the factory then you can be very successful. We had a very adversarial, confrontational position 10 years ago. Now we are possibly seen as one of the most progressive sites, certainly in industrial relations terms, within Michelin and probably within Scotland.'

In addition to direct negotiations between shop stewards and the management, there are communication channels through which the employees' 'voices are heard' within the company. For instance the management has twice surveyed employees' opinions in the past to seek their views on various issues; it also holds frequent team meetings and briefings. The team meetings, especially when they are organised by shopfloor employees at which managers also attend, provide an opportunity to employees to get their voice heard on the issues they choose to discuss.

The issues that employees and management discuss and seek agreement on cover a wide range, from pay and benefits, to working patterns, weekly working hours and overtime, extending the production line, increasing production volume, new projects, lay offs and redundancies, and financing the retraining of the employees who may be made redundant, so that they can find another job.

## ■ CASE STUDY QUESTIONS

**1.** What are the various issues and regulations that Elementis managers take into account when devising their health and safety policies? Can they ignore some or all of them? Why?

**2.** What was the climate of industrial relations like in Michelin in the past and what is it like now? What caused the change?

**3.** How do employees get their views and preferences known to the management?

**4.** What role does the trade union play in this process?

**5.** What main policies are the unions able to influence in Michelin? And how do they inform themselves of relevant issues in order to strengthen their negotiating position?

**6.** In what ways do national and international institutions influence some of the policies and practices that these two subsidiaries employ?

## ■ RECOMMENDED FURTHER READING

Lane, C. (1995). *Industry and Society in Europe: Stability and Change in Britain, Germany and France*. Aldershot: Edward Elgar.

Budhwar, P. S. and Debrah, Y. (eds), (2001). *HRM in Developing Countries*. London: Routledge.

Warner, M. (ed.), (1999). *Management in Emerging Countries*. London: International Thomson Business Press.

Online:

European Union (http://europa.eu.int/)

International Labour Organisation (http://www.ilo.org/public/english/)

### ■ REFERENCES

Bies, R. J. and Greenberg, J. (2002). 'Justice, culture and corporate image; the swoosh, the sweatshops and the sway of public opinion', in M. J. Gannon and K. L. Newman (eds), *Handbook of Cross-Cultural Management*. Oxford: Blackwell.

Brewster, C. (1993). 'Developing a "European" model of human resource management', *International Journal of Human Resource Management*, vol. 4, pp. 765–84.

—— (1995). 'Towards a European model of human resource management', *Journal of International Business*, vol. 26, pp. 1–22.

Burmester, B. (2000). 'Global and regional institutions: the international governance of international business', in M. H. Tayeb (ed.), *International Business: Theories, Policies and Practices*. London: Pearson Education. Chapter 3.

Child, J. and Tayeb, M. H. (1983). 'Theoretical perspectives in cross-national organizational research', *International Studies of Management and Organization*, XII, pp. 23–70.

Davis, L. E. and North, D. C. (1971). *Institutional Change and American Economic Growth*: Cambridge: Cambridge University Press.

DiMaggio, P. J. and Powell, W. W. (eds), (1991). *The New Institutionalism in Organizational Analysis*. Chicago: University of Chicago Press.

Florkowski, G. W. and Nath, R. (1993). 'MNC responses to the legal environment of international human resource management', *The International Journal of Human Resource Management*, vol. 4, pp. 305–24.

Harry, W. (2003). 'Concluding case study: the international manager's world', in M. H. Tayeb (ed.), *International Management: Theories and Practices*. London: Pearson Education Chapter 14.

Lane, C. (1995). *Industry and Society in Europe: Stability and Change in Britain, Germany and France*. Aldershot: Edward Elgar.

Negandhi, A. R., Eshgi, G. S., and Yuen, E. C. (1985). 'The management practices of Japanese subsidiaries overseas', *California Management Review*, vol. 27, pp. 93–105.

North, D. C. (1990). *Institutions, Institutional Change and Economic Performance*. Cambridge: Cambridge University Press.

Strier, F. (1984). 'Quality circles in the United States: fad or fixture?', *Business Forum*. Summer.

Tayeb, M. H. (1988). *Organizations and National Culture: A Comparative Analysis*. London: Sage Publications.

—— (1998). 'Transfer of HRM policies and practices across cultures: an American company in Scotland', *International Journal of Human Resource Management*, vol. 9, no. 2, pp. 332–58.

—— (1999a). 'Foreign remedies for local difficulties: the case of three Scottish manufacturing firms', *International Journal of Human Resource Management*, vol. 10, no. 5, pp. 842–57.

—— (1999b). 'Management in Iran', in M Warner (ed.), *Management in Emerging Countries*. London: International Thomson Business Press. pp. 316–23.

Teague, P. (1993). 'Towards social Europe?', *The International Journal of Human Resource Management*, vol. 4, no. 2, pp. 349–76.

Tsogas, G. (1999). 'Labour standards in international trade agreements: a critical assessment of the arguments,' *International Journal of Human Resource Management* (April).

—— (2000). 'Labour standards, corporate codes of conduct and labour regulation in international trade', in M. H. Tayeb (ed.), *International Business: Theories, Policies and Practices*. London: Pearson Education. Chapter 4.

Turnbull, P. (1986). 'The "Japanisation" of production and industrial relations at Lucas Electrical', *Industrial Relations Journal*, vol. 17, pp. 193–206.

# 4 National Context of HRM: The Case of Seven Major Economies

## Learning outcomes

When you finish reading this chapter you should:
- Be familiar with the main work-related cultural characteristics of some major economies located in different parts of the world
- Know principal HRM and other employee management policies and practices prevalent in those economies
- be able to trace the roots of at least some of these policies and practices in the cultural and non-cultural characteristics of those economies
- have a fair idea of the difficulties and challenges that multinational companies may experience if they set up subsidiaries in those economies
- understand, through a study of the closing case, the challenges involved when a company decides to implement HRM policies and practices originating in countries other than their own.

## Introduction

The previous two chapters discussed major cultural, non-cultural and institutional contextual factors which have a significant bearing on a company's HRM policies and practices. The present chapter examines the implications of these contextual factors for HRM in seven major economies which are different from one another in significant ways.

Between them, they provide a fair representative sample of modern nations ranging from the most economically advanced to those on their way to full industrialisation and economic development. The wide range of HRM and general management styles in these countries serves to highlight the diverse and complex world within which multinational companies operate. Later in the book Chapter 7 will discuss the issues concerned with the applicability of HRM best practices given this diverse and complex world and explore the various strategies that companies can employ to deal with these issues. But for the moment it suffices to say that the economically advanced nations in the sample are not only home to the vast majority of multinational companies but they also host to an equally large number of the companies originating elsewhere. The emerging economies in the sample are major net recipients of foreign investment and host a large number of multinational companies. So there is a constant flow of best practices between these nations in various directions.

To do justice to this issue, each of the economies discussed here would require a book on its own; the coverage here will of necessity be brief. But the recommended further reading at the end of the chapter should help you follow up the chapter's discussions further.

## Major economies and their HRM practices

The United States, the European Union and Japan, the so-called triad, are home to the vast majority of multinational companies; they also host a large number of them. The number of multinational companies originating in other countries is much smaller in comparison, especially in developing countries of Africa, Asia and Latin America, although these host quite a lot of them. The issue of relevance to this chapter is that, compared to the developing nations, the triad countries' multinational firms are more likely to be in a position to decide whether or not to take their home-grown HRM strategies, policies and practices to their host countries. In addition, notwithstanding serious and justified academic and practical challenges, because of the phenomenal success of the triad's companies and also the extensive management research conducted in many of their universities and business schools, companies in most of the rest of the world have looked upon them as models and sources of managerial innovations. It is therefore important to explore HRM and other employee management issues in the triad first and then compare them with the practices in a sample of other countries. The comparison will allow us to examine whether or not the triad's management practices can be successfully transferred to these other nations and indeed between themselves.

For reason of space, six countries and one region will be included in the chapter: US, Japan and UK representing the industrialised and developed world, Turkey, India, Arab Middle East and China, representing the developing and emerging economies. Turkey in addition fulfils another role: it is one of the countries that because of their geopolitical locations, straddling as they do Asia and Europe, have provided a cultural and economic bridge between East and West. As such Turkey is a country where Eastern and Western ideas in many spheres ranging from politics to management styles have been tried out with varying degrees of success.

The discussion of these nations focuses primarily on their cultural characteristics and their implications for HRM, but other contextual factors, such as political economic conditions will be referred to where appropriate. The reason for this is that cultural characteristics change very slowly and can indeed last for centuries in many cases, and therefore their impact on work-related attitudes and values, and in turn on HRM, are long-lasting and more observable in the long-term as well as short-term. Political and economic conditions, on the other hand, are more volatile and can change much more quickly and their long-term consequences for HRM are therefore more tentative and speculative. Who could have, for instance, foreseen in 1988, that within a few years the political economic conditions in the

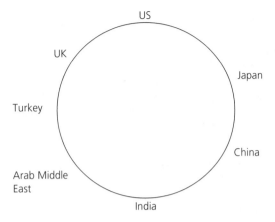

**Figure 4.1** Seven major economies of the world

then Soviet Union and eastern/central European countries would change so drastically that almost all Communist-inspired management practices would be swept aside?

The discussion of HRM in the above nations and their cultural contexts is organised in the following order:

Japan
United States
United Kingdom
Turkey
Arab Middle East
India
China

Figure 4.1 shows that these countries in fact circle the earth and thus encompass and represent the diversity and complexity of our world.

## HRM in Japan

Japan's success in the international market in the past few decades has encouraged many researchers and practitioners to learn about the country's culture and the ways in which its companies are managed. In many countries managers have also tried to emulate Japanese management policies and practices, with varying degrees of success.

Japan, unlike the United states for instance, has a homogenous culture and foreign immigrants make up a very small percentage of its population. As a result, the cultural characteristics attributed to the Japanese are shared by almost all the people, barring some individual and regional variations. As you will notice in Table 4.1, the society as a whole is characterised by a strong sense of group and community. In Hofstede's (1980) study Japan scored 46 on individualism—compare this with the US's 91 and UK's 89. The Japanese loyalty is to the group to which they belong and for which they are prepared to sacrifice their personal interests.

The extent of Japanese collectivism can be illustrated by comparing the in-group in Japan with that of individualistic nations such as Britain and even the collectivist India. The in-group

**Table 4.1** Major Japanese national cultural characteristics and management practices

*National Culture*
- collectivism: group-orientation, a strong sense of community, loyalty to group
- masculine: competitive, ambitious
- endurance: the way of warrior, acceptance of hardship without complaint
- indebtedness: a strong sense of duty and obligation
- absence of horizontal social groupings: vertical stratification by institution or group
- observance of social status: deference to seniors, status clearly signalled in social interactions
- harmony: preference for consensus over conflict
- avoidance of loss of face
- high uncertainty avoidance

*HRM and other employee related values and practices*
- enterprise-based trade unions, cooperative relationship between employees and company, avoidance of open conflict
- emotional and dependent relation between company and employees
- *ringi* method: collective decision making
- quality circles
- implicit discreet performance appraisal
- teamwork: multi-skill work teams, team appraisal and reward
- *nenko*: life-time (or long-term) employment for regular core employees
- seniority-based pay and promotion
- process-oriented
- a strong sense of obligation to colleagues and supervisors
- discrimination against women
- employee-oriented leadership style
- job-rotation, job-flexibility
- employee loyalty and long-term commitment to company

in Britain includes only the immediate nuclear family—spouse, children, and sometimes a spouse's widowed or infirm parent. In India, the in-group not only includes the immediate family, but also the extended one—grandparents, brothers, sisters, uncles, aunts, nephews, nieces, and other relatives and close friends. In Japan, there is an additional member in the in-group: the company for which a person works.

The Japanese are very hard working and, in the words of an expert in the subject (Buruma, 1985, p. 139) have 'an infinite capacity for hardship and pain'. They also have a strong sense of duty and indebtedness, *on*. This sense of obligation and repayment of *on* can sometimes span across generations. The present author was once told by a Japanese acquaintance that his great grandfather had helped build a house for a neighbour. Generations later, the great grandson of that neighbour financially helped my Japanese friend to complete his studies at university. Similar debt repayments can also happen at company levels. It is widely believed that in 2003 Canon agreed to buy Mizuho shares, at the time that the latter was in financial trouble, largely to repay an old debt to Fuji Bank, a member of the same *keiretsu* as Mizuho. Fuji Bank had rescued Canon when it fell into trouble over 30 years ago (*The Economist*, 22 March 2003).

There is an absence of western-style horizontal social class system in Japan. The overall picture of the society is that of vertical stratification by institution or group of institutions. For example, a shopfloor technician does not identify himself with all the technicians in the country or with the working class in general. Rather, he identifies himself with his workplace and all those people who work for it. Japanese enterprise unions, discussed below, are a manifestation of this vertical structure.

The absence of a western-type class structure, however, does not mean an absence of status differentiation and its acknowledgement. Status is clearly signalled in other ways, such as the extent to which one bows when meeting others, sitting arrangements at tables, order of serving meals, the time given to people to speak in groups, and the terms one uses to address people of different ages and professions. The Japanese language itself is such that the relative status of any two speakers is signalled immediately. The correct behaviour is so important that if they do not know each others' professional status, on being introduced to one another they immediately exchange business cards to know where everybody stands (Briggs, 1988).

Trade unions in Japan are company-based. For example, Toyota has its own union, as does Nissan and Hitachi. Compare this with Britain where unions are craft-based and cut across companies and other organisations. For example, fire-fighters have their own union (Fire Brigades Union), coal miners theirs (National Union of Mineworkers), teachers theirs (National Union of Teachers), and so on. The character of Japanese unions and management is moulded by the company culture, and the relationship between the two sides are based on cooperation and harmony.

Another characteristic of Japanese enterprises is the *ringi* method of decision making. This involves a great deal of informal consultation and problem solving, leading to the preparation of a written proposal which is circulated first to those who would be affected by the implementation of the proposal and then to senior management. *Ringi* methods are very time consuming and are thus used for more important decisions only (Misumi, 1984). Employees, especially at operating levels, are also encouraged, indeed expected, to take part in the decision-making processes by putting their suggestions for improvement or new ideas in a 'suggestion box' located prominently in the company premises. Most ideas, however, never make it as far as the top senior managers and are quietly shelved by middle managers unwilling to risk offering their own endorsement. The new ideas that do get through this process are put into effect with speed.

Quality circles are another vehicle for employee participation. A quality circle is a small-group activity in which ordinary blue- and white-collar workers, usually employed on broadly similar work and led by their supervisor, volunteer to participate. Such volunteers are trained in problem-identification and problem-solving techniques. The voluntary nature of quality circles and the devotion that it requires of the participants appear to be in tune with the Japanese collectivist culture. In addition, their success in Japan is sustained by certain other management practices, such as lifetime employment, which creates a stable work environment with virtually no fear of unemployment; the seniority wage system, which encourages loyalty to the firm; and Japanese companies' high levels of investment in employee training.

Life-time employment or *nenko* is not a matter of law, but normal practice in all major enterprises. In its pure form, this would mean that employees are hired on leaving full-time education, and remain with the same company for the duration of their working lives, undertaking a range of jobs and in many cases progressing up the hierarchy. However, *nenko* is operated only by large firms, and offered to no more that one-third of Japan's labour force, the so-called regular employees. Part time, temporary or contract workers, who may be employed on the basis of existing skills, for specific jobs and specific periods, comprise the remaining two-thirds of the workforce.

Workers join the company at a relatively low starting salary, related to age and educational standard, which then rises gradually and by increment until retirement. As Whittaker (2000) points out, the seniority-based wage and promotion system reinforces the long-term employment arrangement. However, although the wage itself is not dependent upon the level of work done, there is a merit element in the pay-packet, which is evaluation-based, and therefore discourages coasting or complacency that might creep in with job security. This merit element takes the form of award of bonuses which relate to individual performance and the company profits, and thus provides an additional monetary incentive since these can in total add up to about a third of the earnings.

The Japanese see their company as a family which is primarily a social entity though operating in an economic environment. This view of the company has arguably resulted in a high level of employee commitment to, and even emotional dependence on it (Hofstede, 1980). The situation contrasts with the West where a firm is overwhelmingly an economic entity and employee involvement with it is non-emotional and strictly contractual. However, economic 'facts of life' in recent years have eroded much of the Japanese employees' long-term commitment to the company. Equipped with technical, linguistic or artistic skills that older workers perhaps never acquired, younger workers are changing jobs more frequently. By instinct, they are job-hoppers, part-timers, moonlighters, and even telecom-muters (*The Economist*, 4 March 1989 and 10 August 1991). There are, however, some executives who try to reinforce corporate loyalty by building ever more luxurious company-owned housing, sports centres and resorts for staff. Such perks are difficult to give up even for the promise of a higher salary. Moreover, employers appear to have fostered loyalty so well that even though job-hopping is increasing, only a small percentage of workers switch companies (*The Financial Times*, 20 February 1991).

Team work and a consensus style of management are often regarded as a distinctive characteristic of Japanese companies. Employees are said to view themselves as members of a community rather than hired labour (Marchington and Parker, 1988). Many observers stress the importance of consensus and teamwork, of managers attempting to seek the approval of their subordinates in reaching decisions, and in the processes attached to discussions between workers and their foremen (see for example White and Trevor, 1983; Bradley and Hill, 1983).

Researchers argue that the early-morning meetings in Japanese companies are not for their obvious media description as fitness and exercise sessions, but for their team building aspects. Employee involvement at the task level is seen as a normal feature of affairs, as too is a commitment to the team (Wickens, 1987). Japanese managers are able to harness this group-orientation, one obvious example being the quality circle, as discussed above.

One of the factors which contribute to the cohesion among team members is their strong sense of obligation, not only to each other but also to their immediate supervisor. In turn, the supervisor's debt to his or her workers develops as a result of their contributions to his or her success. A senior member of staff who attains promotion will not forget the junior member whose contribution was so valuable. It is seldom that a favour will go unacknowledged (Briggs, 1988).

Job rotation, leading to job-flexibility, is another feature of Japanese companies. Unlike American companies, the Japanese do not recruit in order to fill specialised job-slots. New recruits, selected on their broad qualifications, undergo an induction period in which they are socialised into their new corporate 'community' before their initial workplace training. They are then trained 'in-house' by rotation between different departments, dealing with specific company problems. The early stages of rotation for non-manual workers and managers involve also experience of working on the shopfloor. Subsequent assignments reflect long-term human resource development objectives, strategic development and current production considerations. At the end of a long-drawn out process the employees are capable of doing any number of jobs. This system is obviously compatible with and complements the implicit, but not necessarily contractual, long-term employment offered to regular, core employees.

Japanese companies operate a rigidly hierarchical system but the barriers between blue and white collar workers are not synonymous with class, as is the case for instance in Britain. Class markers such as different dining rooms, segmented car parks, and others are absent. Open-plan offices accommodate directors and other senior managers together with the rank and file employees under the same roof (Tayeb, 1994). This illustrates the egalitarian nature of the Japanese management system. Briggs, however, argues that the absence of these class markers is misleading, since status is so clearly signalled in other ways. For instance the finely graded hierarchy which exists within the organisations is explicitly mirrored in the language, and is thus apparent to all.

## HRM in the United States

The US, a nation of immigrants, is truly a 'melting pot' in terms of the diversity of ethnic background and cultural heritage of its people, referred to hereafter as Americans. It is therefore unwise to talk with much certainty about 'American culture', or 'American HRM' for that matter. However, like many other culturally diverse countries (e.g. India and China) one can identify certain characteristics which are more or less common among the people of the country as a whole. Table 4.2 gives a summary of major American cultural values and attitudes and some of their manifestations in American companies.

As the Table shows, prominent among American national cultural characteristics is individualism. Americans are independent, ambitious and individualistic, place a high value on freedom and believe that individuals can shape and control their own destinies. But as Lawrence (2000) points out, American individualism is not expressive and it is not about being different; rather it focuses on achievement, and above all on economic achievement. People pursue mainly their own interests and those of their immediate family—the in-group definitely does not include the workplace. The primary commitment and loyalty of the individuals do not therefore lie with the company or any other larger groupings of which they may be a member. Contrast this with the Japanese culture discussed above. The Americans, however, do display a high level of collectivism and group-orientation in the face of a common threat, for instance, as we all witnessed in the aftermath of the 11 September 2001 terrorist attacks on the World Trade Center's twin towers in New York, and on happy and festive occasions such as the annual national Independence celebrations on 4 July.

Individualism informs and inspires American management and the ethic of personal achievement which runs through it: hard work and long hours when necessary, individual employees' readiness to take decision, personal initiative, strong presentation of personal image, promotion and high incomes as reward for success (Lawrence, 2000). In addition, the individualistic nature of the society encourages managers to promote on the basis of merits as opposed to status, hierarchy, or gender. And unlike for instance many Arab countries where reward and

**Table 4.2** Major American national cultural characteristics and management practices

*National Culture*
- highly individualistic: self-focused, preference to act as individuals rather than as members of a group, yet can be collectivist in the face of a common threat
- small power distance: egalitarian, tend not to treat people differently even when there are great differences in age or social standing
- masculine: ambitious, competitive, goal-oriented, achievers
- low uncertainty avoidance, risk-takers, entrepreneurial
- low context: directness, expressive in communication, do not talk around things, tend to say exactly what they mean
- open: friendly, informal
- ethnocentric: believe their culture and values are superior to all others
- future-oriented: strong belief that present ways of doing things inevitably are to be replaced by even better ways
- readiness to change: try new things, a predisposition to believe that new is good
- 'can-do' attitude

*HRM and other employee related values and practices*
- prefer participative leadership style
- superiors are approachable
- subordinates are willing to question authority
- status based on how well people perform their functions
- performance-oriented
- promotion and reward based on merits as opposed to status, hierarchy, or gender
- live more easily with uncertainty, sceptical about rules and regulations
- value punctuality and keep appointments and calendars
- much more concerned with their own careers and personal success than about the welfare of the organisation or the group
- value success and profit
- acceptance of conflict
- system-driven: conviction that all problems can be solved, system and energy will overcome any obstacle
- proactive: take initiative, aim high, 'go for it'
- result-oriented
- professional: educated and well trained
- strong devotion to managerial prerogative
- hire and fire policies
- communications skill, informal, direct, explicit, often aggressive
- emphasis on entrepreneurship and innovation
- legalist approach to contracts
- informality yet a preference for written rules and procedures
- dislike of trade unions
- preference for HRM over unionisation

promotion are on the basis of loyalty, in the US the reward system is performance oriented and status is based on how well people perform their functions.

The emphasis on individual freedom and success includes freedom to pursue one's career progression by moving from one company to another in pursuit of success. A by-product of employees' careerism in pursuit of success is that their company too feels free to dispense with them in pursuit of its success, that is, it hires and fires people at will and/or when market conditions justify it. For instance, in heavy-engineering firms, such as steel, cars and aerospace, employees are routinely laid off in a slump and rehired when business picks up. Also, large American companies typically hire people to fill particular jobs. Their senior managers know that Americans are mobile people, who have a limited commitment to any particular employer or part of the country. As a result jobs are clearly defined and so are the skills needed to fill them. Contrast this with the situation in many large Japanese companies, discussed earlier, where the relationship between employee and company is based on long-term commitment on both sides and employees are trained to be 'all-rounders' rather than specialists to perform only certain types of jobs.

In this connection, the starkly different approaches which Mazda and Chrysler adopted in reaction to the common threat of bankruptcy in the early 1980s, are interesting. Mazda viewed its workforce as an asset that had to be retained at all cost. Instead of cutting jobs, the firm's managers agreed to a 25% salary cut and a loss of bonuses for four years. Chrysler, in contrast, cut its blue-collar workforce by 28%, its white-collar staff by 7% and its executives' pay by 1–2% (*The Economist*, 24 November 1990).

This kind of attitude to employees is exemplified also in the advice given a few years ago to Germany by the American news magazine *Time*. The magazine identified high unemployment as one of the major problems of the German economy, and advised the politicians to accelerate labour-market reform to allow easier hiring and firing of workers (*Time*, 14 September 1995, p. 28), a policy which goes against the grain in Germany's social-market economic system.

In organisations, Americans prefer participative management; superiors are usually approachable and subordinates are more willing to question authority. Americans live more easily with uncertainty compared with many other nations, a characteristic which facilitates participation in decision-making and risk taking. (US scored 46 on uncertainty avoidance in Hofstede's 1980 study, well below the average for the sample.) Together with individualism, tolerance for uncertainty also accounts for the entrepreneurial and 'go-getter' spirit and competitiveness which underpin the business culture of the country.

A prominent feature of the US business culture is its anti-trade unionism. A vast majority of American employees work in the non-unionised sector, and the power of employers in both organised and non-organised sectors is very high in both political and economic spheres. Also, the opposition of employers to unions has been especially intense since the mid 1970s. Throughout most of the non-unionised sector, redundant workers can be laid off in whatever order the employer desires, and employment contracts terminated for any or no reason. Furthermore, the conditions under which employment takes place are essentially employer-determined, limited only by labour-market forces and the protective labour legislation (Wheeler, 1993), notably the minimum wage law. In addition, many, especially large, American companies prefer to deal with their employees through human resource management policies and practices rather than recognition of unions. HRM in fact has replaced the need for workplace unionisation as far as these companies are concerned.

Americans dislike rules and regulations but do use them in their organisations and in the society at large. This is a culture characterised by, among others, a written constitution, clearly defined roles and functions, minutely spelled-out and legally enforced business contracts and a greater use of written formal rules than many other cultures; a culture which took up Weber's (1947) bureaucratic model and worked it into a model of professionalism.

The Americans' professionalism is also reflected in their business education; they invented MBA and MBO (management by objectives) and coined the term HRM, and arguably invented modern management. The interactive system based on MBO is common in American organisations, and can produce beneficial results such as high output, greater corporate awareness and employee commitment to the company, but can also lead to greater bureaucracy and overproduction in certain areas. However, although MBO schemes have been used by some companies elsewhere outside the US, they do not fit in with the culture of many countries (Hofstede, 1980) and have not been enthusiastically embraced by them.

American companies have some of the highest employee working hours, productivity rates and employee training expenditure in the world. They take training of their employees at all levels very seriously even though the trained employees may later leave if another company offers them better pay, working conditions and promotion prospects.

Most US multinational companies tend to have ethnocentric policies in their HRM, and indeed in many other aspects of their management, in relation to their foreign subsidiaries. They normally allow a limited amount of deviation from their centrally-determined strategy, especially with respect to host-country legal requirements where compliance is not negotiable. They also allow local managers some discretion to make modifications in the implementation of their strategy. For instance, the overall decision on training strategy and policy is taken at the HQ but subsidiaries can choose whether to provide their training programmes in-house or contract them out (Tayeb and Dott, 2000).

## HRM in the United Kingdom

The UK, as its full name implies, is a united kingdom comprising four nations: Scotland, England, Wales and Northern Ireland, each with certain distinctive cultural characteristics. However, they also share many common values and institutions which bind them together. Table 4.3 summarises those common features that are relevant to the focus of this chapter.

The British are highly individualistic and greatly value their individual liberty; at the same time they care for their community and engage in collective action when for instance they disagree with certain government policies. This collectivism is manifested also in the UK's strong trade union traditions whose roots can be traced to the 18th and 19th centuries. Union membership is craft based and cuts across firms and organisations. As a result there are likely to be several unions represented in the same factory or office, bargaining not just with employers but against each other. British unions, unlike their counterparts in some other European countries such as France and (pre-1989) Poland, are more pragmatic in their approach. They fight for better pay settlements and better working conditions within the present economic and social system rather than engage in class struggle and ideological battles for the overthrow of the system. They see their role as one of representing the workforce, pushing for objectives that are consciously desired by the workers themselves. Since the 1980s, a combination of decline in membership and anti-union legislation has greatly diminished the powers of the trade unions.

Individualism appears also to influence the relationship between employees and their bosses and their work organisations. This relationship is strictly contractual. British employees, unlike for instance their Japanese counterparts, do not expect their superiors to look after them and to help them with their personal difficulties. This would be an invasion of their privacy. To them a manager who is concerned with the employees' well being is one who, for instance, provides them with up-to-date equipment so that they can perform their tasks better. In other words, managers and workers have an impersonal and task-oriented relationship with one another (Tayeb, 1994).

British employees, similar to the Americans, are career-oriented and join another company if better prospects beckon. However, unlike in America, managers tend to spend much less

**Table 4.3** Major British national cultural characteristics and management practices

*National Culture*
- individualism: autonomy, liberty, love of privacy, yet caring for community
- small power distance, yet deference and acceptance of inequality, class conscious
- aggressive, yet caring and friendly
- reserve: shy, self-control, self-discipline
- high ideals of conduct both for themselves and for others
- conservatism: dislike of change and uncertainty, aversion to risk, lack of ambition
- tenacity: resilience, resourcefulness
- pragmatism: social-political realism, compromise, flexible, unwritten constitution, common law, prepared to bend the law when it does not suit them
- chauvinism: dislike of foreigners, xenophobia
- honesty, trustworthy, and trusting
- past-orientation: love of age-old traditions, the present is a culmination of past developments, ambivalence towards new technology
- dislike of open conflict

*HRM and other employee related values and practices*
- preference to have freedom to choose their own approach, using individual skills and abilities
- job satisfaction derived from personal sense of achievement and superior's recognition of individual contributions
- leadership style: persuasive
- expectation from subordinate: commitment, initiative, ownership, responsibility, honesty
- deference to authority
- comfortable with minimal amount of rules and procedures
- flexibility yet a preference to work according to the rules
- well educated, skilled and, in certain circumstances, adaptable workforces
- compliance with legislation
- short-term perspective: low expenditure on training and low employee productivity rates compared to many leading economies
- some evidence of discrimination among employees and job applicants on the ground of age, gender or ethnicity, 'glass ceiling'
- formal in communication and interpersonal relationships at work
- ethnocentric attitudes towards foreign counterparts
- conservative approach towards new technology
- contractual, non-emotional relationship with the workplace
- strong trade union tradition
- pragmatic trade unions: fight for better pay and working conditions not ideologically-based class struggle against managers, absence of serious trade union challenge to management's prerogatives and right to manage
- class distinction's reflection within the workplace in the form of hostile them-and-us attitude
- expectation of governmental involvement in employment relationships

on employee training. As a result, the British workforce has far lower productivity rates than the Americans, and indeed workers in many other leading economies.

In Hofstede's (1980) study Britain scored low on power distance relative to many other nations, but people do not really care as much about equality as they do about liberty. Both inside and outside the workplace the Britons are deferential to their seniors; opposition to authority is usually indirect and sometimes wrapped up in humour rather than direct challenge. Yet at the same time, they do not like to be ordered about and hate to be dictated to. In effect, they respect authority only when it is used well.

The acceptance of power inequality is also noticeable in the British class consciousness. Almost everybody one speaks with can place themselves in one class or other. Family background, education, and even accent betray people's social class. In organisations, the class system is mirrored in the different treatments accorded to manual workers and low-level office workers, on the one hand, and to managers and other high-ranking office staff on the other. Managers and other white-collar employees have normally greater advantages over manual workers in many respects, such as power, status, pay, physical working conditions, eating places, rules for lunch and tea breaks, and holidays. Shopfloor workers and low-rank office clerks are subject to a tighter control at work. They have to clock in and out at specific times, work in some cases, e.g. on an assembly line conveyor belt, at a pre-determined speed, and produce a specified number of units per hour and so forth. The managers, by contrast, can come in and go out of the company premises whenever they like and can do their job as they see fit, provided that they achieve their performance targets. Their holiday entitlements, pension schemes, bonuses, share-options and the like are disproportionately far greater than those of the shopfloor employees. This dual-treatment tradition has created a hostile 'them and us' attitude among the workforce which has for a long time bedevilled the British industrial relations.

## HRM in Turkey[1]

Turkey is the world's 7th largest emerging economy and the European Union's biggest trading partner. Because of its geographic position, new business friendly legislation, a growing economy and abundant natural resources (Etkin et al., 2000), Turkey is increasingly attracting foreign capital flow into the economy (Loewendahl and Ertugal-Loewendahl, 2000). As Taner et al. (2000) point out, successive governments have since the early 1980s adopted market-oriented economic policies and liberalisation in foreign direct investment regimes (see also the survey on Turkey in *The Economist*, 8 June 2000).

Built upon the ashes of the Ottoman Empire, modern Turkey is based on legal, political and social reforms introduced and implemented by Mustafa Kemal Atatürk, the founder of the Turkish Republic and its first President. He overthrew the Ottoman dynasty which had ruled over six centuries and created the Republic in 1923.

Like many other nations there is a high level of diversity in Turkish culture (Pasa, 2000), a diversity which is the result of a long history of entanglement with successive civilisations (Yesil, 2003). But there is also a common thread, characterised by nationalism, secularism and statism, which has transformed the country into a western-style and secularly-structured state. Turkish culture is also characterised by a relatively conservative outlook and traditionalism, especially in the rural areas and among the lower socio-economic groups of society. Table 4.4 summarises the common features relevant to this chapter.

Bodur and Madsen (1993) agree with Hofstede's (1980) findings that Turkey is a rather collectivist society with an almost equal level of masculine and feminine values, and with a rather large power distance and strong uncertainty avoidance. Similarly, Pasa (2000) characterises Turkish culture as being conformist, preserving the status quo, collectivist, having high power distance and preserving hierarchy.

However, the socio-cultural environment in the country is changing and according to Aycan (2001) Turkey has become somewhat less collectivist, less hierarchical and less uncertainty avoiding since Hofstede's research. She also argues that Turkish societal and organisational culture is a mixture of 'Western' and 'Eastern' values. However, a recent study by Goregenli (1997) found that dominant collectivist tendencies along with some individualist tendencies remain present in Turkish culture.

---

[1] The section on HRM in Turkey draws on Yesil (2003, Chapter 9) with kind permission of the author.

**Table 4.4** Major Turkish cultural characteristics and management practices

*National Culture*
- high-context culture
- importance of personal and family relationships
- collectivist
- both collectivism and individualism present in the culture
- conservative, conformist, preserving status quo
- strong uncertainty avoidance
- almost equal level of masculine and feminine values
- large power distance, preservation of hierarchy
- nevertheless the socio-cultural environment is changing and as a result the society is becoming less collectivist, less hierarchical, less uncertainty avoiding
- society and culture are a mixture of western and eastern values
- high achievement-orientation

*HRM and other employee related values and practices*
- large power distance between superiors and subordinates
- inequality in wealth and in decision making
- not much dialogue between management and employees
- autocratic leadership style, central decision making, highly personalised strong leadership, limited delegation
- hierarchical leadership and organisational structure
- leadership style characterised by limited information sharing, participation and internal control
- yet at the same time a belief in individual's capacity for leadership and initiative
- managers are high achievement-oriented but low power-oriented, perhaps reflecting the feminine side of the national culture
- high level of tolerance on the part of managers; strong 'empathic' ability

Turkish cultural characteristics can also be observed in Turkish organisations. For example, Bodur and Madsen (1993) argued that in Turkish companies, hierarchy is the way to exercise leadership. Respect for authority is important. High power distance between superiors and subordinates does not allow for equality, either in wealth or in decision making. Autocratic leadership prevails with hardly any dialogue between management and employees. Similarly Pasa (2000) noted that in parallel with national cultural tendencies, Turkish organisations are characterised by central decision making, highly personalised strong leadership, and limited delegation.

Turkish managers also appear to reflect national cultural traits. A recent study (Zel, 1999) concluded that Turkish managers:

- are not very social but they are good at relationships with people,
- prefer to be managed than to manage,
- are not of a 'dominant' personality type,
- have a high level of tolerance,
- have a strong 'empathic' ability,
- like the conceptual rather than the concrete,
- prefer to use 'intuitive' approaches to their decisions,
- use their innovative ability as much as possible but they are also bound to traditional methods,
- are detail conscious,
- do not like to change their jobs often,
- are not risk takers,

- are not good at controlling their emotions,
- take work as an end in itself.

In another study conducted by Kozan (1993) Turkish managers were found to be reluctant to share information, to allow participation and liked internalised control. At the same time they believed strongly in the individual's capacity for leadership and initiative. Arslan (2001) found that Turkish managers reflect high achievement and low power orientation, arguing that this reflects the feminine side of Turkish culture in which a meek or humble personality is valued. However, high achievement orientation was explained by economic and historical conditions. For example the rapid economic growth since the 1980s has contributed to the high achievement orientation. Furthermore, this has been attributed to the characteristics of imperial periods in which ordinary subjects in the Turkish empires, even slaves, were able to move to higher positions, including the top echelons of political power, because of the absence of an aristocratic class (Arslan, 2001).

## HRM in the Arab Middle East

The term 'Middle East' was invented in 1901 by the American Admiral Alfred T Mahan. It was only in 1916, however, that the term was popularised as a result of its official British adoption in correspondence. The term, despite its popular use, suggests a degree of internal uniformity that is unjustified by reality (Ali, 1993). Countries like Cyprus, Turkey, Israel, Egypt, Iraq and Oman are lumped together under this convenient political umbrella.

However, most of the countries in the Middle East are Arab and view themselves as belonging to a community spread nationally and culturally from the Persian Gulf to Morocco in North Africa. As Muna (1980) points out, the nationals of these countries have a common bond: a strong feeling of identity and commonality. They share the same language, religion, and history. While there are elements of diversity in these three bases of identity, the feelings of brotherhood and common destiny among nationals of Arab countries make it possible in the final analysis to refer to them as Arabs. The present section focuses mainly on the people of the oil-exporting countries of the Arab Middle East, referred to hereafter as the Arabs, which have attracted an enormous amount of foreign direct investment (see also the survey on the Persian Gulf region in *The Economist*, 21 March 2002). Table 4.5 shows salient common cultural characteristics and HRM practices in the Arab Middle East countries.

The Arabs are highly collectivist with a strong sense of loyalty to their in-group, whose membership, like the Indian's, goes well beyond the immediate family, to embrace extended family, relatives and friends. Researchers argue that the Arab nations' group-orientation can be traced to their Bedouin tradition, which in turn reinforces customs such as consultation, obedience to seniors, loyalty, face-to-face interaction and networks of personal connections. The loyalty to the group has to some extent resulted in a low level of tolerance for new ideas and challenge of accepted wisdom. Respect for the elders is also fostered by Islam, which in addition encourages dedication to work, cooperation and harmony.

The above characteristics are reflected in organisations in hierarchical and centralised structures, with paternalistic authoritarian management style. Research evidence (Weir, 2000; Mellahi, 2003) shows that subordinates, although they expect to be consulted with, do not expect to participate in the actual decision making as equal partners, which is the

**Table 4.5** Major Arab cultural characteristics and management practices

*National Culture*

Influence of Islam:
- dedication to work, engagement in economic activities is an obligation
- work a source of independence and a means of fostering personal growth, self-respect, satisfaction and self-fulfilment
- obedience to leaders, but blind subservience is not condoned
- emphasis on forgiveness, kind-heartedness, harmony, cooperation and brotherly relationships

Arabic legacy, Bedouin way of life:
- highly collectivist within the in-group (tribe or extended family) and highly individualist with the out-group (non-kin and guest workers)
- loyalty to tribe, pride in tradition, dynasty and tribe
- dependence on relatives and friends
- emphasis on consultation in decision making within the same tribe or extended family but authoritarianism with non-kin (out-group)
- Wasta: face to face interaction, widespread use of personal networks, connections and coalitions
- high uncertainty avoidance: low tolerance for new ideas, low degree of initiative for bringing about change, fatalism, unquestioning acceptance of conventional wisdom, and obedience of justified authority

*HRM and other employee related values and practices*
- a strong preference for participative and consultative style
- dislike of autocratic and authoritarian management style
- but managers tend to adopt an authoritarian management style
- subordinates expect to be consulted about decisions but they do not expect participation in the decision making process
- the last word is always the manager's word
- practice of senior managers getting together on a regular basis with employees and supervisors from various levels
- encourage subordinates to formulate solutions to problems before coming to senior management with a statement of the difficulty
- management culture based on talking, not writing
- explicit decision-making culture based on interpersonal connections
- network takes precedence over loyalty to the firm
- productivity and performance largely disconnected from pay and promotion
- a strong preference for power and role and less for achievement and support
- respect for seniority
- preference for job security
- a lack of relevant human resource management policies and management development and planning
- a lack of delegation of authority, highly personalised superior–subordinate relationships deriving from loyalty to individuals and paternalistic and hierarchical organisational relationships
- widespread lack of use of western style management practices such as assessment centres
- extensive use of expatriate managers
- discrimination between locals and expatriates
- gender discrimination and some degree of occupational segregation
- no serious independent labour union movement/trade union

prerogative of their senior managers. Senior positions are usually held by older people, promotion and pay are more likely to be related to the employees' degree of loyalty to their managers than to their job performance. However, the younger generation managers, most of whom have received higher education either at home or abroad, are more in favour of western-style professionalism than their older colleagues. In Bahrain, for instance, as Weir (2000) points out, the well-educated emerging managerial elite is developing a realistic self image setting strict performance standards, taking advantage of opportunities for professional self renewal. It demands, within the context of the authoritarian and autocratic power structures of Bahraini organisations, inclusion in the decision making process.

The Bedouin tradition of chieftains holding council meetings, *Majlis*, at which the commoners also attended or brought in their petitions, appears to have been carried over to work organisations as well. Here, senior managers get together on a regular basis with employees and supervisors from various levels. Managers normally communicate with their colleagues and subordinates through personal contact, conversation and networking rather than written memos and letters.

One of the main features of many Arab companies is the extensive use of expatriates both at highly technical and professional levels, because of shortage of home-grown experts, and at the shopfloor manual work level, mainly because the locals are not prepared to do low-paid, low-esteemed menial jobs. These expatriates engaged for manual jobs are usually Indians, Pakistanis, Malaysians, Filipinos or citizens of other Arab countries. Expatriates recruited for senior technical and professional positions are mostly from the advanced industrialised countries of Europe and North America.

At high-level positions, the expatriates are very well-paid, and in many cases their pay is exempt from income tax, and their families enjoy living in comfortable and well-appointed accommodation, but their contracts are on a short-term basis with no guaranteed job security or contract renewal. At the shopfloor level, there exists harsh discrimination against expatriates, in terms of pay, working conditions and other employee rights compared to their local counterparts (Harry, 2003). There is also widespread discrimination against women, both domestic and expatriates, especially in terms of job opportunity, recruitment, promotion prospects and pay.

With a few exceptions, no serious independent labour union movement has developed in the Arab world. In those countries where workers are permitted to organise, their unions are either created by the ruling single-party system or are closely controlled by the government.

Muna's (1980) seminal study, whose findings are still valid to this day judging by the research evidence produced since 1980, highlighted other Arab work-related values and attitudes. The Arab executives whom he interviewed admired certain characteristics in expatriates and wanted to see them learned by their employees: high value and respect for time; productivity and hard work; technical know-how and competence; organised and systematic approach to work; conscientiousness and dedication to work; discipline; and accuracy and precision. These are, it appears, the work-related characteristics which Arab managers long for and which they miss most in their people.

Muna also detected the following characteristics among Arab employees:

- Lack of industrial mentality: aversion to systems and procedures; lack of organisation, especially delegation; non-professional attitudes toward business.
- Individualistic approach to work: a preference to work alone rather than be in a team; a tendency to take sole credit for good deeds and to pass the blame to others or to circumstances when things go wrong.
- Dislike of manual work by Arab nationals: young men demand only clerical and administrative work.
- Nepotism and a strong socio-cultural pressure to hire relatives.
- None of the countries included in the study had truly democratic practices such as elections, majority rule, and so on. This was found a continuation of the socio-cultural characteristics of the larger social system of which the organisation was a part.

- A dislike of committee or group meetings and team work in general. Consequently, on the decisions concerning more than one subordinate, the managers seem to prefer individual-to-individual consultation with each subordinate thereby, *de facto* avoiding majority decisions. Moreover, subordinates view a participative management style as a sign of weakness on the part of the senior manager; they expect to be consulted but not to make the final decision.

## HRM in India

India, like the United States, is a complex multicultural society, with many languages, religions and traditions and it is unwise to speak of an Indian culture let alone of an Indian HRM. However, as many researchers and writers on the subject agree (Koestler, 1966; Sharma, 1984; Tayeb, 1988; Sinha, 1990; Mathur et al., 1996), there are certain characteristics that are shared by the diverse peoples of India as a whole, such as arranged marriage, fatalism, expression of emotions, hospitality and friendliness. Table 4.6 lists some of the common work-related values and attitudes generally held by people and their consequent implications for management of employees, as studied by various researchers.

Of the characteristics which are most held in common by Indian people, collectivism is one which can be readily identified as related to work organisation. Indians are said to be

**Table 4.6** Major Indian national cultural characteristics and management practices

*National Culture*
- collectivism: clannish, community conscious, large in-group includes extended family, clan, and friends
- low concern for privacy
- large power distance, obedience to seniors and respect for people in position of power, all wisdom comes from elders
- resourcefulness, hard work, tenacity, ability to cope with adversity
- risk aversion, low tolerance for ambiguity and uncertainty
- emotional dependence
- rigid social stratification: caste system
- acceptance of status quo, preference for conformity
- disciplined, self-restraint, yet emotional and display their emotions in public
- honest, trustworthy, yet considerable corruption in public service
- law-abiding but prepared to bend the rules for friends and relatives
- ambitious and materialistic
- high rate of illiteracy, especially among lower caste people and in rural areas

*HRM and other employee related values and practices*
- entrepreneurial
- preference for paternalistic and authoritarian leadership
- prefer to work under supervision
- contractual relations with the workplace, in-group does not include the workplace, low level of commitment to organisational interests and objectives
- manual workers are unskilled and uneducated
- well educated and highly skilled managers and high-ranking staff
- national and plant based trade unions, confrontational industrial relations
- pro-workers labour legislation
- strong sense of responsibility
- centralised decision making, little or no job autonomy for middle and low ranking staff and shopfloor workers
- low level of formalisation and use of written instructions and rules and regulations especially at the shopfloor, mainly because of workers' illiteracy
- differentiated reward systems and control strategies for white collar and manual workers

'clannish' and community conscious. However, it seems that the 'community' to which an Indian person feels affiliated and in whose affairs he is interested, is his extended family, close circle of relatives and friends, caste and religious group rather than society as a whole. For example, the Zoroastrian community in Bombay have a hospital which, except in emergency accident cases, admits only Zoroastrian patients. Moreover, unlike Japan, this group-orientation does not seem to have been carried over into the workplace, in the form of high commitment to and identification with the interests of the organisation (Tayeb, 1988). Unlike in Japan where the company one works for is a member of a Japanese person's in-group, in India this is not the case. One could argue that the prevalence of corruption and bribery in many public sector organisations is a symptom of this state of affairs. One could also argue that work practices such as quality circles, collective decision making, teamwork, suggestion boxes and morning ceremonies, which presupposes a strong sense of commitment to the company, may not find fertile grounds in India, as they do in Japan.

Large power distance, manifested in the high level of respect for and obedience to older people and those in position of power, is another shared cultural characteristic in India. The acceptance of a rigid caste system which places people in a steep hierarchy of power and privilege is another manifestation of large power distance. Indian people are not so much class conscious as are conscious of their caste and sub-castes. The society is still stratified on the basis of caste membership rather than class as it is known in Western industrial societies. Unlike social class, where people can move up by marriage or by acquiring wealth and getting better jobs, the caste system is rigid in that individuals are born into their parents' caste and die as a member of that caste, no matter what educational qualification, professional status, wealth or anything else they might achieve in life.

Organisations too tend to be hierarchical with a central decision making process and little or no authority delegated to lower ranks. Management style tends to be authoritarian or paternalistic with a clear distinction between white-collar and blue-collar employees in terms of power, pay, working conditions and other privileges.

However, the authority of people in a position of power, be it in the society at large or within companies, does not always go unchallenged. The political regime of the country, though not as egalitarian as those of other leading democracies, is one of the few democratic systems in central Asia. The Indian written press enjoys a high level of freedom of expression and does not hesitate to criticise and challenge government officials and politicians irrespective of their power or popularity.

In the workplace, trade unions represent a countervailing power to management authority. There are no craft unions in India. Trade unions are either plant based or national organisa-tions which are run locally in each state and focus their activities on the interest of their immediate members at the plant or local industry level. There are provisions for setting up works committees in factories and workers participation in decision making at shopfloor and plant levels. However, these committees, and indeed any other forms of workers participa-tion, have not been successful. There are various acts of Parliament which secure minimum wages, regulation for payment of wages, working conditions, equal remuneration for men and women and several schemes providing security to the workers against contingencies, such as industrial accidents. Generally, industrial relations legislation is pro-workers and aims at protecting their employment and general well-being. For instance, until recently the regulations were such that it was virtually impossible for management to sack a worker or reduce his or her wages even if he or she had seriously breached the terms of their contract (Tayeb, 1988). However, since the early 1990s, in parallel with India's gradual opening up of its economy and removing some of the obstacles to foreign investment, the labour market has also to some extent been deregulated. But for various political reasons progress has been very slow (see also the survey on India in *The Economist*, 21 February 2004). It should also be noted that in contrast to Japan's, the Indian industrial relations system is prone to conflict, and mistrust and hostility bedevil the relationships between employees and management from time to time.

India's records on employee productivity, especially at the shopfloor level, are much worse than other Asian emerging economies, mainly because of higher illiteracy rates and lower technical skills at the shopfloor level. India has many excellent universities, and one of the biggest cohort of technically trained manpower in the world. At the lower end of the system, however, India has done less well; its manual workers are among the most poorly trained and unskilled workforce in the region, in spite of the resourcefulness and hard work that many researchers have attributed to the Indians in general (Tayeb, 1996).

Indian people are, in general, resourceful and hard-working, have a keen sense of responsibility, are thrifty and entrepreneurial, and are ambitious and materialistic. However, research shows that, unlike their British and American counterparts who would like to work on their own, they would prefer to work under supervision and seek their managers' approval before making major decisions. This may be a reflection of their deference to and respect for authority rather than inability to accept responsibility as individuals.

## HRM in China

China is one of the world's oldest civilisations and, with over 1.3 billion people, the largest country in terms of population. The country has been under the Communist Party rule since 1921 and has experienced at least two major cultural and economic changes between then and the present time. After World War II, the party under Mao Zedong established a dictatorship that, while ensuring China's sovereignty, imposed strict controls over everyday life and security. Starting in 1978, his successor Deng Xiaoping gradually introduced market-oriented reforms and decentralised economic decision making (see also three surveys on China in *The Economist*, 8 April 2000; 13 June 2002; 20 March 2004). Political controls, however, remain tight even while economic control continues to be relaxed.

As one would expect from the large size of their country, the Chinese are a very diverse nation with a variety of ethnic groups, languages, religions and regional cultures. As in the case of India discussed above, there are however some common cultural threads going through many of the values and attitudes that people hold: a long imperial history and traditional heritage, a communist political regime since 1920s, the predominance of the 'Han' ethnic group, and the overwhelming influence of the Confucian philosophy. You will note in Table 4.7 that all these have left their imprints on the national culture and, at the micro-level, on employee–management relationships and HRM in organisations.

As Fang (2000) points out, Chinese culture has been moulded, among others, by Confucianism, a philosophical doctrine founded by Confucius (551–479 BC). Among the values

**Table 4.7** Major Chinese cultural characteristics and management practices

*National Culture*

Yin and yang philosophy and traditional values:
- opposites are inseparable parts of a larger whole, integrating with each other
- high-context culture: meanings often derive from relationships, authority and context
- reserved, collectivistic, but also individualistic and expressive depending on the circumstances
- personalised loyalty: loyalty to a particular individual
- *guanxi*: personal networking, using extended family and other developed relationships and connections to gain cooperation and to get things done
- attitude to time: both long-term and short-term orientation depending on the situation
- *ji*: a carefully devised scheme with which to cope with difficult situations and gain psychological and material advantages over the opponents

Confucian values:
- moral cultivation, importance of interpersonal relationships, family-orientation, respect for age and hierarchy, need for harmony, and concept of face
- *li shang wang lai*: Confucian attitude toward interpersonal relationships, 'courtesy demands reciprocity'

Legacy of communism:
- state in full political control, but a great deal of economic liberation especially in coastal regions
- centralised economic planning and control structure, unsophisticated legal system, lack of technology and capital, underdeveloped infrastructure, large population, low average education level, low to medium per capita living standard, ongoing reforms, and fast changes
- bargaining as a way of life within bureaucratic institutions

*HRM and other employee related values and practices*
- workers live and work within a Communist structure
- older employees: not proactive or bold when making decisions, and they often do not offer independent opinions on particular decisions
- younger employees: basically more adaptable, and have not been subject to traditional working practices
- local government exerts control on internal affairs such as HRM
- managers are reluctant to share information, to take risky decisions, worry much more about political relationships in organisation, not as much about organisational goals and how to achieve them
- short-term planning horizons
- Communist Party hierarchy in every firm gradually being replaced by the firm's trade union leaders
- managers, especially the young ones, tend to seek their personal gains first in any decision made within the company
- reliance on rules and procedures
- management is centralised, authoritarian, charismatic, personalised, hierarchical, and consensus seeking
- employees lack pride in and identity with their employer organisations
- absence of personal contribution to organisational objectives
- time is not of the essence, not much concern for schedule
- short supply of local managerial and technical skills
- high value on morals, discipline, flexibility, and information collection
- interpersonal relationship (*guanxi*) within the firm
- older managers expect younger members to respect them
- age and seniority are accorded some priority in discussions and decisions
- relationship-oriented approach to conflict management
- social-oriented achievement motivation

that Confucianism espouses are: moral cultivation, importance of interpersonal relationships, family orientation, respect for age and hierarchy, need for harmony, and concept of face.

One of the fundamental tenets of the Chinese culture is the yin–yang philosophy which accepts the simultaneous existence of opposite values and beliefs within a person, and by implications within a culture. The plausibility of this philosophy, as many researchers have pointed out, is also born out by various responses, behaviours and actions of other individuals and cultures elsewhere in the world depending on the specific circumstances and situations in which they find themselves (see for example Tayeb, 2001).

Fang (2003, p. 6) succinctly interprets the yin–yang philosophy within the context of cultural values attributed to the Chinese in general thus:

'The Chinese are, as many cross-cultural studies point out, reserved, long-term oriented, high context, collectivist. But substantial evidences show that the Chinese are also expressive, short-term oriented, low context, individualistic given circumstances. . . . The Chinese [for instance] can be extremely expressive on festive occasions and when they are being put in a contest setting.'

Following such a philosophy, one could argue that although the Chinese are collectivist and group-oriented, they also display highly individualistic tendencies at times. In addition, unlike the Japanese, their work organisations do not seem to be part of their in-groups. Indeed, the persistence of personalised loyalty (i.e. loyalty to a particular individual) in Chinese culture may impede development of organisational loyalty (Castaldi and Soerjanto, 1988). For instance Yager et al. (1994), in their study of foreign joint ventures in China, found that Japanese managers were almost baffled by Chinese workers' display of a lack of pride in and identity with their employer organisations.

Traditionally, Chinese personal networking (*guanxi*) has been important, if not essential, to success, using extended family and other developed relationships and connections to gain cooperation and to get things done. However, the success of Chinese networking skills in building the effectiveness of small businesses, their interpersonal relationships, loyalties, and a system of mutual support do not seem to have been carried over to larger organisations, including joint ventures with foreigners. Yager et al. found that this had some implications for discipline. Industrial discipline, a concept implying not only that workers follow a regimen in their jobs, but also the will of supervisors to exercise sanctions in controlling worker behaviour, was non-existent among Chinese workers. A sense of responsibility to the employer organisation, consistency in work performance and follow-through also seemed to be unusual. There was a pervasive need to build identity to the enterprise.

A combination of *guanxi* and personal loyalty has other interesting implications for employee–management relationships as well. It is, for instance, very common for Chinese managers who leave their company to join another one to invite their subordinates to follow them to the new company. Similarly, it is common for employees to stay in a company mainly because they have strong personal ties with their superiors (Wong and Law, 1999).

The centrally-planned political economic structure of the society has also had profound implications on the ways in which employees behave in their workplace and on their relationships with their supervisors and managers. For example, until recently, a Communist Party hierarchy existed in every plant or firm. Every plant manager had to live with his shadow, the Party boss. Although the formal party control has been relaxed, the plant's trade union leaders behave now much like a party official would have in the past and have the power to veto even top management decisions. It is worth noting, however, that China has no independent trade union truly comparable to those in western or any other democracies (Li et al., 1999).

Local government exerts a lot of control and influence over people and their affairs. For example, people are not free to live wherever they choose. They must obtain a residency permit before they can live officially in a city other than their hometown. Local government plays also an important role in the transfer of people across companies. For instance, the local labour bureau can stop a transfer from one organisation to another if the bureau believes that the requirements of the original employment contract were not met. Also, if foreign companies located in China wish to recruit Chinese national managers, they need to obtain permission from the local government.

Chinese managers, especially the older ones who lived through the Cultural Revolution, are usually not proactive or bold when making decisions, and they often do not offer independent opinions on particular decisions. One study found that Chinese managers reported much stronger reliance on widespread beliefs as a source of guidance in their decision making than did managers in other nations (Smith et al., 1997). Moreover, managers are reluctant to share information and to take risky decisions; they also worry much more about political relationships in organisation than they do about the organisational goals and how to achieve them (Li et al., 1999).

Employees often avoid problems until they are impossible to ignore. When problems are finally addressed, solutions are based on precedent and usually involve a reference to authority. The managers, on their part, tend to rely on rules and procedures. As Weldon and Vanhonacker (1999) point out, the tendency to avoid problems and a lack of creativity have been attributed to various facets of Chinese culture, including traditional socialisation practices where obedience, impulse control and acceptance of social obligations are encouraged, while independence, assertiveness and creativity are not. According to Weldon and Vanhonacker, the following factors have also contributed to this state of affairs:

- the education system, in which students are taught what to think not how to think
- the hierarchical society, where status and precedent must be respected
- experience in state-owned enterprises, were managers made few decisions and were rarely held accountable for results
- the volatility of political life under Mao and the continuing political campaigns.

However, since 1978 and the opening of the economy to the outside world, a great deal has changed. Weldon and Vanhonacker, for instance, observe that the younger people in China today did not experience Mao's reign, they have not worked in state-owned enterprises, and they grew up in the market-oriented economic environment of contemporary China, as opposed to the planned economy their parents experienced prior to economic reforms. The evidence shows that socialisation practices have changed too; parents are now more tolerant of assertive children and feel less strongly that a child must always obey strict rules and regulations, and are more tolerant of children who talk back. Together these changes could produce a generation of young people more likely to adopt a proactive and responsible approach to work.

To end the section on China, it is worth mentioning that a few years ago the present author interviewed, among others, a senior manager of a major multinational company which was in the process of setting up a joint venture in China. This is how he saw the situation with regard to the Chinese employees' work-related attitudes and their productivity within the context of a communist system:

'A standard joke making the round is "How many Chinamen does it take to change a light bulb?" The answer is four in my experience. We needed a light bulb changing in the house and we had four people coming to change it, one to go up the ladder to put it in, one to hand the bulb up to him, one to hold the ladder and one to supervise, you know. So, they do employ everybody but not everybody is all that productive.'

The challenge facing this company, the manager told me, was not to change the cultural attitudes and values of their Chinese workforce, but to help them unlearn unproductive working practices, and replace them with those which are more conducive to greater efficiency. In addition, what the company was aiming for was to recruit young employees who are basically more adaptable and who have not been subject to traditional working practices. The company would then train these employees to work in a different way. The belief was that the Chinese would not have any problem with this approach, because they need to be competitive in the world market, so they would be keen to learn the way their foreign partners do things and maybe within 20 or 30 years they will be doing it even better (see Tayeb, 1998 for more details).

# Implications of national diversity for multinational companies

The above brief tour of six countries and one region around the world demonstrates the degree of diversity and variety that exists between various peoples both at national and organisational levels. As the previous two chapters argued, the ways in which managers run their organisations in general and manage their employees in particular are not divorced from the environment within which they are situated. Multinational companies are no exception in this regard. We shall see in later chapters, especially Chapters 6 and 7, how MNC managers need to modify and adapt their HRM strategies, policies and practices in response to the national characteristics of various countries and regions with which they do business and in which they set up subsidiaries. These adaptation and modification processes are also required when a domestic single-country company decides to import foreign best practices in order to improve its performance. The closing case study at the end of this chapter has been chosen with this point in mind. The case concerns a Scottish company, located within the broader socio-cultural context of the United Kingdom but wishes to implement cell manufacturing, a 'best practice' developed in a Scandinavian country with different national characteristics and way of life from that of the United Kingdom.

■ **CHAPTER SUMMARY**

The chapter built on the arguments advanced in the previous two chapters and highlighted the implications of national culture for employee management and leadership styles in six countries and an Arab region. These major economies were chosen on the basis of the importance of their role in today's international market both as hosts and homes of a large number of multinational companies. The admittedly broad brush discussion of these economies showed the extent to which their HRM policies and practices reflected their deeply-held cultural values and attitudes.

The next chapter will see companies deciding on their internationalisation strategies which will bring them into close contact with precisely the kind of issues which were discussed in this and the previous two chapters.

■ **REVISION QUESTIONS**

1. To what extent are the cultural and other national characteristics of the seven economies studied in the chapter different from or similar to one another?

2. Are these differences and similarities reflected in similarities and differences in their respective HRM and employee management styles? Give examples to clarify your answer.

3. What roles do non-cultural factors, such as level of industrialisation, play in the ways in which organisations in these countries manage their human resources?

4. Imagine you are about to be sent as the HR director of a subsidiary in one of the countries covered in the chapter. Compare the HRM policies and practices prevalent in your home country with those in the country you are going to, and discuss the main challenges you might face if you wish to manage your employees in that country in the way things are done in yours.

# Case study: Litton imports cell manufacturing from Sweden

Litton Interconnection Products (Scotland) is part of a multinational corporation based in North America. It fits in with the corporation's overall profile but is completely autonomous and free to do what it likes, provided that the overall plan and profit targets are met.

The company is the European operation for Litton Inc.'s activities in electronic system packaging and it manufactures board to board and back-plane interconnection systems. These products are sold to major telecommunication, computer, military and transport equipment manufacturers who operate in technologically advanced markets which are subject to constant change. The company uses a system known as Business Process Improvement (BPI) as a vehicle to cope with this continuous-change environment.

The radical element in the implementation of BPI is the appointment of an individual to take ownership of each business process. In this way it has been possible to form cross-functional teams, managed by the process owners, to effect change across departmental boundaries thereby increasing efficiency and, above all, responsiveness to customers.

The current work organisation, based on cell manufacturing, was put in place in the early 1990s when the company was experiencing serious difficulties and there was a question mark over its future. The company had to rethink in a major way and move into new modes of operation. A new managing director was invited from outside to bring in a new vision and to set out new objectives for the company. Customer satisfaction was to become the main focus and aim of the company, to be achieved by being better than their competitors. The objective was to try new/unknown businesses rather than to imitate their rivals. The organisation was seen not as a collection of people but as an organised system where people work together to become a major player in the business. The company aimed at providing the enabling conditions for the employees to live as rich a life as they can as well as focusing on customers and the market.

In order to achieve its new aims and objectives, the company decided to introduce cell manufacturing and in order to implement this new design successfully it embarked on a process of culture change. The company's culture in the past was that of a traditional small electronic firm: success was measured by output, structure was hierarchical, a pyramid. The management team believed this pyramid was wrong and 'threw it out' and put a cell design in its place.

Breaking the old ways was difficult, it created uncertainty, disquiet, shock and 'adhocracy'. Obstacles to this structure came largely from middle managers.

'There were no problems with people in the lower levels, they now have much more opportunity and potentially earn more money. Difficulties were with people who were in positions of control. A couple of people left because they did not fit. Later, the advantages of the new system became obvious and it is no longer an issue.'

Change was introduced literally over a week-end. 'On Friday people left their assembly lines, on Monday they came to find the shopfloor layout organised into self-contained cells.'

## Cell manufacturing in Litton

There are currently ten cells in place under two operations managers, whose official titles are 'business mentors'. Business mentors perform various jobs from operational tasks to personnel, training and customer relations. The skills that functional mentors have and train others on are materials, manufacture, process, quality and the like. Business mentors meet frequently and hold group meetings once a week with their cells.

In addition, there are functional mentors who are experts in specific areas and their role is to train cell members when required. They carry out cross-cell training up to the standard they are expected to be. There is also a design group which consists of highly technically-skilled people and work in conjunction with the cells. Figure 4.2 shows the overall design of cell manufacturing in Litton.

Each cell consists of a self-managed self-directed group of five to ten people who take responsibility for a number of areas. Cell members do not have a leader. The post of supervisors has been abolished and cells are not teamwork in the strict sense. Jobs are flexible and interchangeable, people are multi-functioned multi-skilled, everybody does everything in the cell. They make decisions on the tasks of a given day, and set their goals, scheduling, order entry, materials, control, handling and the like. Mentors might get involved occasionally but cell members basically 'figure out things for themselves' in response to customers' requirements. As one of the business mentors puts it,

'. . . the ownership of the business is given to cell members. People are allowed to maximise their contributions as business owners and hence contribute to the company. Long-term needs of the business is inseparable from the long-term needs of people. If people can express their ideas this contributes to the success of the business. We don't want to control people, we want to control results.'

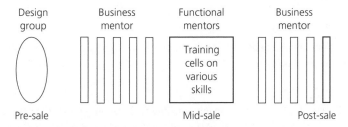

**Figure 4.2** Cell manufacturing in Litton

*Source*: Tayeb (1999), reproduced with permission.

The company has no customer department. Instead cell members interact directly with their customers, brought in by the 'hunters', a group of three employees whose job it is to find new customers. As part of the process of direct interaction with the customer, shopfloor workers even go abroad, when necessary, to visit their customers and discuss with them their requirements.

Each cell looks after a specific customer, such as HP and AT&T. By and large each cell has one major customer, but there are cells which may have more. As customers bring in more and more of their business they get their own cell. If the initial contract is big, then a cell is built specifically for them 'from scratch'. The size of the cell is determined by the customer's requirements.

The management believes the cells' direct contact with customers has improved the company's responsiveness. In the past, for instance, it would take two to three weeks before the customers could have an answer to their queries, now they go directly to their assigned cell. At the same time the direct contact has created an environment which motivates direct labour; it has also reduced cycle time and operating costs.

For the cells to function properly, in addition to bringing in skilled people from outside, the company has embarked on an extensive programme to train the workforce. Functional mentors play a significant role in this respect. The aim of the training programme was, among other things, 'to install in people what you wanted them to do. Their self-confidence had to be rebuilt. What if people do not want to take responsibility? Mentors had to give confidence as well as being experts. We trained our mentors first.'

In addition, the company changed its underlying tradition of 'please the boss' to 'please the customer'. The pay structure and industrial relations have also changed. The distribution of wealth in the company is now based on skills rather than on position on the pyramid.

The implementation of the change was not of course smooth. As was mentioned earlier, the new system was introduced literally over a weekend:

'It created a huge upset, but people gradually got used to it. To begin with there was a lot of kicking and swearing but now they are happy. Before, the pay structure never changed, managers all wanted to tell people what to do, and chaps would hang around until 5p.m. doing nothing. When the new structure was introduced what people found hard was that nobody told them what to do. It took ages for people to realise that it did not matter how long they were in the factory; as long as the customer was happy, they could go whenever they wanted. Now people don't want to go back to the old ways. Those who were not happy to let control go, left the company.'

Litton's performance has improved greatly as a result of the introduction of cell manufacturing. In 1996 there was a 17% growth over the previous year. In the same year their revenue totalled £5.9 from less than £1 million five years ago. Their profit for 1996 grew by 8.3%.

### ■ CASE STUDY QUESTIONS

**1.** Why was cell manufacturing introduced in Litton?

**2.** What problems did senior managers think the company would face and have to resolve while implementing this new working system?

---

Case study source: Tayeb, M. H. 1999, 'Foreign remedies for local difficulties: the case of three Scottish manufacturing firms', *International Journal of Human Resource Management*, 10, pp. 842–57. Reproduced with permission.

**3.** How was cell manufacturing put in place and how did employees react to it?

**4.** How did managers ensure their employees were able to work within this new system?

**5.** What other changes in HRM policies and practices took place as a result of the introduction of cell manufacturing?

**6.** Choose one of the economies covered in this chapter and highlight its main cultural characteristics which might help or hinder the introduction of cell manufacturing there.


### ■ RECOMMENDED FURTHER READING

Hofstede, G. (1980). *Culture's Consequences*. London and California: Sage Publications.

Hickson, D. J. (ed.), (1993). *Management in Western Europe*. Berlin: Walter de Gruyter.

Jackson, T. (2002). *International IHRM*. Sage Publications.


### ■ REFERENCES

Ali, A. J. (1993). 'Preface', *International Studies of Management and Organization*, vol. 23, pp. 3–6.

Arslan, M. (2001). 'A cross-cultural comparison of achievement and power orientation as leadership dimensions in three European countries: Britain, Ireland and Turkey', *Business Ethics: A European Review*, vol. 10, no. 4, pp. 340–45.

Aycan, Z. (2001). 'Human resource management in Turkey: current issues and future challenges', *International Journal of Manpower*, vol. 22, no. 3, pp. 252–60.

Bodur, M. and Madsen, T. K. (1993). 'Danish foreign direct investment in Turkey', *European Business Review*, vol. 93, no. 5, pp. 28–46.

Bradley, K. and Hill, S. (1983). 'After Japan: the quality circle transplant and productive efficiency', *British Journal of Industrial Relations*, vol. 21, pp. 291–311.

Briggs, P. (1988). 'The Japanese at work: illusions of the ideal', *Industrial Relations Journal*, vol. 19, pp. 24–30.

Buruma, I. (1985). *A Japanese Mirror: Heroes and Villains of Japanese Culture*. London: Penguin.

Castaldi, R. M. and Soerjanto, T. (1988). 'Post-Confucianism management practices and behaviors: a comparison of Japan versus China and South Korea', paper presented to the Western Academy of Management Meeting, Big Sky, March.

Etkin, L. P., Helms, M. M., Turkkan, U. and Morris, D. J. (2000). 'The economic emergence of Turkey', *European Business Review*, vol. 12, no. 2, pp. 64–75.

Fang, T. (2000). 'Chinese style of business: *JI* and others', in M. H. Tayeb, *International Business: Theories, Policies and Practices*. London: Pearson Education. pp. 518–26.

—— (2003). 'The moon and sun of culture', unpublished manuscript.

Goregenli, M. (1997). 'Individualist-collectivist tendencies in a Turkish sample', *Journal of Cross-Cultural Psychology*, vol. 28, no. 6, pp. 787–94.

Harry, W. (2003). 'Concluding case study: the international manager's world', in M. H. Tayeb, 2000, *International Strategic Management*. London: Pearson Education. Chapter 14.

Hofstede, G. (1980). *Culture's Consequences*. London and California: Sage Publications.

Koestler, A. (1966). *The Lotus and the Robot*. London: Hutchinson. Danube edition.

Kozan, M. K. (1993). 'Cultural and industrialization level influences on leadership attitudes for Turkish managers', *International Studies of Management and Organization*, vol. 23, no. 3, pp. 7–17.

Lawrence, P. (2000). 'What you see is what you get: thoughts on American management', in M H Tayeb, *International Business: Theories, Policies and Practices*. London: Pearson Education. pp. 487–93.

Li, J., Xin, K. R., Tsui, A., and Hambrick, D. C. (1999). 'Building effective international joint venture leadership teams in China', *Journal of World Business*, vol. 34, pp. 52–68.

Loewendahl, H. and Ertugal-Loewendahl, E. (2000). 'Turkey's performance in attracting foreign direct investment: implications of EU enlargement', The Centre for European Policy Studies working document, No. 57.

Marchington, M. and Parker, P. (1988). 'Japanisation: a lack of chemical reaction?', *Industrial Relations Journal*, vol. 19, no. 4, pp. 272–85.

Mathur, P., Aycan, Z., and Kanungo, R. N. (1996). 'Work cultures in Indian organisations: a comparison between public and private sector', *Psychology and Developing Society*, vol. 8, no. 2, pp. 199–222.

Mellahi, K. (2003). 'National culture and management practices: the case of Gulf Cooperation Council Countries', in M H Tayeb, *International Management: Theories and Practices*. London: Pearson Education. Chapter 5.

Misumi, J. (1984). 'Decision making in Japanese groups and organisations', in *International Year-book of Organisational Democracy*. Volume. 2, Chichester: Wiley.

Muna, F. A. (1980). *The Arab Executive*. London: Macmillan.

Pasa, S. F. (2000). 'Leadership influence in a high power distance and collectivist culture', *Leadership and Organization Development Journal*, vol. 21, no. 8, pp. 414–26.

Sharma, I. J. (1984). 'The culture context of Indian managers', *Management and Labour Studies*, vol. 9, no. 2, pp. 72–80.

Sinha J. B. P. (1990). *Work culture in Indian Context*. New Delhi: Sage Publications.

Smith, P. B., Wong, Z. M., and Leung, K. (1997). 'Leadership, decision-making and cultural context; event management within Chinese joint ventures', *Leadership Quarterly*, vol. 8, pp. 413–31.

Taner, T., Tutek, H., Oncu, S., and Ay, C. (2000). 'Joint ventures in globalisation: a perspective for Turkey', *Advances in International Marketing*, vol. 10, pp. 191–216.

Tayeb, M. H. (1988). *Organizations and National Culture: A Comparative Analysis*. London: Sage Publications.

—— (1994). 'Japanese managers and British culture: a comparative case study', *International Journal of Human Resource Management*, vol. 5, pp. 145–66.

—— (1996). 'India: a non-tiger of Asia' *International Business Review*. vol. 5, no. 5, pp. 425–45.

—— (1998). 'Transfer of HRM policies and practices across cultures: an American company in Scotland', *International Journal of Human Resource Management*, vol. 9, pp. 332–58.

—— (2001). 'Conducting research across cultures—overcoming drawbacks and obstacles', *International Journal of Cross-Cultural Management*, vol.1, no. 1, pp. 113–29.

—— and Dott, E. (2000). 'Two nations divided by a common culture: three American companies in Scotland', in M D Hughes and J H Taggart (eds), *International Business: European Dimension*. Basingstoke: Macmillan. Chapter 5.

Yesil, S. (2003). *Top Management Teams within International Joint Ventures in Turkey: Exploring the Implications of Culture and Demography on Process and Performance*. Unpublished Ph. D. thesis, The University of Nottingham.

Weber, M. (1947). *The Theory of Social and Economic Organization*. New York: Free Press.

Weir, D. (2000). 'Management in the Arab Middle East' in M. H. Tayeb, *International Business: Theories, Policies and Practices*. London: Pearson Education. pp. 501–17.

Weldon, E. and Vanhonacker, W. (1999). 'Operating a foreign-invested enterprise in China: challenges for managers and management researchers', *Journal of World Business*, vol. 34, pp. 94–107.

Wheeler, H. N. (1993). 'Industrial relations in the United States of America', in G J Bamber and R. D. Lansbury (eds), *International and Comparative Industrial Relations*. London: Routledge. Second edition.

White, M. and Trevor, M. (1983). *Under Japanese Management*. London: Heinemann.

Whittaker, H. (2000). 'Management in Japan', in M H Tayeb, *International Business: Theories, Policies and Practices*. London: Pearson Education. pp. 494–500.

Wickens, P. (1987). *The Road to Nissan*. London: Macmillan.

Wong, C.-S., and Law, K. S. (1999). 'Managing localisation of human resources in the PRC: a practical model', *Journal of World Business*, vol. 34, pp. 26–40.

Yager, W. F., Thad Barnowe, J., and Nengquan, W. (1994). 'Human resource management in China: joint venture experiences in Guangdong Province', paper presented to the 4th Conference on International Human Resource Management, Gold Coast, Queensland, Australia, July.

Zel, U. (1999). *Kisiligin Yonetim Performansina Etkileri Orgut Ortaminda Kullanilmasi ve Ulkeler Arasinda Karsilastimali Bir Uygulama*. Unpublished PhD thesis, Hacettepe University, Ankara, cited in Arslan (2001).

# Part II
# HRM in Multinational Companies

# 5 | Going International: Managing HR Across the World

## Learning outcomes

When you finish reading this chapter you should:

- understand why and how some companies engage in international business
- know at what stage of the internationalisation process HRM policies and practices of companies become relevant to their foreign operations
- be familiar with broad HRM strategies that multinational companies (MNCs) may adopt and their respective advantages and disadvantages
- understand the ways in which subsidiaries may influence an MNC's HRM policies in host-countries and elsewhere within the company
- get to know, through the closing case study, the ways in which HRM policies and practices of the Scottish subsidiary of a major Japanese multinational company are shaped and influenced by parent and subsidiary preferences.

## Introduction

This chapter starts off by discussing briefly the major reasons for which some firms engage in international business and the forms that their internationalisation might take. It will be argued that multinational companies' HRM strategies and policies are relevant only to certain forms of internationalisation. The chapter will then discuss HRM issues within the context of parent–subsidiary relationships, by examining various strategic choices available to multinational companies and exploring the factors which might influence these choices. It will be argued that the power and influence of both parent and subsidiaries vis-à-vis one another increase or diminish over time and space, depending on the circumstances under which they operate.

## Going international

Why do some companies decide to expand their operations beyond their home-country and engage in international business?

The prime objectives of any business organisation are: to make profits, to grow and to increase market share and power. Companies engage in international business when the possibility of achieving these objectives are either diminishing at home and/or there are great opportunities abroad.

Market saturation, fierce competition from domestic and foreign companies, high cost of production (wages, raw material, capital, land) and shortage of required managerial and technical skills are some of the reasons why firms might find further investment in home markets less attractive than in foreign markets—the so-called 'push' factors.

Various opportunities and advantages abroad, the so-called 'pull' factors, may also entice companies to internationalise their operations: low production costs, closeness to raw materials, advanced technology, skilled human resources, established customer base, tax incentives in host countries and the like. Sometimes because of a change in foreign governments' political and economic ideologies and policies new markets with exciting opportunities open up. The fall of communist regimes in the late 1980s in the Soviet bloc is a good example. Many MNCs from the industrialised countries, which hitherto had been barred from investment in the countries concerned, took advantage of the change of policies and 'went in'.

It is important however to note that the companies which wish to internationalise can do so only if they have the required core competencies, such as operational capability, managerial skills, ability to work with foreign partners and/or in foreign countries, and so forth.

Having established that they wish and can go international, what forms of internationalisation are available to companies with international ambitions?

Some internationalisation options such as importing, exporting, franchising and licensing do not involve direct investment in other countries and may suit companies which are at the initial stages of the internationalisation process. Other more sophisticated forms, such as joint ventures and wholly-owned subsidiaries, entail progressive business involvement in foreign countries, ranging from investment only, e.g. portfolio investment, to partnership with local companies and to complete managerial and financial control of foreign operations. The decision to adopt any or all of these depends of course not only on the company's internal strengths and capabilities but also on the host-country's policies and preferences.

As we saw in some earlier chapters, although many countries have open-door foreign trade policies and welcome imports from abroad and foreign firms to set up operations within their territories, there are also many which set down various rules and regulations which limit the extent to which foreign companies can get involved in their economy. For example some countries might prefer joint ventures between local and foreign firms, some might allow foreign direct investment provided that all the generated profits be spent in the host-country.

Once a company has gone international in one form or other, what HRM policies and practices should it adopt in a foreign country?

The answer depends on the form of internationalisation and the extent and depth of the company's involvement in the local market. The HRM-related issues in a foreign country are relevant only if the company recruits and manages people in that country. Importing, exporting, franchising, licensing and portfolio investment do not involve employee management as part of a foreign operation in the host-country. There are however some exceptions. For example some multinational restaurant chains like McDonald's take an active role in selection and training of the staff in their foreign as well as domestic outlets. In most cases,

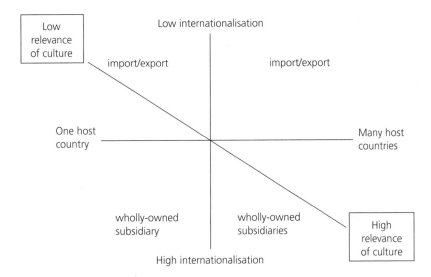

**Figure 5.1** Relevance of host country culture for MNC's HRM policies and practices

however, it is when a company is engaged in wholly-owned subsidiaries and joint ventures that it comes into direct contact with local people (or other nationals) as its employees. It therefore needs to have HRM strategies, policies and practices in place to manage these employees. In such cases, the company becomes deeply engaged in the host country, and its foreign engagement becomes wider as it enters other countries as well. Figure 5.1 illustrates this point.

As the MNC moves from an initial position at the extreme top-left corner of the figure to the extreme bottom-right corner, it becomes deeper and wider involved with foreign countries. As a result, as we shall see later in the chapter, the MNC's HRM policies and practices will become more and more complicated.

The focus of this chapter is on HRM issues within the context of MNCs' relationship with their foreign subsidiaries, generally referred to in the literature as parent–subsidiary relationship. Chapter 8 will deal with HRM issues within the context of international joint ventures.

# Parent–subsidiary relationship

For many years researchers interested in multinational companies' operations in different countries focused mainly on the parent company and the ways in which the headquarters (HQ) ensured various subsidiaries carried out their instructions. It was generally assumed that power and control resided entirely at the HQ and that this would ensure the subsidiaries' operations were integrated in the company as a whole. But later studies demonstrated that the relationship between the parent and subsidiaries are more complex and dynamic, and that the subsidiaries have a degree of autonomy in how they carry out their functions. In addition, as we shall see later in the chapter, in certain circumstances subsidiaries are able to influence the HQ's policies and practices and those of their fellow-subsidiaries within the company.

Here we explore this dynamic and complex relationship from two separate perspectives. In Chapter six we shall discuss the ways in which a balance between the need to maintain subsidiaries' integration within the company, and the need to allow them to be responsive to their particular circumstances and environments.

## Parent company perspective

On the parent company's side, the degree to which freedom of action is granted to subsidiaries depends on the company's overall strategy based in part on its fundamental philosophy, values and beliefs as well as on business imperatives. From a cultural perspective, it is reasonable to assume that companies which start off their life, perhaps as a family-owned entity, in a country where the prevalent value systems encourage respect for other peoples' viewpoints, egalitarian relationships between the partners involved in a social transaction, and, in short, democratic power relationships, such value systems might be reflected in the company's management style and organisational structure. By contrast, if the home country's culture is characterised by non-egalitarian power relationships, a concentration of power and control in the hand of a few 'wise and privileged' people, based perhaps on their wealth and political influence, such characteristics might also prevail in their multinational companies both at home and abroad.

The influence of home-based ways of doing things on those of foreign subsidiaries' may vary depending also on whether or not the parent company managers believe theirs are superior to those of the host countries. The parent's superiority in technological and managerial know-how over its subsidiaries places it in a powerful position, especially in cases where subsidiaries are located in less economically advanced nations compared to the home country. But if a parent company invests in a host nation with the specific intention of tapping into the local managerial know-how and technical skills it is likely that the subsidiary will be given more autonomy and power than would otherwise be the case.

Moreover, whereas parent companies may be willing to decentralise operative and other non-strategic decisions, they might, as Poynter and Rugman (1982) and Crookell (1986) argue, be reluctant to cede the control of strategically important activities to subsidiaries. Most multinational companies used to be, and many still are, unwilling to locate their R&D activities in their foreign subsidiaries. The reason, as Tayeb (2000) argues, may not entirely be on the ground of a lack of expertise in host nations, as evidenced by many Japanese and American firms which do not take their R&D functions to the countries with equal if not better records in scientific research and innovation and skilled workforce. R&D functions represent the heart and brains of a company, as it were, as do strategic industries for nations—one may not want such a source of life and power to be owned and/or controlled by foreigners.

Major strategies, in the HRM area and other activities, are initiated by the parent company at the headquarters. All the decisions, from the internationalisation of operations and the selection of host countries to the form of internationalisation and the kind of people to be employed, are naturally considered as the parent company's prerogative. They invest huge amounts of money and energy and need to ensure that everything possible is done properly to achieve the company's goals and objectives. The management structure of the

**Table 5.1** HRM strategic options

| Strategic option | Implications for HRM | Consideration for host-country culture and institutions |
|---|---|---|
| Ethnocentric | Export home-country style to subsidiaries | Ignore |
| Polycentric | Adapt HRM policies and practices to local conditions | Take employees' different cultural backgrounds, and national institutions into consideration |
| Global | Have a global company-wide HRM style | Create a cultural synergy, build up a strong organisational culture |
| Hybrid | Different strategies for different subsidiaries | Take employees' different cultural backgrounds, national institutions, and subsidiaries' characteristics into consideration |

company is also designed by the HQ in such a way as to facilitate the implementation of its strategies.

But what HRM strategic options are available to MNCs and what factors influence their ultimate choice?

Multinational companies have three broad strategic options to choose from: ethnocentric, polycentric, and global (Perlmutter, 1969). These strategies would lead in turn to (i) the firms having HRM policies which would resemble that of their home-country styles, or (ii) would be similar to the host countries' indigenous styles or (iii) a company-wide style irrespective of home- and host-countries' preferred and prevalent styles. In practice however, as Table 5.1 shows, MNCs might in certain circumstances pick and mix and opt for a hybrid strategy.

## Ethnocentric strategy

The first instinct of a multinational company might be to manage employees and other resources and functions of its foreign subsidiaries according to its home-base models and ways of doing things, because they are 'logical', work well, and are familiar. Moreover, some international companies, especially those from more advanced countries, often resist adapting to cultural differences because they believe their own way is superior to that of others. The logic of local practices, in many cases tried and tested over centuries, is sometimes lost to a parent company from a different national background.

One of the advantages of this strategy is that the HRM practices that have been proven to lead to higher performance at home might also lead to similar results abroad. It also enables the company to have a coherent and unified approach to its HRM preventing harmful contradictions, imbalance and disarray.

This strategy, however, has proved difficult to implement, even though many multinationals, especially those originating in the US, have in the past advocated and tried it out. It has for some times been recognised, by both researchers and practitioners, that such a rigid strategy cannot really be implemented without allowing some degree of modification and flexibility. The main reason is that the complex and diverse world in which the subsidiaries are located imposes its own imperatives which cannot be ignored. As we saw in earlier chapters, you cannot for instance require the subsidiaries located in a collectivist culture to have a motivation policy which works well in the individualistic culture of the parent company, and vice versa.

## Polycentric strategy

The pure version of this strategy implies that MNCs would allow their subsidiaries freedom to act as they see fit with due consideration for local conditions, and to follow, if they so wish, the HRM policies and practices prevalent in their respective host countries—'when in Rome do as the Romans do'.

This strategy is normally accompanied by a decentralised organisational structure and few international HR policies and guidelines for 'best practices'. The parent company might preserve for itself only a few areas, for example, recruitment of senior executives and issuing advice on key appointments at the subsidiary level. GEC and American Express (Evans and Lorange, 1989) are among the well-known companies which have adopted a polycentric strategy.

The advantage here is that the subsidiaries' HRM policies and practices are in tune with their own local culture and environment and are therefore easier to implement and get results. A major disadvantage is that some local management practices might be undesirable and harmful (for example corruption and nepotism) and it would not make sense to emulate them. In addition, the subsidiaries might become 'loose cannons', acting not in harmony with the rest of the company but independently and sometimes in conflict with its overall interests and objectives.

## Global strategy

This option envisages a strong organisational culture in which a synergy between various best practices regardless of their country of origin is created and incorporated in the company's 'ways of doing things'. For instance, if teamwork has been proven to lead to better performance in a collectivist culture, and individual-based performance appraisal has worked in individualist cultures, why not marry them together. The company can have a mixed-mode working pattern in which a group of employees work together as a team, say in cells (see case study in Chapter 4), but they will be individually rewarded if they work hard to increase their own productivity. Some companies such as IBM, Hewlett-Packard and Proctor & Gamble (Evans and Lorange, 1989), follow this strategy and are known to have a strong organisational culture which acts as a glue to link the various parts of the company together regardless of their geographical dispersion.

A global strategy is by implication accompanied by a centralised hierarchical structure in which control over the subsidiaries' HRM policies are laid down in detail for all subsidiaries and exercised through such means as formalised rules and regulations, standardised procedures and manuals, annual budget, various achievement targets and monitoring mechanisms. Such policies normally cover all areas of HR functions such as recruitment and promotion, union recognition, remuneration, working conditions, performance appraisal, training, pension scheme, and employment termination.

For a centralised strategy such as this to work companies usually put in place extensive employee training and retraining to eradicate the working habits that are perceived to be harmful and encourage those which are conducive to the achievement of company goals and objectives as a whole.

An obvious advantage of the global strategy is cohesion and consistency of approach across the company, like a well-conducted orchestra in which all the musicians play the same symphony and are in tune with one another. The main disadvantage is that it tends to ignore the reality on the ground, so to speak. Various subsidiaries are quasi-independent organisations which develop their own organisational culture over time and will acquire certain features which are more in tune with the local ways of doing things than the headquarters' preferences.

The above three strategic options, although they have commendable merits, share in common a simplistic perception of the real world in which MNCs have to operate and the complex issues that they have to tackle all the time. Various studies have shown that the strategic management of a subsidiary, especially its workforce, from a distance is a complicated affair. The choice between the above strategies does not simply depend on the philosophy and preferences of the parent company, but also on a number of other factors some of which could be beyond the parent's control, such as host country conditions (see also Björkman and Furu, 2000; Tayeb, 2000; and Wallace, 2000).

Another complicating factor is specific areas of HRM practices. Rosenzweig and Nohria (1994) studied practices regarding time off, benefits, gender composition, training, executive bonus, and executive participation in a large sample of foreign subsidiaries in the United States. They found that the degree of conformity to local practices diminished as one went down along these functions, with the time off showing the highest and the executive participation the lowest degree of conformity.

The discussion so far leads us to conclude that, in practice, many MNCs are inclined to adopt a more sophisticated hybrid strategy, than any one of the three discussed above.

## Hybrid strategy

In this option, the parent company treats each subsidiary individually on a case by case basis. For example, an ethnocentric approach might be adopted with respect to some subsidiaries and a polycentric one for others, depending on their individual circumstances and characteristics. In addition, the strategy towards any one subsidiary might change over time. For instance a newly-established subsidiary might be tightly controlled from the HQ, but as its management team and other employees acquire the necessary skills and experience, the parent company would loosen the rein and at some point in time let go of a lot of control over its activities.

The choice of strategy depends also on how the foreign subsidiary is set up. In a green field site, the expatriate managers have more room to exercise their choice. The Japanese multi-national firms operating green field plants in many parts of the United Kingdom, for example, have been able to bring in many of their HRM practices to their brand new subsidiaries. But if the subsidiary is created by taking over an already existing local company, the new firm is more likely to resemble other fellow firms in the country, initially at least until gradually the parent company organisational culture asserts itself (Tayeb, 1994).

The examples given in Table 5.2 show how a parent company might choose different HRM strategies on the basis of local conditions, such as the labour market.

Also, as we shall see in Chapter 7, there is a qualitative difference between HRM strategies and policies on the one hand, and HRM practices on the other. Whereas multinational companies might find it feasible to have company-wide *strategies* and *policies* of a global or ethnocentric nature, they might find it necessary to be responsive to local conditions when it comes to HRM *practices* and therefore adopt a polycentric style.

**Table 5.2** Some local factors which might influence MNCs' HRM strategic choices

| Local conditions | Parent-company strategy |
|---|---|
| The workforce does not enjoy much power<br>The workforce is unskilled and uneducated<br>Job opportunities are scarce<br>Unemployment rates are high<br>Economic down-turn | Ethnocentric<br>Global |
| Employees are highly educated and skilled<br>Employees are aware of their rights<br>Pro-workers rules and regulations<br>Low rates of unemployment<br>Economic boom | polycentric |
| Foreign subsidiary is a green-field site<br>Employees are young, with little or no work<br>  experience, no organisational cultural baggage | Ethnocentric<br>Global |
| Foreign subsidiary acquired through a take-over<br>  of an existing company<br>Employees resistant to new management style<br>Heavy organisational cultural baggage | Polycentric<br>(initially at least) |
| Subsidiary located in a technically and<br>  professionally advanced industrialised country | Polycentric |
| Subsidiary located in a developing country and<br>  less advanced in technical and professional<br>  management issues | Ethnocentric<br>Global |

## Subsidiary perspective

The above discussion on various HRM strategies that may be adopted by parent companies shows clearly that the host country in which subsidiaries are located cannot be ignored. In this section we will discuss why the subsidiaries themselves also cannot be treated as passive recipients of HQ instructions.

### Host-country culture

As we saw in earlier chapters, national cultural characteristics, including those related to HRM and management–employee relationships, vary a great deal across the world. Moreover, many of these cultural characteristics are deeply-rooted in centuries-old traditions, history and shared experiences. The fact that a foreign multinational takes over a company or sets up one from scratch, cannot easily obliterate its host-country employees' cultural attitudes, values and beliefs, certainly not from a distance and through rules and regulations. People will always find a way of avoiding instructions and procedures which run contrary to their deeply-held values and traditions, and assert their own individuality. As a result, strategies which on paper ignore local culture in practice may be diluted and modified to allow a relatively tension-free atmosphere in which the local employees can work. NCR's plant in Scotland (Tayeb, 1998) illustrates this point.

A few years ago, when NCR holding company was taken over by AT&T, the new parent company management introduced a programme of 'common bond'. The idea was to create a common identity within each subsidiary and throughout the company worldwide, and to remove or at least reduce status differentiation among the workforce. The programme however caused a serious offence to the workforce, at the root of which was seen to be the parent company's perceived insensitivity to the host culture.

As part of the programme, there would be explicit emphasis on such concepts as respect for individuals, dedication to helping customers, highest standards of integrity, innovation, and teamwork. To bring the message home a one-day mass meeting was organised in a special venue and the programme was introduced to the workforce. Posters were put up everywhere in the company buildings to remind people of this new creed, but they were for all intents and purposes ignored and the programme as a whole was received coldly by the workforce. This was not because people did not agree with what such concepts signified. Rather, they had been offended that the new parent company had felt necessary to tell them such ideals should be aimed and pursued in the company. As one of those who was present at the mass meeting put it:

'A lot of people, and I include myself, said "I really am offended, in fact almost insulted, that they feel they've got to do this with us". Because my firm belief, being in this job and having been in it all the years I've been here, is that unless we operated for example, with integrity, we wouldn't have lasted. The company wouldn't have lasted the 50 years that it's been in Dundee [Scotland]. If we had not applied the principles of the common bond across the board during those 50 years, then we wouldn't be celebrating the 50th anniversary this year. So that came over from the US and I don't think it was well received. I think a lot of people said this is an absolute nonsense, I mean coming to teach us at this stage in the game is just crazy stuff, it's quite offensive. I think they consider it in the US to be still alive and kicking, but as far as I'm concerned, we operate the way that we've always operated, and that probably incorporates what they call the common bond.'

AT&T and NCR parted ways later and the common bond posters were taken off the walls of the Dundee subsidiary.

## Host-country institutions

We saw in Chapter 3 the powerful influences that political, economic, legal and other societal institutions can sometimes have on the internal affairs of organisations, especially their HRM policies and practices. To the extent that the host country institutions are different from those of the parent company's, the subsidiaries are able to diverge from the parent company and modify its instructions and rules to make them compatible with the local conditions, and in some cases even ignore them, either by mutual consent or unilaterally. Power of trade unions, industrial relations legislation, health and safety regulations, and workers rights are some of the major areas over which there are huge differences between various countries. For instance, as we saw earlier in the book, in Germany the right of employee participation in decision making is enshrined in the works councils that all major companies are by law required to have and in the UK a minimum wage regulation is in place. UK and German sub-sidiaries of multinational companies will abide by the laws and regulations of their own country, regardless of the parent company's wishes. And in practice the parent company gives its consent as well.

Generally, compared to the HQ, subsidiaries are better placed to judge the local political and legal situation and make appropriate decisions, especially with regard to sensitive issues. For instance, in some countries many HR practices are influenced by religion and laws derived from religious traditions. In Saudi Arabia for instance, women are barred from senior positions in companies, and such rules apply as much to the subsidiaries of foreign MNCs as to domestic firms.

Also, subsidiary managers, especially in some nations in south east Asia and the Middle East, where informal connections and personal networks greatly enhance the chances of success and getting things done (see also Chapter 4), will have the upper hand vis-à-vis their HQ managers hundreds of miles away, socio-culturally as well as geographically. The familiarity with the local conditions goes of course beyond informal relations. Knowing one's own country's legal systems, being in touch with political events, being aware of the latest changes in laws, rules and regulations, and keeping abreast of the latest developments in fads and fashions and customers' tastes, are also contributory factors to the balance of power within the parent–subsidiary relationship (Tayeb, 2000).

## Market conditions and subsidiary mandate

An aspect of a foreign subsidiary's experience, which could earn it autonomy, is related directly to its local business environment. Building on Porter's (1990) model, Birkinshaw and Hood (1998) argue that some of the factors which contribute to the presence of a subsidiary mandate are local market competitiveness, demanding customers and strong supporting and related industries in the local business environment. Such an environment, as is for instance the case in Japan and many similar advanced capitalist nations, could help local managers gain invaluable experience and training, which would in turn place them in an advantageous position.

In a study conducted by the present author, she found that the Scottish subsidiary of Total, a major oil company, had to deal constantly with a competitive local labour market. This had given it valuable knowledge and experience which in turn enabled it to diverge from the parent company policies in certain HR areas and make decisions autonomously as it saw fit.

One of the local managers interviewed, talking about pay and benefits structure, commented thus:

'In our case after over 20 years the Centre [parent company HQ] recognises that we are a reservoir of expertise. People come into and go out of this reservoir. They also recognise we do certain things here that they do not yet do in Paris [HQ's location]; they are interested in and keep track of what we are doing.

We keep an eye on our competitors here and keep up with them. If we don't pay the local rate [which is much higher than in Paris] we won't be able to attract and keep talented skilled professionals. They [Centre] like to have a window to the Anglo-Saxon world, they would like to know what Mobil, Texaco and BP are doing here. In France there are only two oil companies, EIF and Total, there is nothing else. They know we have a sophisticated grading system and we also have a feel for local market. Our skills in coping and dealing with competition are useful to the Centre.'

## Subsidiary location

Research evidence shows that many subsidiaries located in industrialised nations have managed to earn their mandate largely because of managerial and technical competence and skills of their workforce. As the HR manager of the French company Total put it to the present author:

'There is also the 1st world–3rd world case in this regard. They [HQ] are quite comfortable with us here to do our own thing, but when they want to set up a subsidiary in Myanmar, for example, they take the French system there and they *will* implement it there. . . . In Indonesia they did the same initially; now after many years they have almost completed the localisation process, to comply with local environment and legal requirements, among other things. . . . When setting up new subsidiaries they are more directive, because no infrastructure is in place.'

However, as we saw in Table 5.2, unfavourable local economic conditions such as recession and high rates of unemployment can adversely affect the subsidiaries' power and influence, regardless of their excellent locally-acquired experience. In such cases the parent company can dictate terms, both in strategic spheres and with respect to operative decisions.

Regional political economic conditions within the same country can also at times influence the extent to which home-country practices can be implemented in the subsidiaries. Beechler and Yang's (1994) study of a sample of Japanese companies operating in the United States provides an interesting example.

The study concerned five manufacturing and five service subsidiaries of Japanese multinational companies. The service companies were based in New York City. Their environment was characterised, among other things, by a heterogeneous workforce in terms of culture, religion, race and gender; a fiercely competitive labour market; a high rate of labour turnover; and a need for a highly skilled specialised workforce. Under these circumstances, the Japanese firms had to depart from a large number of their home-country practices, such as job flexibility, long-term training, group-based promotion and benefit payment, seniority-based wage agreements, and concern for employees. Instead, after initial unsuccessful experiments with these practices, they adopted American styles of human resource management. They opted for recruiting highly specialised employees, no on-the-job training and job rotation, and aimed at high profit rather than concern for employees.

The five manufacturing firms were located in Tennessee, with an environment characterised, at the time, by low labour turnover, a relatively uncompetitive labour market, and a homogeneous and less individualistic workforce, compared to the New York City environment.

Here, although the unionised plants offered more resistance to the introduction of Japanese management practices than did the non-unionised ones, the managers were able to implement more successfully some of their home-based human resource management practices. They recruited the workforce after lengthy screening and pre-employment training procedures. They introduced quality circles, an emphasis on process-based control and quality rather than quality inspection, flexible job rules, job rotation, work teams, and uniformity between blue- and white-collar workers.

## Dependence on local resources

In cases where the foreign operation depends on local resources, such as a skilled workforce, raw materials, capital and distribution networks, the subsidiaries can earn a great deal of decision making power and autonomy. They are on the spot, have access to a lot of information and know how to go about doing things. As a result, they are better able to identify and employ the local resources than their bosses at the HQ.

## Reverse diffusion

Sometimes subsidiaries are able to come up with new initiatives and implement innovative HR practices independent of the company-wide HR strategies and policies. If such local initiatives turn out to be successful, in terms of employee higher productivity and ultimately

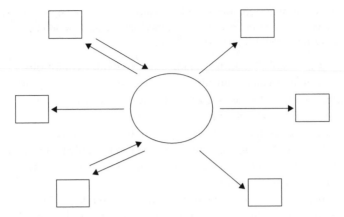

**Figure 5.2** Parent–subsidiary relationship

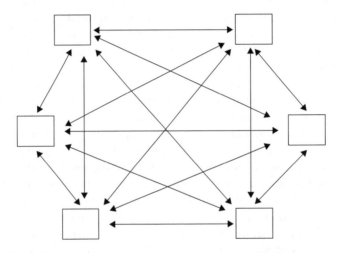

**Figure 5.3** Subsidiary–subsidiary relationship

increased profits, the parent company might be inclined to adopt such initiatives in other subsidiaries or even at the HQ and home-country plants (see also Figures 5.2 and 5.3).

A few years ago, the local Scottish plant manager of Michelin, a French multinational company, decided to embark on a cellular manufacturing (CM) initiative which required the removal of shift managers and implementation of self-managed teams during night shifts. Once Scotland started the programme other sites in the UK also followed. The HQ's most senior manager (one of the owners) was unaware of this and learned about it only informally and by accident. He was reportedly livid—he had always seen the shift managers as absolutely necessary to the factory operations. He sent some HQ people over to Scotland and demanded explanations. A working party was then set up to evaluate the risk to the company and its culture. The HQ's eventual conclusion was that CM made a positive contribution to the company's working practices and even recommended it to other subsidiaries to emulate. The home-based plants too have implemented similar working arrangements (Tayeb and Thory, 2000).

It is due to the very nature of relationships between the parent company and its subsidiaries that tension and conflict become inevitable, as there is both the need to maintain the integrity of the corporation as a coherent, coordinated entity, and at the same time to allow for responsiveness to their differentiated environments (see for instance Prahalad, 1976; Prahalad and Doz, 1987; Welch, 1994). Chapter 6 will discuss in detail the issue of differentiation and integration and explores the ways in which multinational companies may maintain a balance between the two.

## ■ CHAPTER SUMMARY

This chapter began by discussing the rationale for internationalisation of MNCs operations and the ways in which they might go about it. We also learned that HRM issues are essentially of utmost relevance to international joint ventures and wholly owned subsidiaries. This is because the MNCs recruit and manage a foreign workforce when they adopt these two modes of internationalisation.

The HRM issues were discussed from two separate but obviously intertwined perspectives—parent and subsidiary. From a parent company's vantage point, the chapter discussed various strategic options and other factors which might influence the ways in which the HQ would manage their employees around the world. The chapter then explored the characteristics of ethnocentric, polycentric, global strategies and evaluated their merits and disadvantages. It was argued that because of the complexity of the real world in which MNCs operate they might in fact adopt a hybrid strategy and even at times deal with their various subsidiaries on a one-to-one basis, that is, the parent may choose to adopt different approaches to different subsidiaries because of the different environments in which they operate and the different issues that they face.

From the subsidiaries' perspective, it was argued that various factors such as the host-country's socio-cultural and political economic characteristics, and the subsidiaries' own experience and capabilities, tend to increase their influence and autonomy. These factors could earn the subsidiary a mandate to interpret the company's overall HRM strategies and policies in a way that would be more compatible with 'the facts on the ground'.

## ■ REVISION QUESTIONS

1. To what extent MNCs' HRM strategies and policies are relevant to their operations in host-countries?

2. What are the main strengths and weaknesses of ethnocentric, polycentric and global HRM strategies?

3. What is a hybrid strategy and why might a company wish to adopt it?

4. Imagine you are the HR director of a foreign company subsidiary in your country. In what major HR areas would you consider to be in a better position than your bosses at the headquarters to decide on policies and practices in the subsidiary?

# Case study: Seiko Instruments

The Seiko Group, established in 1937, consists of three distinct companies—Seiko Corporation, Seiko Instruments Inc (SII) and Seiko Epson Corporation. They operate independently but function as a cohesive unit in the design, production and marketing of the timepieces that established the Seiko name. The company has around 70 subsidiaries worldwide with over 10,000 employees. Through its global network, Seiko Corporation markets the timepieces produced by SII and Seiko Epson. In 1988 Seiko completed the world's first automated assembling system for multipurpose, small-lot production of watch movements.

The Scottish plant was founded in March 1990 and has 110 employees. The location was chosen because it is close to European markets, has a stable skilled workforce, and other Japanese companies had a successful experience in Scotland. The subsidiary manufactures thermal printers and watch components.

The organisational structure is constrained by British standards in some respects, in common with other Japanese companies operating in the UK.

## HR strategy

The General Manager (GM), who is Scottish, has worked on the site for over 10 years and in all those years there have been only two visits by a personnel representative from Japan. The main objectives of the visits was for the HQ to survey the Japanese employees working overseas.

'The corporation's stance is basically that in the overseas countries the personnel function should operate entirely autonomously. It's fairly bizarre to have identical policies and procedures in sites in as diverse locations as Japan, China, Thailand, Malaysia and the UK. Generally the company tries to treat its employees fairly well and it's left up to local personnel to follow local standards.'

'If it wasn't for Mr X [a Japanese senior manager] you wouldn't know you worked for a Japanese company. There isn't really anything Japanese about it at all. I say to people: you will probably find this company is not like your typical Japanese company.'

Most personnel policies of the Scottish site are made locally; the site is given targets and a free range to achieve them 'the Scottish way'. The company's policy is to respect local ways—they try to adapt to local management practices 100 percent within the Scottish location. People management is designed locally, mainly by the General Manager. They have constructed a policy manual and handbook containing mostly local practices. They are first written in draft, involving all the managers at this stage, agreed upon, and then formalised. Then they are placed on notice boards and employees are notified. Revisions are initiated as required by legislation, for example changes in working practices. The GM has spent some time working in the US (California) with Seiko and has introduced some Californian practices into the site.

## Recruitment

All practices are driven from the Scottish site. In Japan they select school leavers for operators. Initially, the Japanese Manufacturing Manager had a preference for school leavers and teenagers and wanted the Scottish site to recruit them. He was involved in the recruitment of the first 90 employees who fulfilled this age criterion. When these 90 young recruits were assessed on, for example, how they behaved against their elders on site, they were considered unreliable and 'unaccustomed to this kind of work'. Absenteeism was a problem at this stage.

He believed that 'they had no work ethic at this age'. The Personnel Manager at the time was the only personnel manager of a Japanese company in Livingston to say 'I will not employ school leavers and teenagers'. He thinks the policy of recruiting school leavers works in Japan because youngsters are more obedient and better educated.

## Overseas training

Watch manufacturing has been in operation for over four years. A lot of initial training was done in Seiko's subsidiaries in Singapore and the far east; a lot of overseas trainers came over, and worked with the operators for about 3 months. The on-site practices have been refined over the years. Production supervisors go over to Japan every year to learn new processes. If the Scottish site had a disastrous manufacturing problem a Japanese would come over. Recently they have had an engineering design problem in the printers section and quality people came over from Japan. They stayed for three days to sort things out.

What has been brought from overseas is mainly knowledge. When the watch manufacturing was set up there were no processes in existence. Twenty four employees were sent over to Japan to learn how to operate the equipment. They came back and eventually increased the number of people in the area and developed their own systems.

The senior manufacturing engineer goes to Japan for training and looking at business opportunities, and to Singapore for transfer of production lines and further training.

Generally, no one goes over to Japan to train. Although things are changing—they are becoming more interested in what Scotland is doing with regard to technical processes. Scotland has taken Japanese ideas and is now running some of their machines more efficiently.

## Training differences between Japan and Scotland

In Scotland the company encourages people to develop at operator level, both in-house and in colleges and other educational establishments, and finances their further education.

In Japan, because employees stay in the company a long time, they have large, established internal training and recognised formal qualifications. They have extensive support resources, for example engineering and technical support. Rank and file employees do not go to college or university, because they are not available to everyone at the company's expense, but sometimes managers do attend short courses in these establishments. However, the company will pay up to 50 percent of the cost of out-sourced English classes if employees wish to learn the language.

## Team working

The subsidiary management has introduced the Japanese way of teamworking. The local managers know the Japanese practices such as total quality management and quality circles, and use them in a modified way. The management does not push Japanese quality initiatives; they are happy for the employees to apply the tools they prefer. Also, in Japan they run quality circles after working hours on a voluntary non-paid basis but the Scottish managers would not be able to implement them here because the operators would want to be paid overtime.

In addition, the managers believe that such practices as twice daily exercises in the office, customary in the Japanese sites, would not work here 'because the company is not a school or army'.

## Consensual decision making

The GM's observation from working in Seiko plants in Japan is that Japanese style consensual decision making offers unsatisfactory compromises. He says decisions take more time to be made. Also, if junior Japanese managers are involved they will not speak their mind because they feel inhibited, for cultural and traditional reasons. In the Scottish site employees are more frank.

'I would imagine that having worked here for a number of years our boss probably prefers what he may have initially interpreted as a fairly antagonistic discourse—it's a bit more stimulating and actually more things are aired and moved forward.'

## Pay and benefits

These are all decided locally. There is considerable competition for skilled local staff. Seiko in Livingston competes against the likes of Motorola and Sky for employees. Consequently their pay is competitive, with rewards for hard work. They also offer paternity leave, pensions, life assurance and sick pay.

## Industrial relations

The Scottish site is not unionised, but the Japanese sites have company-based unions. Moreover, in Scotland there are grievance procedures in place to enable the employees to file claims against their boss, but such a system does not exist in the Japanese sites. Senior managers believe that the history of local trade unions still make the employees suspicious of management, even today. The management have to work harder to gain trust and get people to buy in and get them to come up with ideas and work on problems themselves.

In Scotland they make employees redundant if they have to. In Japan Seiko does not do this. The company offers jobs for life, and if need be transfers employees to holding divisions rather than make them redundant.

■ **CASE STUDY QUESTIONS**

1. Why has the parent company adopted an HRM strategy which would allow overseas subsidiaries to perform their personnel function autonomously?

2. In what respect is the Scottish subsidiary's recruitment policy different from its Japanese parent company, and why?

3. Why has the local management team decided not to implement some of the Japanese parent company's practices in Scotland?

**4.** In what ways have the local political economic conditions enabled the subsidiary to act locally as they see fit and thereby go against the headquarters' current HR policies?

**5.** To what extent does this case confirm or reject the discussions about parent–subsidiary in the main body of the chapter?

### ■ RECOMMENDED FURTHER READING

Birkinshaw, J. and Hood, N. (1998). 'The determinants of subsidiary mandates and subsidiary initiative: a three-country study', in G. Hooley, R. Loveridge, and D. Wilson (eds.), *Internationalisation: Process, Context and Markets*. Basingstoke: Macmillan.

Tayeb, M. H. (2000). *The Management of International Enterprises: A Socio-Political View*. Basingstoke: Macmillan.

### ■ REFERENCES

Beechler, S. and Yang, J. Z. (1994). 'The transfer of Japanese-style management to American subsidiaries: contingencies, constraints, and competencies', *Journal of International Business Studies*, vol. 25, pp. 467–91.

Birkinshaw, J. and Hood, N. (1998). 'The determinants of subsidiary mandates and subsidiary initiative: a three-country study', in G. Hooley, R. Loveridge, and D. Wilson (eds.), *Internationalisation: Process, Context and Markets*. Basingstoke: Macmillan.

Björkman, I. and Furu, P. (2000). 'Determinants of variable pay for top managers of foreign subsidiaries in Finland', *International Journal of Human Resource Management*, vol. 11, no. 4, pp. 698–713.

Crookell, H. H. (1986). 'Specialisation and international competitiveness', in H. Etemad and L. S. Sulude (eds.), *Managing the Multinational Subsidiary*. London: Croom Helm.

Evans, P. and Lorange, P. (1989). 'The two logics behind human resource management', in P. Evans, Y. Doz, and A. Laurent (ed.), *Human Resource Management in International Firms: Change, Globalisation, Innovation*. Baskingstoke: Macmillan. pp. 144–61.

Perlmutter, H. V. (1969). 'The tortuous evolution of the multinational corporation', *Columbia Journal of World Business*, vol. 4, pp. 9–18.

Porter, M. E. (1990). *The Competitive Advantage of Nations*. Basingstoke: Macmillan.

Poynter, T. A. and Rugman, A. R. (1982). 'World product mandates: how will multinationals respond?', *Business Quarterly*, vol. 46 (Fall), pp. 54–61.

Prahalad, C. K. (1976). 'Strategic choices in diversified MNCs', *Harvard Business Review*, July–August, pp. 67–78.

—— and Doz, Y. L. (1987). *The Multinational Mission: Balancing Global Demands and Global Vision*. New York: Free Press.

Rosenzweig, P. M. and Nohria, N. (1994). 'Influences on human resource management in multinational corporations', *Journal of International Business Studies*, vol. 25, pp. 229–51.

Tayeb, M. H. (1994). 'Japanese managers and British culture: a comparative case study', *International Journal of Human Resource Management*, vol. 5, no. 1, pp. 145–66.

—— (1998). 'Transfer of HRM policies and practices across cultures: an American company in Scotland', *International Journal of Human Resource Management*, vol. 9, no. 2, pp. 332–58.

Tayeb, M. H. (2000). *The Management of International Enterprises: A Socio-Political View*. Basingstoke: Macmillan.

—— and Thory, K. (2000). 'The internationalisation of HRM policies and practices: the case of Japanese and French companies in Scotland', paper presented at the AGRH (Association Francophone de Gestion des Ressources Humaines) Conference, 16–17 November, Paris.

Wallace, T. (2000). 'Societal effects meet sectoral effects: work organization, competencies and payment systems in the Volvo Commercial Vehicle Division', *International Journal of Human Resource Management*, vol. 11, no. 4, pp. 714–35.

Welch, D. (1994). 'HRM implications of globalization', *Journal of General Management*, vol. 19, pp. 52–68.

# 6 | Differentiate or Integrate? That's the Question

## Learning outcomes

When you finish reading this chapter you should:
- know about a major managerial preoccupation of multinational companies (MNCs), i.e. differentiation and integration 'dilemma', especially with regards to HRM
- be familiar with the current theoretical debates within the international management literature and its origins
- be able to explore and assess the ways in which MNCs might choose to deal with contradictory demands of differentiation and integration policies
- get some idea from the closing case study how in practice a major MNC maintains differentiation and integration of activities of one of its subsidiaries.

## Introduction

The last chapter discussed major HRM issues of concern to multinational companies from both parent and subsidiaries' perspectives. The chapter ended by arguing that the relationship between the parent company and its subsidiaries is inherently prone to tension and conflict. This is because of the geographically and culturally differentiated nature of a multinational firm and at the same time the need to keep it as a consistent 'whole' so that it can rationalise the use of its resources and serve its large and complex market more effectively.

The present chapter will elaborate on this issue further and explore the ways in which multinational companies maintain a balance between the two. The chapter will conclude by suggesting various mechanisms that MNCs might employ to do just that. Figure 6.1 maps out the main issues addressed in the chapter.

## Differentiation and integration

The concepts of differentiation and integration, originally a focus of debate among sociologists, were first discussed within the context of management and organisation studies by Lawrence and Lorsch (1967). They argued that for an organisation to perform effectively in diverse environments, it must be both appropriately differentiated and adequately integrated in order that the separate units and departments are coordinated and work towards a common goal.

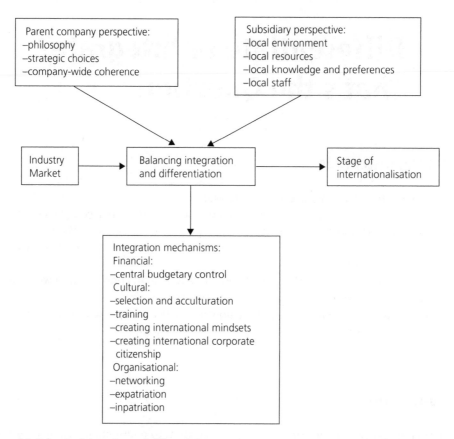

**Figure 6.1** Balancing integration and differentiation

For example, in a typical manufacturing company the marketing department faces a different segment of the firm's external environment (e.g. customers) than that with which an R&D department normally deals (e.g. scientific community, universities). Since it is crucial for each department to interact with its own segment of the external environment freely and appropriately, the departments must be given autonomy and freedom of action. But of course there is a danger that the employees and managers working in various departments immerse themselves in their 'little world' to such an extent that they might lose sight of the overall interests and objectives of the firm. In pursuance of their immediate objectives they might indeed unwittingly act in detriment to the interests of the company as a whole. For instance, the Research and Development department might work on and produce a technologically advanced and interesting product, but the Marketing department will later on find out that there is no significant consumer demand for it. In a company with an integrated strategy the two departments will work in tandem from the start—they coordinate their strategies and activities and move forward side by side, not one in front of the other.

In order to prevent such conflicting loyalties and strategies, integrating mechanisms should be employed, e.g. a strong organisational cultural identity, central budgetary control, moving employees around the departments. As we saw in Chapter 4, Japanese organisations in general are very good at the last of these.

In the context of internationalisation, Lawrence and Lorsch's (1967) model has been developed in order to explain the dynamics of managing organisations operating across national borders.

Doz (1976) described the need for differentiation in political terms, emphasising the tension that exists between the 'economic imperative' (large scale efficient facilities) and the 'political imperative' (local content laws, local production requirements). Prahalad (1976) developed a typology of multinational companies which stressed the 'need for managerial interdependence' (integration) versus the 'need for managerial diversity' (local responsiveness), so highlighting the need for differentiation on a geographical basis.

In order to maintain an equilibrium between these two conflicting forces, Prahalad and Doz (1987) suggested a multifocal solution where the focus of decision making shifts between the international and local depending on the problem under consideration. They argue that the mindset of managers should have a global framework balancing the needs between local responsiveness and a global vision of the firm.

Arguing in the same vein, Welch (1994a) states that the global organisation is faced with a paradox: on the one hand it needs to develop control and coordination mechanisms consistent with effective and efficient global operations; on the other, it needs to be responsive to national interests which may impede worldwide activities. Applied to human resource management, a multinational firm, intending to maintain its overall identity and strategies, could benefit from global, geocentric orientation in personnel policies and practices. But in order to remain at the same time responsive to local variations it should have a polycentric (locally specific) orientation. This, Welch suggests, requires the multinational to operate at two levels: maintain an HRM orientation that enables local concerns to be addressed, yet develop a team of international staff who can be moved into and out of the various worldwide activities of the firm, and thus help bind the organisation together.

It is worth noting that the 'push' towards integration comes not only from within the firm, but also, indirectly at least, from the outside interests, such as clients and suppliers. In this connection, Nahapiet (1998) points out that as clients integrate their activities across borders they often look to their service providers to do the same, and as companies globalise, they generally seek suppliers who can cater for them as a single entity and provide them with a consistent and coordinated cross-border service. Moves to regional and global branding, for example, require corresponding support teams at regional and global levels—both in the client company and the supporting advertising agency. Similarly, the growing regional or global concentration of specialist functions in areas such as research and development and manufacturing often calls for regional or global consulting teams.

The distinction between culture-specific and universal aspects of management may also be relevant to the debate regarding the management of foreign subsidiaries in general and the question of differentiation and integration in particular. A recent case study in three American subsidiaries and affiliates located in Scotland (Tayeb and Dott, 2000) provides a good example here. The study found the so-called 'soft' aspect of management, such as inter-personal relationships and communication, HRM and industrial relations issues, were influenced by the local culture and handled according to locally accepted norms and traditions, even though in some cases the parent companies were unhappy with the outcome. Certain culture-free and so-called 'hard' aspects of management such as strategy, budgetary control, hierarchical structure and use of standard procedures and rules, were decided by parent companies and implemented more or less unchallenged and unchanged in the Scottish plants.

The study showed that the American multinational companies' preferred way of organising and controlling their subsidiaries in Scotland was to delegate as much autonomy as possible to the local management in charge, but at the same time this decentralisation was accompanied by detailed written policies, rules and regulations. This is not dissimilar to the policies and practices employed by most large-scale organisations, multinational or otherwise, with a wide range of functions and operations. In other words, the three multinational companies involved in the study had differentiated those aspects of their subsidiaries' management which were closely affected by local socio-cultural conditions, but had maintained the integration of the company as a whole by centrally controlling those organisational aspects which were relatively culture-neutral.

As we saw in Chapter 5, the relationship between parent company and subsidiaries is dynamic and changes over time and space. Similarly, we can argue here that the balance between differentiation and integration represents a dynamic, fluid and continuously-changing state, often resolved on a one-to-one basis—that is, at any point in time the specific relationship between the parent company and each individual subsidiary ultimately determines how the issue of differentiation and integration is managed (Tayeb, 1998). This view is in line with Ghoshal and Bartlett's arguments (1990) but contrasts with the view held by some other researchers (e.g. Hulbert and Brandt, 1980) who see multinational firms as homogeneous entities, especially with regard to parent–subsidiary relationships.

What the above and similar arguments point to is that multinational companies do not adopt either integration or differentiation as an HRM strategy, rather they try to accommodate both by maintaining a balance between the two, and that this balance is crucial to their success. But is this balancing act relevant and important to all companies with international interests?

# The relevance of integration and differentiation dilemma

The importance and relevance of the question of integration and differentiation varies from company to company depending on a number of factors, such as their level of internationalisation, their industry, the market they serve and the kind of employees they have.

## Stage and form of internationalisation

As we saw in Chapter 5, there are various forms in which companies might choose to expand internationally. These forms could range from import and export to franchise and license to joint ventures and wholly-owned subsidiaries. Some firms might stop at any of these stages, some might go on from one stage to another, accumulating experience until they arrive at the wholly-owned subsidiary level. Others might leap-frog some of these stages and reach where they want to be more quickly. Once there, some companies might like to expand only in a few countries; others might go for a global worldwide market presence.

Figure 5.1 in Chapter 5 showed the extent to which national culture is relevant to any of the above stages and forms of internationalisation. Figure 6.2 here uses the same idea in

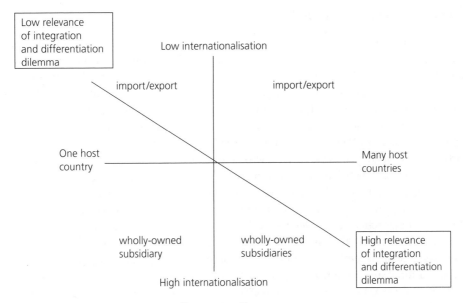

**Figure 6.2** Relevance of integration and differentiation dilemma

order to argue that the deeper and wider a firm is internationalised the more complicated and bigger its problem of differentiation and integration becomes.

As the figure shows, the question of integration and differentiation of HRM function across borders does not even arise for firms which do not have any significant operational units abroad (e.g. those which export or licence the manufacturing of their products). These firms' interests and affairs abroad are normally handled by local facilitating agents, such as sales representatives and distribution networks. They themselves do not directly employ and manage local people. In contrast, to those companies engaged in the most advanced and complex form of internationalisation—that is a fully fledged subsidiary, either wholly-owned or in partnership with others—a viable and effective international HRM policy is of utmost significance. Here the issue of integration and differentiation lies at the heart of the company strategy.

It is important to note, however, that international companies, even when they are in similar stages of internationalisation, vary quite considerably with regard to the ways in which they approach their overall HRM policies and practices. After all, every company is a unique entity. As Weber and Festing (1994) suggest, even companies who have extensive worldwide activities can pursue different international HRM policies and practices which are equally efficient for their needs. An example can be drawn from the management consultant companies. Although these enterprises are working throughout the world they usually do not pursue sophisticated international HRM activities. An important contribution to the coordination of such a company is the standardisation of qualifications and the exchange of knowledge. Another typical situation can be found in the supplier industry for cars. Usually, suppliers—say the company which makes car radios—follow the car industry. It is important to produce and deliver the products within the different countries, but in most of these cases there is no need for a high degree of local responsiveness or global integration (Weber and Festing, 1994).

## Industry and markets served

The industry in which a firm is engaged and the nature and scope of the competition it faces, given that industry, is an important consideration when deciding on an appropriate overall HRM strategy and the balance between integration and differentiation. We saw earlier that the most complex form of internationalisation for a firm is to have manufacturing or service plants and units in foreign countries. But there are various 'shades' within this category of internationalisation, depending on the nature of the market they serve.

Porter (1986), for instance, makes a distinction between two extreme types of industries in terms of the competition that they face, with a wide range in between: (a) the multidomestic industry, where competition in each country is essentially independent of competition in other countries, such as retailing, distribution, and insurance; (b) the global industry, where the firm's competitive position in one country is significantly influenced by its position in other countries, such as commercial aircraft, semiconductors, and copiers.

Porter further argues that an international company's overall strategy depends on how closely its industry resembles one or the other of these two types. In a multidomestic industry international strategy consists of a series of more or less independent domestic strategies. In a global industry a firm must in some way integrate its activities on a worldwide basis to capture the linkage among countries. This is so because the global industry is not merely a collection of domestic industries but a series of linked domestic industries in which the rivals compete against each other on a truly worldwide basis.

Commenting on the relevant human resource implications, Dowling and Schuler (1990) note that in a multidomestic industry, the role of the human resources department will most likely be more domestic in structure and orientation. The main role of the human resources function would be to support the primary activities of the firm in each domestic market to achieve competitive advantage through cost reduction and efficiency or value added to products and services. In a global industry human resources function needs to be coordinated across all affiliates and structured in such a way as to deliver the international support required by primary activities of the firm (see also, Schuler et al., 1993).

One could follow up the above arguments by saying that for the companies which operate in a multidomestic industry and adopt a multidomestic HRM strategy, the dilemma of differentiation and integration is almost irrelevant. Their HR policies and practices do not have to be integrated in any significant manner across various subsidiaries. These can be fairly differentiated to meet the demands of their specific local environment without damaging the interests of the company as a whole. By contrast, to the firms operating in a global industry the integration and differentiation dilemma is of utmost relevance, and the 'right' balance must be struck between the two to ensure the achievement of their overall goals and objectives.

## Characteristics of employees

The kind of employees a company has in its various subsidiaries influences the degree to which it would let go of control with little fear of disintegration of HRM strategies and policies of the company as a whole. Highly skilled, experienced, and fully committed and loyal employees are more likely to keep the interest of the company within their sight even if they are hundreds of miles away from its central office. Compare these with a subsidiary in which a vast majority of employees do not have sufficient skills or experience, or have a reputation for being corrupt, or have little to gain from loyalty to the company over and above a bear minimum. In cases such as these, the headquarters might exercise a great deal of control over the foreign unit. The advantages of integration here far outweighs those of differentiation, from the parent company's perspective at least.

The balance between integration and differentiation also depends on whether or not managers and employees working in a subsidiary are willing to accept centralised control over the ways in which they run their unit. Rosenzweig (1994) for instance found local staff in a large number of European multinational companies' subsidiaries in the United States were very reluctant to give up their autonomy and independence to the staff in their parent companies' headquarters. Sir John Harvey-Jones, the former Chairman of a British multi-national company, says of Americans that they are:

'. . . convinced that the sole aim of everybody outside America is to force them to operate in a way which is inappropriate to their country. No matter how many times you tell them that you do not wish to introduce British management style in the USA, they are convinced that every move you make is a step in that direction; an effort to introduce greater centralisation and rigidity in order to curb their freedom of action. This syndrome has . . . occurred in practically every company of every nationality that operates in the USA and is . . . something to do with American culture and the very high value that they put on headroom.' (Harvey-Jones, 1988, pp. 160–161)

Similarly, Welch (1994b) reports of an Australian bank which took over a similar organisation in Britain. In the now British subsidiary of the bank there was some resentment that a 'colonial' bank was the purchaser. And one manager commented 'Australians coming to tell us what to do, what did they know?' (p. 155).

# Mechanisms to achieve integration in highly differentiated and global companies

Multinational companies, especially those whose operations are run on a global basis and serve global markets, use various formal and informal devices in order to integrate their activities and their HRM across their subsidiaries. Many traditional devices such as budgetary control, formalised rules and regulations, performance criteria and intra-firm accounting practices can be put in place to make subsidiaries to work towards a common goal and to coordinate their activities. These devices can be grouped broadly into financial, organisational, cultural and HR categories.

## Financial mechanisms

Parent companies can redirect priorities and coordinate prioritised activities through central budgetary control. Financial limits can be imposed on recruitment for certain jobs (e.g. unskilled manual work), funds may be made available for employee training in certain skills (e.g. operating sophisticated computerised machines), performance related bonuses can be given for excellence in certain areas of activities (e.g. team working, problem solving) and so on.

## Organisational mechanisms

Company-wide accounting practices, rules and regulations governing managers' and employees' jobs and conduct, hierarchical command structure, clear and detailed job descriptions and authority boundaries are some of the ways in which parent companies ensure similarities of purpose and behaviours among their subsidiaries. One of the many managers interviewed in the present author's project said that in her company, Sun Microsystems, 'there is a worldwide code of conduct for answering phone calls received from outside the company'. You yourself may have experienced this sort of standardisation of procedures when ordering a product online through the Internet. If you order for example a book using any of the outlets of the Internet-based multinational company Amazon—e.g. amazon.com based in the US, amazon.co.uk based in the UK, amazon.fr based in France and amazon.de based in Germany—you will observe that the same procedures are followed everywhere, not only in the case of certain actions and steps which are automated and do not require direct employee involvement but also in cases for which humans are directly involved, such as packaging, invoicing, and responding to individual queries and issues which are personal to your custom and will have to be dealt with by an employee at the other end.

## Cultural mechanisms

In Chapter 5 we saw that some companies adopt a global strategy, which involves creation and maintenance of a strong organisational culture and which aims to provide a company-wide 'way of doing things'. Within the context of the current chapter, organisational culture can be considered as a powerful integration mechanism.

Organisational culture is a concept which, like its two constituent parts (i.e. 'organisation' and 'culture'), is difficult to define. Schein (1985), a writer who has contributed most significantly to the study of organisational culture, proposes his own definition, after a brief critical assessment of what other writers have offered.

He argues that organisational culture should be viewed as a property of an independently defined stable social unit. Organisational culture refers to basic assumptions and beliefs that are shared by members of an organisation. These operate unconsciously, and define in a basic 'taken-for-granted' fashion an organisation's view of itself and its environment. These assumptions and views are based on shared experiences and have worked for long enough to come to be taken for granted and be dropped out of awareness. Organisational culture, in this sense, is a learned 'product' of group experience and is therefore to be found only where there is a definable group with a significant history.

In the same vein, Denison (1990) sees organisational culture as a code, a logic, and a system of structured behaviours and meanings that have stood the test of time and serve as a collective guide to future adaptation and survival.

Similarly, Tunstall (1983) describes corporate culture as a general constellation of beliefs, mores, customs, value systems, behavioural norms, and ways of doing business that are unique to each corporation, that set a pattern for corporate activities and actions, and that describe the implicit emergent patterns of behaviour and emotions characterising life in the organisation.

There have also been studies which have explored and discussed the surface levels of culture (e.g. rites, stories, legends etc.) and examined their relationship with deeper levels of values and beliefs (see for instance Martin et al., 1983; Sathe, 1983; Trice and Beyer, 1984).

The origins of corporate culture could be traced, among other things, to the founder or founders of the organisation—their value systems, attitudes, beliefs, philosophy, and likes and dislikes. For instance, the founders might value hard work, honesty and punctuality, and believe in caring for employees and being responsive to their customers' needs. They bring these values and beliefs with them to the organisations they set up. Many internationally known multinationals such as Toyota and Hewlett-Packard owe much of their current culture and philosophy to their original owners.

In addition to the founders' values and beliefs, organisational culture, as a living entity, reflects the learning and retention that have occurred over time, solutions to problems which have worked well enough to be considered valid and therefore to be taught to new members as the correct way to perceive, think and feel in relation to those problems (Schein 1985; Denison, 1990).

But how do companies maintain the continuity of their culture given that new recruits keep coming in and replace those who leave? Here is where the HR function contribution is crucial right from the start, at the selection and recruitment stage and beyond.

## HRM mechanisms

### Staff selection and acculturation

Multinationals select staff from three sources: their home country, a subsidiary's respective country, other subsidiaries' countries. Usually a mixture of these sources are present in the company but the crucial point is the positions allocated to each of them. A vast majority of companies fill the most senior and important positions by nationals of their home country—i.e. staff from their headquarters, the so-called expatriate managers. As Welch (1994*b*) points out, one can find a few firms whose management has been delegated to non-home country staff (Philips, ABB, Heinz, Unilever, and IBM for example) but while these may indicate a trend they tend to be exceptions rather than the rule.

The expatriate senior managers fulfil at least three crucial roles: they run the subsidiary on behalf of the head office in its image, so to speak; they pass on the company's values and philosophy and management style to the subsidiary; they act as a conduit for central control and coordination (see also Chapter 9).

Blue-collar workers, white-collar employees and lower-managers are normally selected from the subsidiary's host country. Some multinational companies prefer to recruit local school leavers without significant work experiences for these positions, and then train them for the job. Many Japanese companies take this route (Tayeb, 1994). Yager et al. (1994) report a similar picture from multinational firms operating in China. They consistently prefer untrained young workers recruited from the countryside and trained from scratch. These people are considered to be unspoiled by experience in state-owned plants, and counterproductive work habits do not have to be unlearned.

Middle management posts are given to highly educated, and experienced staff from the host nation and other subsidiaries' countries. These managers normally undergo extensive training in the headquarters and/or designated educational centres, usually in the company's home country. McDonald's for example has a worldwide management training centre, Hamburger University, located in Oak Brook, Illinois, United States. Established in 1961, it is designed exclusively to instruct personnel employed by McDonald's Corporation or employed by McDonald's Independent Franchisees in the various aspects of the business. At the time of writing, more than 65,000 managers in McDonald's restaurants have graduated from Hamburger University (www.mcdonalds.com/corporate/careers/hambuniv/, accessed 15 September 2003).

## Staff training

For local managers, some companies arrange extensive training, which might include spending a period of time working at the head office to learn from the parent company staff. This learning process not only includes technical and managerial skills but also organisational culture and management style.

Workers and lower staff members are normally trained on the job in the host country by expatriate trainers and/or at local educational establishments. Sometimes technical staff are sent abroad. Some Japanese, American and European multinational companies, for instance, train their subsidiaries' local engineers back in their home country.

## Internationalisation of staff

For the employees of an international company to feel part of a whole enterprise it would be necessary to develop an international mindset. That is to say, to think internationally and company-wide while acting locally in their immediate workplace. Most firms combine various methods to internationalise their staff, especially managers. Here is what Derr and Oddou (1993) found in their study.

To prepare their young expatriate managers, companies like ICI and Natwest in the UK, Philips in the Netherlands, and Groupe Total in France conduct extensive international in-house seminars. These courses typically cover national culture differences, local politics and laws when conducting business abroad, family adaptation and international finance. Some firms send their managers, spouses and even children to special language courses so they can be briefed on culture and customs and start learning the target language. Still other companies provide special training, once the expatriate and his or her family have arrived at their new post. Some European companies take a front-end approach by selective recruitment; they look for young men and women who already possess fluency in at least two languages, demonstrate cross-cultural ability and have a serious interest in working globally.

Philips uses cross-national teams as part of its managerial training and development programmes. Three task forces of eight people each (called 'octagons') work together for six to eight months on a specific study assignment. After a two-week seminar in Eindhoven, in Holland, senior management presents a number of important global projects; each group chooses one. The task force participants devote about 29 percent of their time to those projects, meeting regularly in various European locations. At the end of the project, the group presents its report to Philips' top-level managers, who consider carefully the possibility of implementing their recommendations.

Some companies might also choose to bring foreign nationals into their headquarters for a short- or medium-term assignment which would involve them in decision making, a process known as *inpatriation*. The head office would also be a forum in which they could share their more global perspectives with the parent company staff and expose them further to international views and values.

Extensive travels including long business trips and international networking and teleconferencing are among other methods which serve as a mechanism to implement and sustain the process of internationalisation of management staff (Derr and Oddou, 1993).

It is, however, important to note that internationalisation policies normally involve only senior and upper middle managers. Most lower managers and other employees and workers are relatively unaffected by these policies. This is so because those who occupy lower levels of the organisational hierarchy are rarely in a position to make decisions which would affect the company as a whole. Their authority is more likely to be limited to day-to-day functions of their own departments or their subsidiary at the most.

## Non-traditional mechanisms to achieve integration

So far in this section we explored various widely used traditional devices to create and maintain integration. Increasingly companies are attempting to address the tensions caused by the concern for differentiation and integration from novel perspectives. Rather than trying to balance the contradictions by, for example, trading some degree of integration for some degree of responsiveness, the best global competitors are instead attempting to maximise both these dimensions. This approach, as Pucik (1998) points out, represents a shift away from structural solutions to the challenges of global business organisation. It replaces the continuous oscillation between centralisation and decentralisation with an acceptance of the global organisation as a fluid and dynamic network. Networking focuses on the management process, not on organisational structure and procedures. Another significant nontraditional integrating mechanism is relationship management. Both of these approaches are discussed below.

### Multinational companies as differentiated networks

The use of networking has been suggested as a means of examining how global businesses relate to their subsidiaries and other internal units as well as the outside world (Ghoshal and Bartlett, 1990; Forsgren and Johanson, 1992). Networking is increasingly replacing the traditional hierarchical structure as a means of maintaining integration while remaining responsive to local conditions.

Ghoshal and Bartlett (1990) liken the multinational company to a network of relationships between and among parent and subsidiaries. In addition, each subsidiary as well as the HQ are embedded in their own respective local networks of organisations and institutions with which they develop their own linkages and relationships. Given the cultural, political and legal diversity of the nations within which various units of a multinational firm are situated, the network density within each host country and as a result across the firm varies from location to location.

Further, the authors argue, the allocation of a company's resources, such as production equipment, finance, technology, marketing skills and management capabilities, to various subsidiaries depends on a number of criteria, including their local networking density. For instance, in some locations internal interactions within the local organisation sets may be high, but external linkages within other organisation sets may be low. In such locations, the multinational firm may provide all the required resources in appropriate measures so that its local subsidiary can build and maintain linkages with key members of its own community. By comparison, the organisation sets in some other countries may be sparsely connected internally, but different elements of the local environment may be strongly connected with their counterparts in other countries. For such locations, the company may create a resource structure that is concentrated and specialised. In some cases the location of the specialised resource may reflect the desire to access special resource niches, but in other cases the location choice may be motivated by modalities of the external network.

## Relationship management

Relationship management, is in essence at the heart of networking among various units of a multinational firm, provides among other things consistency and coherence through establishment of strong and integrated relationships within the company regardless of specific geographical locations. It fosters integration and coordination and creates and supports a sense of common purpose, trust and cooperation among all units.

Relationship management is an approach rooted in continuity, interdependence and partnership over time and demands a significant investment in getting to know and understand one another. It seeks to establish strong and integrated relationships with individuals on a company-wide basis (Nahapiet, 1998).

A major objective of such networks of relationship is to spread around value systems to which the firm would wish to subscribe and which form the basis of its organisational culture. However, the extent to which values could be shared throughout the firm, is not certain (see for instance Ghoshal's [1986] attempt at establishing the extent of normative integration in a sample of companies). Moreover, organisational culture, as a form of normative integration mechanism, may not be able to eradicate people's culturally-rooted values and attitudes, it may only encourage them to subscribe to certain expected practices (Hofstede et al., 1990).

In any case, creating such inter-unit networks across nations is not easy. The individuals and units involved have to face not only different national cultures, with different perceptions of power, approaches to efficiency, methods of cooperation and so on, but also an unfamiliar professional culture, as an example given by Chassang and Reitter (1998) demonstrates. In one international manufacturing firm the German and Spanish units complained about the UK 'procurement' culture. The relationship between some UK units and their internal suppliers was managed not by the project managers in charge of the final assembly but by a procurement department that also dealt with external suppliers. The internal suppliers were treated in the same formal, contractual and at times aggressive manner as external ones. What is more, each unit was required to supply components according to convenient splits in the equipment to be produced but with no regard to the technical interfacing between elements. The procurement officers had no technical expertise and therefore adopted a purely purchasing-oriented approach more appropriate for standard components that can easily be integrated into a final product. There was no attempt to act together to anticipate and solve common problems. This gave rise to disputes over changes and delays as technical interfacing became an issue later in the assembly process.

As Nahapiet (1998) points out, a different mindset is needed to participate in global relationship management, the key features of which are realistic expectations, a cosmopolitan and collaborative outlook, high levels of trust and a willingness to learn from one another.

Also, some multinational companies might develop a structure which Bartlett and Ghoshal (1989) describe as *differentiated network* (see above), and which is suggested with regard to resource configuration (Ghoshal and Bartlett, 1990). But one can just as easily apply it within the context of attempts to create shared values. That is value systems created in certain parts of the company, say among the subsidiaries located in Anglo-Saxon regions, may reflect the region's historical and cultural heritage, those created in the Arab Middle East and other Muslim nations may be coloured by their Islamic heritage.

## ■ CHAPTER SUMMARY

This chapter discussed mainly the question of differentiation and integration, one of the major issues confronting firms with international business, especially those with foreign affiliates and subsidiaries in which local people are employed.

It was argued, along with many scholars and writers in the field, that, while it is imperative for such firms to maintain their integrity and 'wholeness', in terms of overall direction and strategic thrust, it is very difficult, if not impossible, to remain indifferent to local variations in customer base, clients, employees, suppliers and other contacts. These local variations are, of course, rooted in age-old national cultures and other socio-political and economic institutions and policies, some of which may result in practices and policy preferences totally in opposition to what the parent company might have in mind.

It seems, on the whole, that the culture-specific aspects of international firms, such as leadership and human resource management style, negotiation, advertising, and relationships with suppliers, in short those parts of the operation which bring people and their values and attitude into contact with one another, tend to be differentiated in response to local conditions. But universal, culture-free aspects of firms, such as divisionalisation of operations, budgetary control, financial targets to be achieved by senior managers and related periodical progress reports and the like, are ripe for maximum integration and harmonisation across all the units, affiliates and subsidiaries.

The balance between these two considerations is further informed by the companies' extent and form of internationalisation, their industry and the markets they serve, and the kind of staff they are able to recruit.

International firms can employ various internal mechanisms, such as selection procedures, training, and internationalisation of staff, to help them implement their preferred HRM strategies and policies.

Management of human resources in a single company with operations across different nations is complicated enough. It becomes far more complex and sometimes well nigh impossible when two or more companies join forces (including employees) and embark on a joint venture. Chapter 8 examines the tensions and difficulties involved in such an operation as far as human resource management is concerned.

## ■ REVISION QUESTIONS

**1.** What is meant by differentiation and integration and how does it apply to HRM?

**2.** What factors determine the relevance of this issue to multinational companies?

**3.** What are the major traditional and non-traditional mechanisms of maintaining integration while allowing for a degree of differentiation?

**4.** If you were in charge of HRM department of a multinational company which of the above would you choose and why?

# Case study: News International plc

News International plc in the UK is part of the News Division of News Corporation, an Australian multinational of which Mr Rupert Murdoch is the majority shareholder. Although it trades on the Australian stock market and its share capital is Australian it is based in the US (New York).

News International (NI) publish a number of national UK daily and weekly papers and has also set up an Internet based media company. NI's head office (HO) is in London and has plants in Wapping (publishing and production), Glasgow (publishing and production with sales, advertising, editorial team) and Liverpool (production). The Chairman and Chief Executive report directly to New York. This case study is based on interviews conducted in the Glasgow plant, which was set up in 1986 and has approximately 200 employees.

## Relations with the head office

Editors are relatively free to get on with what they want to do. However, occasionally they have to drop what the teams are doing to follow an initiative from the HO, for example feasibility studies for new ventures/features. In addition the editors have regular contacts with HO, 4–5 times a day, by telephone.

'There is a desire, and the necessity, throughout the plant not to be totally independent from the rest of production [in Liverpool], just as Scotland is not totally independent from the rest of the UK, but I think we like to reflect what's going on in Scotland. There is a psychological thing about it—we are Scots, we want to print Scottish newspapers, we want to do all our Scottish newspapers here and we don't want to be beholden to Liverpool or elsewhere to do it for us.'

Vice President (VP) for HR in New York periodically comes over to the UK (once a year or so). The HR director in London will report to the worldwide structure and has regular contacts with the VP of News Corp in New York. The US are kept informed of what the UK are doing, but do not direct new HR initiatives from the US.

Glasgow managers are constantly in dialogue with London, individuals come up to Glasgow and go down to London. There is also a sharing of experience in such areas as employment law. If the UK/Glasgow need to tap into company resources in order to handle changing legislation in the UK, they would be able to discuss it with the HO through the HR director in London. The HR director would then be able to inform them of directives or trends that have occurred elsewhere around the globe.

Glasgow receives quarterly newsletters from the US and Australia. There are also three-month international staff exchanges with the US and Australia.

## HRM policies and practices

Policies are generally developed in London in consultation with Glasgow. HR manager reports to GM in Glasgow and HR Director in London.

Budget, including HR budget, is controlled from London, and ultimately Mr Murdoch, who makes decisions on capital expenditure overall. Editors are given the budget at the beginning of the financial year, and there is no negotiation with the HO, which holds the purse strings (e.g. contract agreements for staff) and has the final say.

'We don't tend to generate [HR] policies. We are not a great policy company as it happens. Because of the nature of the business and because of who is in command of the organisation, despite its size it's quite an agile organisation. If Rupert Murdoch decided tomorrow that instead of going in this direction he wanted to go in that direction, then the company is pretty quick at turning around. It's not a huge tanker that takes 22 miles to turn around. Despite its size it is surprisingly light on its feet.'

However, there are occasions when policies are amended or tailored to suit the Glasgow site. There are also some policies which are devised locally; the 'giving-up-smoking' campaign for example was a Scottish initiative.

## Selection and recruitment

Operational tests and psychometric inventories are used in the selection process. The HR manager works with line managers to help them to get a clearer picture of what they specifically want in terms of skills and personal attributes. From that they develop a template of what type of person they want. In general, aside from specific skills and competencies, they look for 'get up and go', 'can do' attitude which reflects the company's ability to move quickly. They assess this by exploring the candidate's past experience—culture of the previous work place, aspects of personality, e.g. enthusiasm, not being rule-bound. They look for a cultural fit albeit not a precise fit.

In Glasgow they use personality questionnaires more than in London. There is greater scope for line managers' decision making and the site allows for greater relationships between line managers and the HR manager. It is difficult to apply London's practices fully to all sites, there is some resistance.

## Induction training

Induction training, especially for advertising staff, occurs in London usually over two weeks. The new recruits are sent down to London to learn about the system and the bigger picture, which are considered as being beneficial and useful. They then return to Glasgow and get some further training. Glasgow is responsible for induction of staff in sales and commodity, some of which is done locally, and some nationally.

The company does not have a regular induction training for health and safety, but there are ad hoc training sessions when required. Such induction courses are tailored to local Glasgow needs, because of the specific hazards on site, such as noise, chemicals, manhandling, VDUs and heavy machinery.

## Training and development

There are central policies and a central development programme in HO based in London but Glasgow would have an input into these.

'Normally training initiatives are driven by London, but the Glasgow site has started new management development projects that are locally driven. Instead of sending employees down to London, Glasgow has decided to run the same course jointly with other UK subsidiaries of News Corporation, at which trainers from London teach. This joint training programme is locally driven as opposed to having been decided at the Corporation level. The programme is not different from the ones run in London. It simply makes financial sense to do it this way.'

In terms of contents, standards and accreditation procedures and requirements, there are no differences between Glasgow and HO programmes.

Sometimes Glasgow uses Wapping plant's training facilities, and sometimes Wapping in-house trainers are sent off to Glasgow. The day that some of the interviews for this case study were conducted a trainer from Wapping was on the Glasgow site training local staff in presentation skills. The Glasgow site also has its own locally written health and safety handbook.

## Pay and benefits

HR practices mainly come from London. With the newspapers there is a commonality in terms of structure and pay bands but these are regionally adjusted. There is also a central grade structure which again reflects local rates and local supply and demand.

A company-wide bonus is paid once a year in October. Sometimes a discretionary bonus is given if staff bring in a good story.

## Career development

Employees in editorial offices have the chance to move to London. They like to have people who have worked in Scotland because it gives them a better insight into how things operate. The job is sold on possible moves to London.

## Industrial relations

Glasgow has been working very closely with their American colleagues to get a better understanding of 'fairness at work' legislation and the shifting balance of trade unions. The company will do everything that the law says but if they (Glasgow) have a choice of union vs non-union, they would prefer to work directly with the employees rather than a third party, i.e. unions. The US have been watching the site closely and they have been able to give advice about their experiences and that of other sites all over the world.

The HO in the US is very highly unionised, so the model they use is totally different from what is used in the UK.

## Staff handbook

Generally the content of the handbook is driven by HO, but there is always room for Scotland to make some changes, usually by rephrasing some paragraphs and sections to reflect how things work in Glasgow. For example car parking facilities are provided for all staff in London, but not in Glasgow, or there is an on-site dentist in London, but not in Glasgow. So the wordings of the handbook have been adapted to account for these differences.

## Organisational culture

The culture of the Glasgow site is very close knit. Everyone knows each other. Senior managers know the home addresses of a lot of employees without having to look up the records, partly because of the site's small size (200 employees).

There are no hard and fast rules on dress code—usually smart/casual dress. Advertising and sales dress smartly because they are meeting clients. Production staff come into the offices in their overalls, sometimes quite inky, but they change to something smarter when attending meetings.

The site benefits from the Scottish work ethic. 'Scots are by nature hardworking', but Mr Murdoch also drives a hardworking culture from the top. He looks for people who are keen because, he believes, they will work long hours.

### ■ CASE STUDY QUESTIONS

**1.** What are the main areas of activities which are differentiated as far as the Glasgow site is concerned?

**2.** And what areas are integrated in the Corporation's overall scheme of things?

**3.** What principal factors have contributed to this state of integration and differentiation?

**4.** What mechanisms does the Corporation employ to reinforce its integration and differentiation policies?

### ■ RECOMMENDED FURTHER READING

Birkinshaw, J. (1996). 'How multinational subsidiary mandates are gained and lost', *Journal of International Business Studies*, vol. 27, pp. 467–96.

Nohria, N. and Ghoshal, S. (1997). *The Differentiated Network: Organizing Multinational Corporations for Value Creation*. San Francisco: Jossey-Bass.

Rosenzweig, P. (1994). 'Why is managing in the United States so difficult for European firms?', *European Management Journal*, vol. 12, pp. 31–8.

### ■ REFERENCES

Barlett, C. A. and Ghoshal, S. (1989). *Managing across Borders: The Transnational Solution*. London: Century Business.

Chassang, G. and Reitter, R. (1998). 'Steering between chaos and tyranny', *Financial Times*, 7 March, Survey page 12.

Denison, D. R. (1990). *Corporate Culture and Organizational Effectiveness*. New York: Wiley.

Derr, C. B. and Oddou, G. (1993). 'Internationalising managers: speeding up the process', *European Management Journal*, vol. 11, pp. 435–42.

Dowling, P. J. and Schuler, R. S. (1990). *International Dimensions of Human Resource Management*. Boston: PWS-Kent.

Doz, Y. (1976). *National Policies and Multinational Management*. DBA dissertation. Cited in J. Roure, J. A. Alvarez, C. Garcia-Pont, and J. Nueno (1993). 'Managing international dimensions of the managerial task', *European Management Journal*, vol. 11, pp. 485–92.

Forsgren, M. and Johanson, J. (1992). *Managing Networks in International Business*. Philadelphia: Gordon & Breach.

Ghoshal, S. (1986). *The Innovative Multinational: A Differentiated Network of Organizational Roles and Management Processes*. Unpublished doctoral dissertation, Boston: Harvard Business School.

Ghoshal, S. and Bartlett, C. A. (1990). 'The multinational corporation as an interorganizational network', *Academy of Management Review*, 15, 4, pp. 603–25.

Harvey-Jones, Sir John (1988). *Making it Happen: Reflections on Leadership*. London: Fontana.

Hofstede, G., Neuijen, B., and Ohavy, D. (1990). 'Measuring organizational cultures: a qualitative and quantitative study across twenty cases', *Administrative Science Quarterly*, vol. 35, pp. 286–316.

Hulbert J. M. and Brandt, W. K. (1980). *Managing the Multinational Subsidiary*. New York: Holt, Rinehart and Winston.

Lawrence, P. and Lorsch, J. (1967). *Organizations and Environment*. Cambridge, Massachusetts: Harvard University Press.

Martin, J., Feldman, M. S., Hatch, M. J., and Sitkin, S. B. (1983). 'The uniqueness paradox in organisational stories', *Administrative Science Quarterly*, vol. 28, pp. 438–53.

Nahapiet, J. (1998). 'Strategies for the global service', *Financial Times*, 6 February, Survey page 10.

Porter, M. E. (1986). 'Changing patterns of international competition', *California Management Review*, vol. 28, no. 2, pp. 9–40.

Prahalad, C. K. (1976). 'Strategic choices in diversified MNCs', *Harvard Business Review*, July–August, pp. 67–78.

—— and Doz, Y. L. (1987). *The Multinational Mission: Balancing Global Demands and Global Vision*. New York: Free Press.

Pucik, V. (1998). 'Creating leaders that are world-class', *Financial Times*, February, Survey page 4.

Rosenzweig, P. (1994). 'Why is Managing in the United States so Difficult for European Firms?', European Management Journal, vol. 12, pp. 31–8.

Sathe, V. (1983). 'Implications of corporate culture: A managers guide to action', *Organisational Dynamics*, Autumn, pp. 5–23

Schein, E. H. (1985). *Organizational Culture and Leadership: A Dynamic View*. San Francisco: Jossey-Bass.

Schuler, R. S., Dowling, P. J., and De Cieri, H. (1993). 'An Integrative Framework of Strategic International Human Resource Management', *Journal of Management*, vol. 19, pp. 419–59.

Tayeb, M. H. (1994). 'Japanese managers and British culture: a comparative case study', *International Journal of Human Resource Management*, vol. 5, no. 1, pp. 145–66.

—— (1998). 'Transfer of HRM policies and practices across cultures: an American company in Scotland', *International Journal of Human Resource Management*, vol. 9, no. 2, pp. 332–58.

—— and Dott, E. (2000). 'Two nations divided by a common culture: three American companies in Scotland', in M. D. Hughes and J. H. Taggart (eds), *International Business: European Dimension*. Basingstoke: Macmillan. Chapter 5.

Trice, H. M. and Beyer, J. M. (1984). 'Studying organisational cultures through rites and ceremonials', *Academy of Management Review*, vol. 9, pp. 653–69.

Tunstall, W. B. (1983). 'Cultural transition at AT&T', *Sloan Management Review*, vol. 25, pp. 15–26.

Weber, W. and Festing, M. (1994). 'Essentials and limits for IHRM practices', paper presented to the 4th Conference on International Human Resource Management, Gold Coast, Queensland, Australia, July.

Welch, D. (1994*a*). 'HRM implications of globalization', *Journal of General Management*, vol. 19, pp. 52–68.

Welch, D. (1994*b*). 'Determinants of international human resource management approaches and activities: a suggested framework', *Journal of Management Studies*, vol. 32, pp. 139–64.

Yager, W. F., Thad Barnowe, J., and Nengquan, W. (1994). 'Human resource management in China: joint venture experiences in Guangdong Province', paper presented to the 4th Conference on International Human Resource Management, Gold Coast, Queensland, Australia, July.

# 7 Knowledge Transfer within a Multinational Company

## Learning outcomes

When you finish reading this chapter you should:

- know about organisation knowledge base and its significance for a company's competitiveness in business
- be able to distinguish between two major types of organisation knowledge and their sources
- understand the complex issues involved in dissemination of knowledge within and between organisations
- be familiar with the current debates on cross-cultural transfer of HRM within multinational companies and the factors which help or hinder such transfers
- know about various strategies that multinational companies can employ to disseminate best practices between their subsidiaries and units
- understand, through the closing case study, the practical issues involved in knowledge creation and knowledge transfer in a foreign subsidiary of a Japanese company.

## Introduction

Chapter 4 discussed the socio-cultural characteristics of six countries and one region and demonstrated their implications for HRM and other employee management practices in those nations. The chapter concluded by pointing out that the diversity of cultural characteristics will also have implications for MNCs regarding the transfer of their HRM policies and practices to their overseas subsidiaries. The present chapter will develop that theme further by putting it within the wider debate on knowledge transfer within MNCs.

The chapter will briefly discuss major theories and arguments related to knowledge and knowledge transfer in companies in general and MNCs in particular. It will then focus specifically on the issues and challenges associated with the transfer of HRM policies and practices within multinational companies. The chapter will also argue that the direction of this transfer, as was pointed out in Chapter 5, is not only from the parent to subsidiaries, but also from the subsidiaries to the parent and between various subsidiaries. Various mechanisms of knowledge transfer and the complications involved will also be addressed.

# Organisational knowledge and its significance

Organisations, like individual human beings, learn and acquire expertise and knowledge on how to deal with different issues and situations internally through experimentation with innovative ideas, in-house training, and externally through formal and informal interaction with the outside world. The know-how thus created and/or acquired gets accumulated over time and form the organisation's collective knowledge base.

The nature and sources of organisational knowledge and its transfer in multinational corporations have received a great deal of attention in recent years (Gupta and Govindarajan, 2000), largely because of the significant role knowledge plays in companies' competitive advantage. Some researchers even argue that knowledge is the only source of competitive advantage over rivals (Nonaka, 1991).

In addition, MNCs are no longer seen as repositories of their national imprint but rather as instruments of knowledge transfer across subsidiaries, thereby contributing to further knowledge development. A common theme in this line of research is that MNCs might develop knowledge in one location and then exploit it in other locations, implying internal transfer of knowledge by MNCs. Therefore, the argument goes, MNCs' comeptitive advantage depends, in part at least, on their ability to facilitate and manage inter-subsidiary transfer of knowledge. Hedlund (1986) and Bartlett and Ghoshal (1989), for example, focused on how to organise and structure MNCs in order to facilitate the internal flow and transfer of knowledge in MNCs.

But why is organisational knowledge considered as a major factor contributing to MNCs' competitiveness in business?

Factors which contribute to competitiveness of companies keep shifting all the time depending on general circumstances and changes in market conditions. There was a time when access to cheap natural resources or other factors of production would give a company, or a nation for that matter, an advantage over its competitors. Then came a time when the ability to manage and utilise such factors properly would differentiate between the competing actors. In our time added to all this is the knowledge and information factor, as crystallised in the skills to produce and use electronics technology and to process information, for example. Companies which have access to these new factors are more likely to succeed in the international market place compared to those which do not (Tayeb, 2000). In other words, successful companies are those that consistently create new knowledge, disseminate it widely through the organisation and embody it in new technologies and products. Japanese companies' spectacular success in the 1970s and 1980s has for instance been attributed to their skills and expertise at 'organisational knowledge creation' (Nonaka and Takeuchi, 1995).

However, it is important to note that creation of knowledge, though necessary, is not sufficient to make a company successful. The knowledge must be efficiently and effectively shared and utilised across the organisation, especially in the case of multinational companies, where different units and subsidiaries are spread over a vast geographical area (see for instance Porter, 1986; Gupta and Govindarajan, 2000).

But where does company knowledge actually reside?

Identifying and examining the roots of organisational knowledge is problematic because the content, processes and the networks that exist are often difficult to define. Whereas both researchers and practitioners would readily agree that organisational learning is important, it would be difficult to describe exactly how learning occurs and is accumulated as knowledge at various levels and the processes that exist to support knowledge development (Pollard, 2001). However, it is fair to say that employees of a company carry in their heads, if you like, their know-how, innovative ideas and solutions to problems of all sorts. Such an argument is in line with the theory of human capital. The main assertion of this theory, as Sparkes and Miyake (2000) point out, is that people possess skills, experience and knowledge that have economic value to firms. The theory was originally developed in the context of the economic value of education, measured by expenditure and return on investment. Empirical work has consistently indicated a positive relationship between the two (World Bank, 1998). The importance of investment in human capital is also stressed in non-economic and more subtle ways:

'Some of the value is added directly by transforming the firm's product, but much of it is less tangible consisting of solving problems, co-ordinating the work of departments, and exercising judgement in novel situations.' (Snell and Dean, 1992, p. 469)

An effective and coherent organisation makes proper use of the human capital, this 'well' of knowledge, through appropriate company-wide dissemination processes and mechanisms. Here is where the role of HRM policies and practices becomes paramount—more on this later in the chapter.

## Sources of organisational knowledge

Although an internal element necessarily enters into the production of all organisational knowledge, as Foss and Pedersen (2002) argue, it makes sense to distinguish between the following types of knowledge, derived from different knowledge sources:

### Internal knowledge

This knowledge is generated through investing in the internal production of knowledge, such as research and development. It is the kind of knowledge that has been highlighted in resource- and knowledge-based theories of the firm (Foss, 1997). In this literature, the focus has been on the production and organisation of knowledge that is embodied in bundles of routines of a highly tacit and social nature. Teams of individuals operate it for some strategic purpose.

### External knowledge

This is to a large extent created on the basis of knowledge inputs from relations to external partners, and can be further divided into two categories. The first category, 'network-based knowledge', is acquired and accumulated through long-term interaction with specific external parties, such as customers and suppliers, and the use of that knowledge in the company's activities. The second category, 'cluster-based knowledge', is based on knowledge inputs from, for example, a well-educated work force or local knowledge institutions, such as technical universities.

As Foss and Pedersen (2001) argue, no knowledge is entirely generated internally, and in fact there may be significant complementary relations between internal and external knowledge sources. For instance, a company's R&D department recruits its scientists and researchers from the larger community in which it is located and the staff are constantly in touch with what happens in the outside world and absorb from it the latest developments in the field. Nevertheless, it makes conceptual and empirical sense to say that some knowledge is largely internally produced, while some other knowledge is strongly based on external knowledge inputs.

## Tacit and explicit knowledge

According to Nonaka and Takeuchi (1995) and Weggeman (1997), tacit knowledge is person-specific and consists of personal experiences, skills and attitudes and is therefore hard to formalise or communicate to others. Explicit knowledge, by contrast, is independent of the person who holds it and can therefore be easily communicated and shared in the form of hard data, scientific formulae, codified procedures, or universal principles (Kogut and Zander, 1992, 1995).

Some researchers such as Burton-Jones (1999) go on to argue that only tacit knowledge, whether alone or in conjunction with explicit knowledge, can give a firm a sustainable competitive advantage. Tacit knowledge, once acquired, can be developed as a company resource which is very difficult for rivals to copy; and therein lies true competitive advantage (Holden, 2002). It is worth mentioning here that in the period between the mid-1980s and mid-1990s many companies embarked on extensive down-sizing of their manpower. As a result they also lost much of the sources of their tacit knowledge. They had to recover some of it through contracting out part of their activities back to the people they had sacked (see various issues of *The Economist* of the period).

The distinction between tacit and explicit knowledge is important in connection with dissemination and circulation of knowledge within an organisation. As Pollard (2001, p. 74.) points out:

'The difference between tacit and operational knowledge is a fundamental issue in considering knowledge transfer. Operational knowledge can be transferred through written routines and instructions but tacit knowledge is often highly content-specific; existing in an individual's memory as accumulated beliefs and experience, and often only invoked when circumstances dictate. This experience can only be effectively transferred to others through some measure of personal interaction. It should be noted, however, that explicit and tacit knowledge is not a dichotomy, rather the opposite ends of a continuum.'

Finally, Nonaka and Takeuchi (1998) suggest that a key challenge for organisations is how to convert tacit knowledge into explicit knowledge that can be incorporated more easily into organisational knowledge and also simplify technology and knowledge transfer.

# HRM and organisational knowledge

The theory of human capital, referred to above, has led many authors to highlight the role of HRM in creating and sustaining the competitive advantage of companies and indeed even nations (Kydd and Oppenheim, 1990; Martell and Carroll, 1995; Leonard-Barton, 1992; Tayeb, 1995).

HRM for instance can help improve the transfer of knowledge, especially in the form of technological and managerial know-how. In addition, development of human resources in the context of knowledge transfer is often treated as building the capability to absorb and utilise knowledge (Lall, 1994). In essence, as Sparkes and Miyake (2000) note, the creation, management and transfer of knowledge is inseparable from the influence of the HRM practices of a company:

- some of the issues associated with manufacturing technique are closely linked with human resource management practices.
- human resource development is the core activity of building capacity to absorb knowledge.
- human resource management is inseparable from the study of knowledge transfer, because tacit knowledge is embedded in people. In other words, HRM is indirectly managing tacit knowledge.

Selection, training, motivation, creation of an atmosphere of trust and sharing vision, inter-unit transfer of employees are some of the major HRM functions which facilitate the creation, maintenance and transfer of human knowledge base in a company (see also the case study at the end of this chapter).

# Transfer of knowledge between and within organisations

Within the organisation and management literature, some researchers have suggested their own definition of knowledge transfer. Rogers (1983) for example defines it as an attempt by an organisation, or a unit within the organisation, to copy a specific type of knowledge from one organisation or unit to another. Kostova (1999) defines organisational knowledge transfer as the degree to which organisational practices are implemented and internalised by the recipient firm.

The most common form of transfer, as Giroud (2000) points out, is technology transfer and has been widely covered in the literature and often related to the growth of the electronics industry in East Asian countries.

Knowledge transfer comprises transfer of technology, managerial and technical know-how, and marketing skills from one firm to another for possible benefits through long-term relations and the exchange of information. Channels of technology transfer include foreign direct investment, turnkey operation, purchase of machinery and equipment, licensing and management agreements, technical assistance contracts, direct employment of foreign experts and training of local staff.

In addition, companies through subcontracting relationships with their suppliers in home- and host-counties can transfer technical, financial, and managerial knowledge to other firms. In most cases, the company will supply blueprints to its suppliers. It may further provide special tools. In the case of subcontracting, the partner may take part in the capacity and production planning of the subcontractors (Halbach, 1989). Support is frequent for the learning of specific process technologies, but upgrading of technological know-how to product design is limited (Wong, 1991).

# Transfer of knowledge within MNCs

The literature on knowledge transfer within multinational companies, with a few exceptions, addresses the issue of knowledge transferability largely from two angles: the nature of knowledge to be transferred and absorptive capacity of the recipients of knowledge and motivational factors. These will now be explored.

## The nature of knowledge to be transferred

Tacit knowledge, as we saw earlier, is context and person specific, it cannot easily be codified. Therefore it is less easily transferable from one part of an MNC to others, compared to explicit knowledge which is 'codifiable' and therefore more easily transferable.

A related argument has been put forward by Foss and Pedersen (2001) with regard to their distinction between internal and external knowledge, mentioned above. According to their view, internal knowledge is likely to be more easily transferable than external knowledge, because it is more likely to lie at the core of the MNC's knowledge structure and is more likely to be at least partly developed through interaction with its units. By contrast, external knowledge lies outside the core of company's knowledge structure and is likely to be less easily transferable than internal knowledge. This is because this type of knowledge contains many elements that make it hard to transfer to other MNC units: it is largely derived from specific problems and needs of the external parties with which the subsidiary interacts, and/or it consists of knowledge of local skill levels, tastes, regulatory authorities, etc., much of which may be hard to transfer or is of little use to other units.

## Absorptive capacity of the recipients of knowledge and motivational factors

Absorptive capacity has been defined as the 'ability to recognize the value of new external information, assimilate it, and apply it to commercial ends' (Cohen and Levinthal, 1990, p. 128) and is argued to be the receiving unit's most significant determinant of internal knowledge transfer in MNCs (Lane and Lubatkin, 1998; Gupta and Govindarajan, 2000).

Motivational factors associated with the parties involved have been viewed as another separate group of factors influencing knowledge transfer (Szulanski, 1996; Lane and Lubatkin, 1998; Gupta and Govindarajan, 2000). As Szulanski (1996) points out, motivation to acquire and receive knowledge is important since new knowledge may disrupt current organisational practices and working routines. Knowledge acquisition and reception may require substantial investments in time and effort. It is fair to assume that subsidiaries differ in both their absorptive capacity and level of their motivation, and this affects the effectiveness of MNC internal knowledge transfer to subsidiaries.

In this connection, Szulanski (1996) explored 'internal stickiness' of knowledge, that is factors that impede transfer of knowledge within a company. He identified two sets of factors that create internal stickiness of knowledge in firms and impede their internal transfer: motivational factors and knowledge-related factors. The latter stem from the tacit, context-specific and ambiguous kind of knowledge which is difficult to transfer from one location to another, while the former is related to the motivation to apply the necessary time and resources to conduct the transfer.

Most researchers treat the absorptive capacity as a cognitive barrier distinct from motivational factors. However, Minbaeva et al. (2001, p. 3) argue that subsidiary absorptive capacity is a function of both competency and motivation. In other words, subsidiary absorptive capacity has to be examined along two dimensions—*ability* to recognise the value of new information, assimilate and commercialise it and *drive* to do so. In other words, it is the interactive effect of *ability* and *drive* that actually matters for knowledge reception.

The major ingredient missing from the above arguments is the complex and diverse socio-cultural and political economic context within which multinational companies and their subsidiaries operate. The knowledge transfer between parent and subsidiaries and between subsidiaries takes place within this complex and diverse context, which could help or hinder the transfer process. This raises the question: Is any organisational knowledge culture-free and therefore transferable across the world irrespective of its country of origin?

# Transferability of knowledge across national borders

As Hofstede (1980) points out, what is appropriate knowledge in one country may not suit the needs of firms in other countries. Factors such as different language, business culture, and institutional framework make up a 'psychic distance' as perceived by managers (Johanson and Vahlne, 1977; see also Chapter 8 for a discussion of 'psychic distance'). As the psychic distance between nations increases it is more difficult for firms to acquire knowledge from abroad (Mowery et al., 1996). Thus, a clash between national cultures may jeopardise the international transfer of knowledge. By contrast, geographical proximity and cultural affinity could help knowledge transfer between countries and organisations (Galbraith, 1990; Lester and McCabe, 1993; Epple et al., 1996).

However, transfer of ideas and models in the field of management, and in fact other collective and individual human activities, across borders is not of course new. In ancient times, great empires learned from one another as well as from those peoples that they conquered. In more recent times, colonial powers took with them their administrative skills and procedures to their colonies. Indian civil service is well known to have been modelled after that of the United Kingdom during the British rule. Even now, decades after independence, the traces of the British system are still discernible in the Indian bureaucracy.

The Iranians, although they never were a colony, have had for centuries close cultural and commercial ties with France. When early in the twentieth century they wanted to modernise their institutions, they imported ideas from that country, especially in such areas as education, civil service and legal systems.

Nations can therefore learn from others those practices which have proved successful elsewhere. However, in some societies the extent to which non home-grown practices can be adopted is limited compared to other societies. This is because national culture and other societal institutions can enhance or diminish a country's ability to avail itself of foreign options (Tayeb, 1995). A comparison between Japan and India clarifies this point further.

India and Japan are both collectivist cultures, but the two societies differ from one another in almost all other aspects of their economic, political and cultural lives. Japanese societal mix of harmonious industrial relations, highly educated and skilled work-force and a relative cultural homogeneity and a sense of collective identity, has enabled the managers to capitalise on and incorporate their employees' collectivism in their management practices, such as flexible working arrangements, quality circles and collective decision making. In India, a societal mix of confrontational industrial relations, cultural heterogeneity and inter-communal hatred and conflicts, a rigid caste system, corruption in certain quarters, massive poverty and a high rate of illiteracy, especially among manual workers, has diminished the managers' ability to transform their collectivist employees into a highly committed work-force who would consider their company as part of their in-group and who would put the interests of their company before theirs. As a result, such practices as quality circles which depend on employee loyalty and commitment are beyond the reach of most Indian managers (Tayeb, 1995).

Governments can help improve a nation's ability to learn what is fashionably referred to as 'best practices' from successful societies. This could be done for instance by providing a suitable environment, through educational and training policies, in which people may learn the new skills required to operate new techniques. However, it is important to be aware of incompatibilities between foreign management practices and local social and cultural characteristics. This is particularly important for developing countries (see also below).

The debate about beneficial or harmful effects of transfer of certain technologies and practices from MNCs to their host countries is beyond the scope of this chapter. Suffice to say that, given the socio-economic-political embeddedness of technologies and management practices, a certain amount of modification and adaptation is needed to make them workable in the recipient countries and beneficial to the indigenous population.

Although many issues related to learning foreign practices apply to almost all countries, the case of former communist countries and developing nations merits special attention. This is especially crucial in the case of developing countries whose cultural make-up and socio-economic needs are widely different from those of the home-countries of a vast majority of MNCs.

## Developing countries and foreign knowledge and practices

The question of transfer of management practices is of crucial importance especially for the less developed nations. Many of these countries, in an attempt to upgrade their organisational systems and to improve their performance, import various management techniques from the more advanced industrialised nations, especially the United States, without due regard to their own socio-cultural and technological conditions. If these imported techniques are not modified and adapted to the local conditions, both in cultural terms and in terms of the availability of human skills (through training), the transfer process will almost certainly fail (Tayeb, 1992).

Imagine a company operating in the Middle East decides to import certain US-grown practices such as participative management style. The Americans themselves have, in general, the cultural prerequisites to function under this style, both as managers and as subordinates. The Middle Eastern employees and their managers' traditional upbringing has not, in general, prepared them for a participative management style (see Chapter 4). There is of course nothing inherent in the participative management style which is beyond the ability of an average citizen of the Middle East countries to learn. But it will take time, determination and political will at both national and organisational levels.

It is also important for developing nations, in parallel with learning from abroad, to build on their own resources and develop compatible indigenous management practices. In other words, the transfer of management practices should not replace but in fact complement local practices that are a culmination of the specific context of a particular society. As Marsden (1991) points out, current development efforts should focus on building institutional capacity through the encouragement of local self-reliance. For these nations, the West, or Japan for that matter, is not the only source of valuable innovation and creativity. 'Local', 'traditional' or 'folk' knowledge is no longer the irrelevant vestige of 'backward' people who have not yet made the transition to modernity. Rather, they are the vital well-spring and resource bank from which alternative futures might be built.

## Ex-communist countries and foreign knowledge and practices

Many companies in the ex-communist countries of central and eastern Europe are tempted to import some of the capitalist countries' management practices. In addition, multinationals with wholly-owned subsidiaries or joint ventures located there are keen to take their home-grown practices with them. However, the process of transfer from capitalist countries to ex-communist ones is a great deal more complicated than when the transfer takes place between two capitalist countries.

This is because in capitalist countries companies generally perform *similar functions* but maybe in *different ways*. But in ex-communist countries, when they were under communist rule, companies did not perform certain functions at all. In other words, the difference between capitalist and communist countries is not only that of *style* but also of *substance*. For instance, an average manufacturing company in any capitalist country, will have functions such as marketing, research and development, accounting, personnel/HRM, as a matter of course. In the ex-communist countries, before the 1989 changes, many of these functions were either out of the company's control or were not performed at all.

In addition, companies based in a capitalist country have already developed these functions in accordance with its existing socio-economic structure. When importing new management and organisational practices from abroad the companies may only need to make certain adjustments to make them workable, and to train their employees to work in new ways. In ex-communist countries, by contrast, companies have to start by adapting their existing functions to their new domestic economic conditions, then learn to perform new sets of functions which would be necessary to survive in the market. Then at a later stage they have to decide whether for instance to go for Japanese or German or American styles of doing things, or none at all.

From a western multinational company's perspective, when deciding to transfer its home-grown practices to central and eastern European countries, there is yet another added complication: the cultural heterogeneity of these countries. It is true that the Soviet Union imposed on these countries similar political economic structures and institutions, but national character, which lies behind people's behaviours, is more than just the sum of a nation's social institutions. Culture, in term of values, attitudes and beliefs, is a deeply-rooted construct which may not necessarily be eradicated by an imposed regime. The stories of invasions, occupations, and colonisation of various countries throughout history tell us as much. Therefore the effect of national cultures as well as former political economic structures of the ex-communist countries must be taken into account when transferring organisational knowledge there from elsewhere.

# Transfer of managerial know-how and HRM across national borders

## Vehicles of transfer

There are two major means by which HRM and other management policies and practices 'travel' between various nations: multinational companies, formal or informal education.

### Multinational companies

Multinational companies are a powerful vehicle for transfer of knowledge not only to their subsidiaries but also to their local suppliers, and indirectly as a role model to other firms operating in their host countries and elsewhere. Production technology, such as electronics, and management practices, such as teamwork (Lall, 1993; Chen, 1994; Buckley et al., 1997; Tayeb, 1998), are examples of such transfers.

A multinational company 'exports' its management practices to the host country through its subsidiaries. As we saw earlier in the book, parent–subsidiary relationship is more complicated than a simple flow of instructions from the headquarters to subsidiary managers. Nevertheless, the parent company can influence and shape, among others, the subsidiaries' HRM, on major issues at least. For instance, the parent can through various means control the number of people employed, decide on broad training requirements, establish some form of performance appraisal systems, and change working patterns.

Also, HRM can travel from subsidiaries to the HQ and between the subsidiaries. For example, a subsidiary in Taiwan could experiment with cell manufacturing and teamwork and thereby reduce the number of overlapping functions. Another subsidiary located in Indonesia might learn about this and try it out, or the HQ might encourage all other subsidiaries and affiliates, including those based in the home country, to do the same.

MNCs can indirectly enable the transfer process through being looked up to as a role model by the host-country firms and those in other countries. Japanese companies are a good example here in that their reputation for efficiency and quality products have encouraged many companies to try to emulate them. Just-in-time, quality circle, teamwork are but a few examples of working practices which have travelled from Japan to many parts of the world in this way. International joint ventures also provide similar opportunities for people to learn from foreigner firms.

Sometimes there may initially be scepticism and resistance by local firms towards such foreign imports. The present author in a series of interviews in the mid-1980s found such sentiments, accompanied by disparaging remarks, among some British senior managers towards Japanese management styles in two-way and three-way joint ventures involving Japanese partners located in south east and south west Britain. However, now two decades or so later, such practices are seen as a useful means to increase employee productivity and achieve efficiency in production processes.

Transfer of HRM policies and practices through the above routes are not always possible. For example many countries with protectionist economic policies do not allow foreign firms to set up subsidiaries, or engage in joint ventures with local firms, and thereby bring in their 'ways of doing things' with them. As a result, local firms will not have the opportunity to explore and, where appropriate, to emulate foreign practices.

### Education

In many countries, universities, colleges and high schools teach various management subjects. There are many courses and modules through which students can learn about international business, international HRM and management practices in various countries. Also, as part of their employee development and training schemes, many companies require their employees to attend in-house and/or external courses to learn various practices. If you meet senior HR managers in their offices you are very likely to find their bookshelves lined with books and professional magazines on HRM and personnel management.

International professional and academic conferences, conventions and other networking forums are also other ways of learning from others. However, there are some limitations here in that some countries for various political and economic reasons do not allow their citizens, including managers, to participate and engage in such open networking activities and exchanges of views. As a result cross-national transfer of HRM policies and practices or even information about them can be somewhat hampered.

### Transferability of HRM policies and practices

Until a decade or so ago it used to be, and still is to some extent, the United States which would inspire managers around the world. In recent years, the economic success of Japan has enticed academic researchers and practising managers to look to that country's companies as a model and source of inspiration for management practices and techniques.

For some time now there has been a lively debate within the cross-cultural management discipline with regard to the effect of national culture on transfer of HRM and other management practices.

From a purely culturalist point of view, organisations and management styles are, as Crozier (1964) puts it, 'cultural solutions to social problems'. In which case, an Iranian organisation has nothing to learn from an American company, because the two countries are culturally poles apart (see for example Meyer and Rowan, 1977; Hofstede, 1980; Lincoln et al., 1981; Laurent, 1983).

Proponents of the universalist approach would argue that business is business wherever you go. Managers have to deal with customers, competitors, unions, creditors, and so on, regardless of where they are located (e.g. Kerr et al., 1952; Cole, 1973; Hickson et al., 1974; Form, 1979).

Then, there are those who argue that technology carries with it its own imperatives: for an assembly-line car manufacturing technology to be utilised properly a certain organisational design and management style must be adopted. An electronics company on the other hand would find a different design more appropriate. And so forth (Woodward, 1965).

The reality, what managers actually do, however, is too complicated to fit any one of the above or similar black and white prescriptions (Tayeb, 1988). It is true that HRM, like many other aspects of organisations, are embedded in the socio-cultural and political economic context within which they operate. In theory, unless all the elements of this context are also simultaneously transferred, HRM policies and practices cannot successfully travel between various nations. In practice, however, this is not the case. Human beings over centuries of existence have developed certain practices that are common to almost all civilised communities even though in some cases these practices have different local 'colours'. For instance, all companies in all countries have at least one day (or half a day) off in every working week. In many Muslim countries this weekend break is on Friday so that people can attend day-time Friday prayers in mosques. In Christian countries Sunday is in most companies the weekly day off, when practising Christians go to church for worship. In addition, given the right circumstances, we are all capable of learning all sorts of things from other human beings even if they live hundreds of miles away from us in a totally different country. We can certainly adapt and modify some of these practices to suit our own specific 'context' so as to make them workable and acceptable by our compatriots.

HRM policies and practices are no exception. Some practices can be transferred almost without any change from one country to another. Some must be modified to become workable in another setting. Some are more deeply culture-specific and may not always be transferable. Some practices are part and parcel of a coherent overall strategy, a 'package', and cannot therefore be transferred successfully in isolation and without the rest of the package going with them as well.

In addition, certain aspects of organisations are more likely to be universal and easily transferable, e.g. factory lay-out. There are areas which are more culture-specific, e.g. the relationship between a senior manager and his subordinates and cannot easily be transferred between nations. In some cultures, for instance, the senior manager has absolute power over his subordinates and expects obedience; in some other cultures the subordinate is able to challenge the superior if he or she makes wrong decisions.

In terms of transferability, broadly speaking HRM policies and practices can be grouped into three categories:

- Policies and practices which are more or less universal and thus easily transferable.

Examples:
  physical lay-out of shop floor/office

  formal hierarchical structure

  use of technology (subject to skill availability)

  contractual based employment

  holiday entitlement

These and many similar practices can be observed in all companies around the world or can easily be applied, given willingness on the part of managers and employees.

• Policies and practices which are culture specific but can be transferred after some modifications and adaptations to suit local conditions.

Examples:
  quality circle

  team work

  performance appraisal

  motivation

  leadership style

Some of these practices, notably quality circle, were based on the ideas about total quality management advocated by an American scholar, W. E. Deming, but they evoked little interest in the US. However, they were enthusiastically embraced by major Japanese companies, which modified them and turned them to workable practices by building upon some of their indigenous cultural traits and traditions, notably collectivism and group orientation. These and similar practices helped bring about Japan's post-war production miracle. Interestingly, their success captured major Western companies' imagination and in the 1980s there was a strong drive to import these practices back to the West. Here too the pure Japanese versions became workable only after some modification to account for western culture. For example, team work in Japan is accompanied by team performance appraisal; in many individualist countries of the West this would be unworkable. So although many companies especially in the West now tend to group their shopfloor employees into teams which would be responsible for the entire stages of production (from collecting of the raw materials to the packaging of the final product), the employees' promotion, pay increase and bonuses are still largely based on individual performance.

• Policies and practices which are so entrenched in the home-country culture that are difficult to transfer to other nations.

Example:
  company songs

  morning/afternoon exercises

Many Japanese companies are said to have a company song which the employees sing in a morning ceremony conducted at the start of working days. There are also office exercises and rituals like bowing to colleagues before setting down to work. While these may be instrumental in fostering team spirit, cohesion and cooperation in Japanese companies they are also more in tune with Japan's traditional culture and customs. But they have not found fertile grounds elsewhere in the world, not even in other collectivist cultures, such as India and Iran, and no serious attempts appear to have been made to emulate them.

Finally, it is important to make a distinction between *strategies*, *policies* and *practices* when discussing cross-cultural transfers of HRM. Generally speaking, it is easier to transfer a company's HRM strategies and policies to host countries than its practices. Here is an example to illustrate this point.

Strategy:  We need to increase employees' productivity

Policy:  We should give higher rewards to high performing employees, in order to implement this strategy

Practices: (a) In our Japanese subsidiary, performance appraisal should be discrete and based on team productivity records

(b) In our American subsidiary performance appraisal should be explicit and based on individual employee's productivity records

The above example shows that there is some element of universality in strategies and policies, devised in the headquarters which would make sense in many cultures. But when it comes to their implementation elsewhere, e.g. subsidiaries or host country domestic firms, cultural differences and preferences 'intervene' and 'call' for modification and adaptation.

## Transfer strategies

We saw in Chapter 5 that parent companies have at their disposal various HRM strategies with regard to their subsidiaries. We also saw how subsidiaries can influence such strategies both directly and indirectly. In practice, the chapter argued, the pure ethnocentric approach, that is a wholesale transfer of parent company home-grown HRM style, is not workable. Neither is the pure polycentric approach, that is allowing the subsidiaries to do as they wish. A synergistic approach (Adler, 1995) is probably one of the more practicable ways of transferring HRM between parent and subsidiary. This approach entails using best practices of both home and host countries. For instance, if the host-country employees' culture is collectivist and group oriented, why not turn this into a mutual commitment between employer and employees. If the home-country culture is characterised by participation and respect for other people's views, why not encourage and train the subsidiary's group-oriented employees to participate formally in the decision making process.

Whatever transfer strategy a parent company might adopt, the ways in which these strategies are actually conveyed to the subsidiary may vary from company to company, rooted to some extent in the home-country culture.

Oki, a Japanese company with a subsidiary in Scotland investigated by the present author, adopts a very subtle way of transferring HRM policies and practices and at the same time also encourages the host-country managers to consider its own local policies and practices in a new way.

Here the HR Director of the subsidiary describes graphically the process by which parent company's ways of thinking have been introduced into the Scottish site. In the early days when they talked about giving bonuses, HR Director submitted a proposal to give staff a bonus of around £250 because they had met all their targets in the first period.

'It was agreed that we would give bonuses and I said I would arrange for payroll to pay these and the Japanese MD was horrified, he said "what do you mean? You've talked to me about how these people should be congratulated and looked after. If you put it in their pay packet who is going to shake their hands and say thank you? Why don't we give them cash?" I automatically thought it was nonsense because no one uses cash in the UK [as a form of reward], certainly not pound notes, or £5 as the case may be. What he was really getting at is that the real point of contact was to thank personally rather than just shove something in the payroll. My conditioning for many, many years had been you reward someone by throwing cash in their pay packet.'

Compare this with the description of an expatriate manager's approach in the Scottish subsidiary of Wyman-Gordon, an American company; he is trying to encourage his Scottish employee to get on with his ideas the way it is done in the HQ back in the US:

'One American manager was sitting in his office; the then Production Control Manager approached him with his proposed forge plan on a sheet of paper. The American read it, carefully folded the piece of paper into a paper aeroplane, threw it out the door-way, and said "follow it".'

And here is a French company's approach, which shows intolerance of deviation from HQ policies. Note specially the contrast with the Japanese way of showing disagreement with the local managers.

A few years ago the Scottish site of Michelin, a French MNC, replaced assembly-type production methods with team-based cell manufacturing without informing the HQ. Mr X, a 72 year old at the time and an owner of the company, found out accidentally that the Scottish subsidiary in Dundee was taking managers off the shifts as part of the new system (he saw the managers as 'the guys who did the business'). He was livid:

'Mr X bumped into someone in the UK who said 'You want to see what Dundee are doing' and immediately he said "What? You've done what?" and started flying people over for Dundee to explain themselves.'

It is of course difficult, if not impossible, to say whether these different approaches are rooted in the managers' respective home-country culture, or their company's organisational culture or something else. What is clear however is that they employ different ways to transfer HQ's preferred HRM policies and practices.

### ■ CHAPTER SUMMARY

This chapter discussed the issue of transfer of HRM policies and practices in multinational companies within the wider debate on knowledge and its transfer between organisations. Having examined the significant role that knowledge plays in the success of modern companies, the chapter identified the sources and types of organisation knowledge. It then explored the complex issues involved in cross-organisation and cross-country transfer of knowledge. The discussion was then focused on the transfer of HRM policies and practices within multinational companies. It was argued that the success or failure of such transfers to a large extent depends on the socio-cultural make-up of the recipients on the one hand, and the cultural embeddedness of the transferred practices on the other. The farther apart the 'exporter' and 'importer' of HRM practices are from one another (large psychic distance) the more difficult it would be to transfer such practices from one to the other. It was however argued that employee training could facilitate such transfers, once the usefulness of certain foreign practices are established.

### ■ REVISION QUESTIONS

**1.** What is organisation knowledge and where does it come from?

**2.** Why should companies be concerned about their knowledge base and how can they create it and improve its quality?

**3.** What are the major impediments to transfer of management know-how across nations?

**4.** How would you go about importing and implementing foreign best practices to your company if you were in charge of such matters?

## Case study: Transfer of knowledge in OKi—training and development

Oki was founded in 1881, and was established as a company in 1949. It has 24,000 employees worldwide, with sites in Japan, Thailand, US and Europe.

Oki (UK) Ltd at Cumbernauld, Scotland, manufactures and supplies all the Oki dot matrix printers for the European markets and some of the corporation's page printers and fax machines. It is recognised as one of the most cost-effective manufacturing plants of its kind, achieving some of the highest quality levels within the international electronics industry.

The Scottish subsidiary which employs 3,000 people opened in 1987 and is the oldest Oki printer factory in the UK. Since then it has won a number of UK and Scotland national awards, including 'sharing good practice in management' in 1994 and 'Scottish national training award' in 1995.

### Training strategies and policies

Employee training is very much a part of the overall company strategy and various approaches and methods are used to implement a comprehensive training programme.

'We start from a very high level strategy: where are the visions, the thrusts and what are the deliverables. We filter that down into what we should be doing. That's typically how you develop a training plan.'

Training and development policies are driven by the Scottish site. In the early days they were driven by Japan but this has changed completely. The site's annual training budget is £280,000 (excluding trainer salaries).

## Training new recruits

Off-line training is booked for all new employees for 5 days (induction). No matter what position they are recruited for, all the new recruits go through the same induction course. The first objective is to put them at ease by using icebreakers, such as company presentation, including cultural aspects and activities of the site; they watch a video on the company and the Scottish site made by the BBC. Quality issues are then introduced. The induction course is very similar to that of the parent company in Japan. The process of induction is based on teamwork. They have changed and modified the induction as a result of invited feedback from new employees who have been through the course.

Following the induction course, the next few days are spent on on-the-job training. New assembly employees are asked to strip down a product and reconstruct it from scratch. The trainer would explain all the components. In the configuration section of the shop-floor, they are given a ready made product and are asked to configure it for a specific country.

## Training programmes

In 1994, 4,500 man-days were spent in 'off the job' training. Up to 30 per cent of staff are currently engaged in higher education, in most cases helped and supported by the company. There are a lot of training and development opportunities. Technical training includes apprentices, in line with the Government's Modern Apprenticeship scheme (7 apprentices in total). They have put 10 technicians through 'Train the Trainer' courses to pass on their skills effectively to the apprentices. They will then train up these technicians to achieve D32 and D33 (higher level qualifications). Other managers have these qualifications too. The site is considering developing Scottish Vocational Qualification frameworks for operators as well. Someone from the manufacturing department is studying Information Systems because they have skills in this area and a post may arise in the future, others are doing courses to get Higher National Certificate in Electronics. The company pays for it all. 'You pay it back if you fail the course'—which serves as a good incentive. One technician interviewed has been doing college courses with Oki for the past 6 years.

A lot of operators have on-the-job training. The site has developed competencies for jobs and have a training matrix e.g. for technicians there are 3 posts: technical operator, technician, training technician—each is graded on a scale of 0–3. 3 is fully competent and can train others. They then developed a two-week training course, at the cost of £30,000, so that everyone has the same skill level. The next stage is to individualise the training programme.

The company has experienced no problems in imparting knowledge to subordinates. There are career development opportunities, and the culture and philosophy promote shared learning.

Team leaders can go on personal development training programmes—the Leading Edge project. This involves team leaders and managers (middle to senior management staff) going on an 'outward bound' course—identifying their strengths and weaknesses. They have to make all their own meals etc. This is a 4–5 day programme and the outcome is a development plan. Individuals also have to manage a project in the community, e.g. building a garden for a school, developing disabled facilities for charities. In year 2000 they developed and implemented a school millennium project for 10 year olds. It created a huge amount of pride.

The project lasted for about six months. About 30 people have been through the Leading Edge programme over the last 3–4 years.

The company has strong links with a local college—Coatbridge College. They have lecturers who come on site to run the courses in the evenings from 5.30pm to about 7.30pm. It costs a little more but it means that employees can finish the course a little earlier than if they ended their shift, drove to the college then travelled back home afterwards. The courses can also be more tailored to Oki. There is a good take-up of courses every year. Generally the local external environment has been very supportive towards Oki's training and development—as illustrated by the adaptation of some of their specialist courses to Oki's needs.

A training needs audit is conducted through appraisals and discussions with department managers every 6–12 months. In addition, when individuals apply to go on training objectives are formulated and then improvements are identified against targets after training is completed. This is then followed up with a training evaluation form which asks how far the objectives have been met and what they are actually doing that is different now. This information is then compiled into reports on general improvements for each individual, and fed back to the managers.

## Training for job flexibility

The company has a flexibility programme in place in many areas; it identifies what training employees require. They spend a lot of money on training but do not take more than 25 per cent of employees off-line training at any one time. The ultimate objective is to get all operators on each shop-floor station trained in every job, every skill and every department; they are also sent over to Japan if necessary.

Employees on their part want their job to be varied and flexible—'it's boring to do the same job every day'. They want the flexibility as much as the organisation does. If an employee wishes to develop their skills for their present or future role the opportunities are available.

Managers sometimes face resistance when someone is moved to a new position:

'They will have made friends on the old line, and it's nerve racking learning a new job. But employees realise in some cases they have to move because there is no longer a job for them in their current role.'

## Company knowledge base

The knowledge base of Japanese managers is much wider compared to the Scots. In Japan (HQ) every January the company announces employees' career promotions or moves. It is common for one manager to go from one department to a completely different function. Over time this creates an incredible knowledge of customers, products, processes from a wide perspective; they quite easily cross the boundaries between suppliers and customers. In Scotland this is not the case. Here they allocate the right number of people to each department and there are no buffers. Promotions are functionally driven, university courses and schools too are geared towards functional specialisation.

'If you ask employees in Japan [HQ] what they do, they say "I work for Oki"; in the Scottish site they would say "I am an engineer".'

## ■ CASE STUDY QUESTIONS

**1.** What are the main mechanisms employed by Oki (Scotland) to create and strengthen its knowledge base?

**2.** What are their major external and internal sources of knowledge?

**3.** How successful or otherwise has the subsidiary been in implementing parent company practices? What factors have helped or hindered the process?

## ■ RECOMMENDED FURTHER READING

Nonaka, I. and Takeuchi, H. (1995). *The Knowledge Creating Company*. Oxford University Press.

Kostova, T. (1999). 'Transnational transfer of strategic organisational practices: a contextual perspective', *Academy of Management Review*, vol. 24, no. 2. Online edition.

Tayeb, M. H. (1998). 'Transfer of HRM policies and practices across cultures: an American company in Scotland', *International Journal of Human Resource Management*, vol. 9, no. 2, pp. 332–58.

## ■ REFERENCES

Adler, N. J. (1995). *International Dimensions of Organizational Behavior*. Boston: Kent Publishing. Second edition.

Bartlett, C. A. and Ghoshal, S. (1989). *Managing across Borders: The Transnational Solution*. London: Century Business.

Buckley, P. J., Campos, J., Mirza, H., and White, E. (1997). *The International Transfer of Technology by Smaller Firms*. London: Macmillan.

Burton-Jones, A. (1999). *Knowledge Capitalism: Business, Work, and Learning in the New Economy*. Oxford University Press.

Chen, E. K. Y. (1994). *Transnational Corporations and Technology Transfer to Developing Countries*. London: Routledge.

Cohen, W. and Levinthal, D. (1990). 'Absorptive capacity: a new perspective on learning and innovation', *Administrative Science Quarterly*, vol. 35, pp. 128–52.

Cole, R. E. (1973). 'Functional alternatives and economic development: an empirical example of permanent employment in Japan', *American Sociology Review*, vol. 38, pp. 424–38.

Crozier, M. (1964). *The Bureaucratic Phenomenon*. London: Tavistock.

Epple, D., Argote, L., and Murphy, K. (1996). 'An empirical investigation of the micro structure of knowledge acquisition and transfer through learning by doing', *Operations Research*, vol. 44, pp. 77–86.

Form, W. (1979). 'Comparative industrial sociology and the convergence hypothesis', *Annual Review of Sociology*, vol. 5, pp. 1–25.

Foss, J. (1997). *Resources, Firms, and Strategies: A Reader in the Resource-Based Perspective*. Oxford University Press.

Foss, N. J. and Pedersen, T. (2001). 'Transferring knowledge in MNCs—the role of sources of subsidiary knowledge and organizational context', *Journal of International Management*, vol. 8, no. 1, pp. 49–68.

Galbraith, C. S. (1990). 'Transferring core manufacturing technologies in high technology firms', *California Management Review*, vol. 32, no. 4, pp. 56–70.

Giroud, A. (2000). 'Japanese transnational corporations' knowledge transfer to South East Asia: the case of the electrical and electronics sector in Malaysia', *International Business Review*, vol. 9, pp. 571–86.

Gupta, A. K. and Govindarajan, V. (2000). 'Knowledge flows within multinational corporations,' *Strategic Management Journal*, vol. 21, pp. 473–96.

Halbach, A. J. (1989). 'Multinational enterprise and subcontracting in the third world: a study of inter-industrial linkages', Working Paper no. 58, Multinational Enterprises Programme, ILO. Geneva: International Labour Office.

Hedlund, C. (1986). 'The hypermodern MNC: a heterarchy?', *Human Resource Management*, vol. 25, pp. 9–35.

Hickson, D. J., Hinnings, C. R., McMillan, C. J. M., and Schwitter, J. P. (1974). 'The culture-free context of organization structure: a tri-national comparison', *Sociology*, vol. 8, pp. 59–80.

Hofstede, G. (1980). *Culture's Consequences*. California: Sage Publications.

Holden, N. J. (2002). *Cross-Cultural Management. A Knowledge Management Perspective*. Harlow: Pearson Education Limited.

Johanson, J. and Vahlne, J. E. (1977). 'The internationalisation process of the firm: a model of knowledge development on increasing foreign commitments', *Journal of International Business Studies*, vol. 8, no. 1, pp. 23–32.

Kerr, C. J., Dunlop, J. T., Harbison, F. H., and Myers, C. A. (1952). *Industrialism and Industrial man*. Cambridge, MA: Harvard University Press.

Kogut, B. and Zander, U. (1992). 'Knowledge of the firm, combinative capabilities, and the replication of technology', *Organization Science*, vol. 3, pp. 383–97.

Kogut, B. and Zander, U. (1995). 'Knowledge and the speed of transfer and imitation of organizational capabilities: an empirical test', *Organization Science*, vol. 6, pp. 76–92.

Kostova, T. (1999). 'Transnational transfer of strategic organisational practices: a contextual perspective', *Academy of Management Review*, vol. 24, no. 2, Online Journal.

Kydd, C. and Oppenheim, L. (1990). 'Using human resource management in Japanese industry', in M Aoki and R Dore, *The Japanese Firm: The Sources of Competitive Strength*. Oxford University Press. pp. 41–65.

Lall, S. (1993). 'Promoting technological development: the role of technology transfer and indigenous effort', *Third World Quarterly*, vol. 14, no. 1, pp. 95–109.

—— (1994). 'Technological capabilities', in J.-J Salomon, F. R. Sagasti and C. Sachs-Jeantet, *The Uncertain Quest: Science, Technology and Development*. Tokyo: United Nations University Press. pp. 264–301.

Lane, P. and Lubatkin, M. (1998). 'Relative absorptive capacity and interorganizational learning', *Strategic Management Journal*, vol. 19, pp. 461–77.

Laurent, A. (1983). 'The cultural diversity of western management conceptions', *International Studies of Management and Organizations*, vol. 8, pp. 75–96.

Leonard-Barton, D. (1992). 'The factory as a learning laboratory', *Sloan Management Review*, Fall, pp. 23–38.

Lester, R. K. and McCabe, M. J. (1993). 'The effect of industrial structure on learning by doing in nuclear power plant operation', *The Rand Journal of Economics*, vol. 24, pp. 418–438.

Lincoln, J., Hanada, M., and Olson, J. (1981). 'Cultural orientations and individual reactions to organizations: a study of employees of Japanese-owned firms', *Administrative Science Quarterly*, vol. 26, no. 1, pp. 93–115.

Marsden, D. (1991). 'Indigenous management', *International Journal of Human Resource Management*, vol. 2, pp. 21–38.

Martell, K. D. and Carroll, S. J. Jr. (1995). 'The role of HRM in supporting innovative strategies: recommendations on how R&D managers should be treated from an HRM perspective', *R&D Management*, vol. 25, no.1, pp. 91–104.

Meyer, J. W. and Rowan, B. (1977). 'Institutionalized organizations: formal structure as myth and ceremony', *American Journal of Sociology*, vol. 83, pp. 340–63.

Minbaeva, D., Pedersen, T., Björkman, I., Fey, C. F., and Park, H. J. (2001). 'The MNC knowledge transfer, subsidiary absorptive capacity and HRM', Working Paper 14–2001, Copenhagen Business School.

Mowery, D. C., Hoanne, E. O., and Silverman, B. S. (1996). 'Strategic alliances and inter-firm knowledge transfer', *Strategic Management Journal*, vol. 17, pp. 77–91.

Nonaka, I. (1991). 'The knowledge-creating company', *Harvard Business Review*, vol. 69, no. 6, pp. 69–104.

—— and Takeuchi, H. (1995). *The Knowledge Creating Company*. Oxford University Press.

—— and Takeuchi, H. (1998). 'The knowledge-creating company', in C. Mabey, G. Salaman, and J. Storey (eds), *Strategic Human Resource Management*. London: Sage.

Pollard, D. (2001). 'Learning in international joint ventures', in M. H. Tayeb (ed.), *International Business Partnerships: Issues and Concerns*. Basingstoke: Palgrave (Macmillan). Chapter 4.

Porter, M. E. (ed.) (1986). *Competition in Global Industries: A Conceptual Framework*. Harvard Business School Press.

Rogers, E. M. (1983). *Diffusion of Innovation*. New York: Free Press. Third edition.

Snell S. and Dean, J. (1992). 'Integrated manufacturing and human resource management: a human capital perspective', *Academy of Management Journal*, vol. 33, no. 3, pp. 467–504.

Sparkes, J. R. and Miyake, M. (2000). *International Business Review*, vol. 9, pp. 599–612.

Szulanski, G. (1996). 'Exploring internal stickiness: impediments to the transfer of best practice within the firm', *Strategic Management Journal*, vol. 17, Winter special issue, pp. 27–43.

Tayeb, M. H. (1988). *Organizations and National Culture: A Comparative Analysis*. London: Sage Publications.

—— (1992). *The Global Business Environment*. London: Sage Publications.

—— (1995). 'The competitive advantage of nations: the role of HRM and its socio-cultural context', *International Journal of Human Resource Management*, vol. 6, no. 3. pp. 588–605.

—— (1998). 'Transfer of HRM policies and practices across cultures: an American company in Scotland', *International Journal of Human Resource Management*, vol. 9, no. 2, pp. 332–58.

—— (2000). *The Management of International Enterprises: A Socio-Political View*. Basingstoke: Macmillan.

Weggeman, M. (1997). *Kennismanagement: Inrichting en besturing van kennisintensieve organisaties*. Schiedam: Scriptum Management (In Dutch). Cited in S. Mulders, J. Bucker, and R. Schouteten, 2003, 'Knowledge management as a means to improve intercultural co-operation in multinational companies: a case study', paper presented at the 7th Conference on International HRM, Limerick, Ireland. June.

Wong, P. K. (1991). 'On the transferability of management systems: the case of Japan', in P. J. Buckley and J. Clegg (eds), *Multinational Enterprise in Less Developed Countries*. London: Macmillan.

Woodward, J. (1965). *Industry and Organization: Theory and Practice*. Oxford University Press.

World Bank. (1998). *World Development Report 1998/1999: Knowledge for Development*. Washington DC: World Bank.

# 8 | HRM in International Joint Ventures

## Learning outcomes

When you finish reading this chapter you should:
- understand why some companies engage in international joint ventures (IJVs)
- know about the overall performance records of IJVs and major reasons behind them
- be familiar with the debates regarding the implications of national and organisational cultures for IJVs and their HRM policies and practices
- know the main ways in which IJVs may be able to overcome some of the cultural issues and problems they face
- through the closing case study, have some knowledge of major issues concerning knowledge transfer in IJVs.

## Introduction

International joint ventures have been increasing in numbers in the past two decades or so along with the burgeoning of international trade and opening up of the markets previously closed to foreign investment. Joint ventures between two or more companies from different national backgrounds are in many ways mini-MNCs located in the same country, but because of their multi-parentage status their management is much more complicated and prone to frequent bouts of tension. The management of human resources in such companies brings to a head, among others, different national and organisational cultures of the parents and their leadership style preferences. The institutional and other characteristics of the IJVs' host nation also have a major role to play. Issues such as the choice of company language too can become a source of tension and complication. This chapter deals with the above and other relevant issues, but starts with a discussion of why some companies engage in international joint ventures in the first place.

## Going international in partnership with others

International strategic alliances have been growing in importance in recent years as a choice vehicle for companies to expand their product, geographic or customer reach (Contractor and Lorange, 1988; Gugler, 1992). Between 1990 and 1995 the number of domestic and cross-border alliances grew by more than 25 per cent annually (Bleeke and Ernst, 1995).

As the terminology implies, the companies involved in a strategic alliance join together in an exercise of shared strategies and vision, usually in order to be able to handle their environments and markets more effectively, but they do not share financial and managerial activities. The companies may own a certain proportion of each other's shares, but they do not become or create a jointly-owned entity and do not lose their independence. They may even exchange senior executives on a reciprocal short-term 'visit' basis and develop common career management learning and development policies, but they do not merge their employees. An example of a successful international strategic alliance is that between the UK's British Airways and Australia's Qantas. Here the two airlines aim at developing and sharing common strategies, core values, information systems and exchange of expertise in a two-way manner.

Joint ventures are a form of strategic alliance where the partners involved move a few steps further than sharing visions, strategies and markets. They create a new company in which they share assets and ownership, pool together their skills and knowledge, mix employees, and engage in joint management. As a mechanism for growth and expansion, international joint ventures are suitable for smaller companies as well as large corporations because small businesses may be able to expand more quickly or create market opportunities beyond their present internal capacity.

The setting up and management of the new organisation are usually subject to a formal agreement between the partners in terms of funding and operation, but the degree of formality may vary from case to case. Each of the partner organisations shares the decision-making activities of the venture (Geringer, 1988, 1991) but the extent to which the parent companies engage in decision making depends on the nature of the venture (Datta, 1988; Kogut and Singh, 1988; Glaister, 1990).

## International joint ventures and the rationale behind their formation

International joint ventures, formed by organisations in two or more countries, have become a widespread form of cross-border business cooperation. Researchers have offered various models and theories as to why some companies decide to engage in international joint ventures. One such model suggests that IJVs offer unique benefits of cross-culturally meshing each organisation's complementary skills, assure or speed up market access transnationally, leap-frog the host nation's technological gaps, and strategically respond to increasingly intense national and global competition (Killing, 1982; Beamish et al., 1994).

Another model proposes that international joint ventures have proliferated because individual companies recognise that expansion into new markets can be resource-intensive and risky. Traditional models of acquisition and merger are less attractive, especially if the venture is product- or time-dependent. Companies may meet significant resistance to opening new markets in foreign countries, as governments strive to protect local firms (Datta, 1988). Such governments may require a stake in international joint ventures or insist that local companies have a significant holding of the new company equity.

Glaister and Buckley (1996) identify five major perspectives: mainstream economics orientation, the transaction cost approach, resource dependence, organisational learning, and strategic positioning. The mainstream economics approach treats the extension of the firm by alliance as a means to obtain economies of scale and some control over inputs at a low cost. Transaction cost explanations can be achieved by emphasising the use of alliance as a means of reducing cost, specially the transaction cost involved in extending vertical links and in transferring technology (negotiation and re-negotiation of contracts, the creation of trust between partners). The resource dependency explanations are to extend the firm's domain of control through vertical links and risk sharing. The transfer of technology and exchange of patent motives are the implied motives of organisational learning. Strategic positioning suggests that alliances are formed by the desire to shape competition and consolidate the firm's market position.

There are obviously certain advantages in setting up joint ventures with local businesses, such as the partner's knowledge of the local scene and, in some cases, its political connections and ability to work with the bureaucracy and handle myriad other issues. In Russia for instance, as Tallman et al. (1997, p. 185) point out, 'IJVs . . . combine the capabilities of foreign companies with local knowledge and contacts, as well as a certain amount of legal protection, thereby reducing uncertainty and potentially providing decreased costs and increased revenues.' In addition, in some 'risk-prone' countries entering into joint ventures with local partners reduces the risk of nationalisation without compensation or other politically and economically motivated threats to the foreign partners' investment. These and similar considerations inform multinational firms' proactive strategic decisions leading to engagement in IJVs as opposed to other forms of foreign investment (Porter and Fuller, 1986; Harrigan, 1988; Hébert and Beamish, 1997).

Table 8.1 summarises some of the major motives for creation of international joint ventures.

## Performance record of joint ventures

Joint ventures, and indeed other forms of strategic alliances, have had a mixed record. As Bleeke and Ernst (1995) point out, the term alliance can be deceptive. In many cases, an alliance really means an eventual transfer of ownership. The median life span for alliance is only about seven years, and nearly 80 per cent of joint ventures—one of the most common alliance structures—ultimately end in a sale by one of the partners.

**Table 8.1** Rationale and motives for IJVs

- risk reduction
- product rationalisation and economies of scale
- exchanges of complementary technologies and patents
- coping with or blocking competition
- overcoming government protectionist policies
- getting access to foreign markets
- facilitating initial international expansion
- vertical quasi integration
- diversification
- consolidation of market position
- obtaining lower cost locations
- technology development
- market power
- market development
- resource specialisation
- large projects

Many reasons such as strategic misfit, preoccupation with short-termism, and incompatible organisational and human resource management policies have been offered by researchers as the causes of the relatively high failure rate of alliances. For instance, Niederkofler (1991) argues that a major cause for cooperative failure is managerial behaviour. In nature, cooperation differs fundamentally from competition. Whereas *competitive* processes are well understood and practised daily, the key success factors in *cooperative* processes are widely ignored. In the same vein, Harrigan (1986) asserts that alliances fail because operating managers do not make them work, not because contracts are poorly written.

Harrington's (1988) research suggested that common areas of joint venture failures include the following:

- partners would not get along
- market disappeared
- managers from disparate partners in the venture could not work together, what was thought to be good housekeeping by one partner did not prove to be as good as expected
- partners who were to contribute information or resources could not deliver through their personnel
- partners reneged on their promise.

Harrington's suggestion means that common management activities, business undertakings, programming goals and profits, and common risks and opportunities require the attention of managers and other employees of the partner organisations not only at the negotiation stage in the alliance partnership (Datta, 1988), but also throughout its life span. As Faulkner (1995) puts it, long-term success, whilst obviously reliant upon the economic benefits, is also particularly strongly dependent upon the attitudes of the partners towards each other, how they manage the joint enterprise, and on the degree to which the partners adopt a positive learning philosophy, thus enabling the alliance to evolve.

However, a note of caution regarding the failure records of international joint ventures is in order. International alliances, especially joint ventures, are in principle similar to single-parent profit-oriented companies when it comes to definitions and criteria of their performance: making profits, increasing market share, fighting off competition and meeting other strategic and operational objectives. But the nature of the 'beast' is somewhat different and, as a result, what might be perceived as failure or success in a straightforward manner in single-parent firms might be a complex matter in IJVs (Tayeb, 2001).

Take the much debated issue of IJVs termination for example. A single-parent company's termination signals its ultimate failure, but for some IJVs it may even be considered a success, that is if they were meant to be disbanded having successfully achieved their objectives set by the parents.

Another example: a judicious take-over of a company by another one in most cases is hailed as an exciting, shrewd move by a successful bidder, usually resulting in an over-night increase in the share prices of both companies involved. But a joint venture which is taken over by one of the partners and turned into a wholly-owned subsidiary may be considered a failure in certain quarters, both academic and professional.

A third example: in many single-parent companies, instability, symbolised for instance by continuous re-organisation, restructuring, changes of strategies, in proactive or passive response to the changes in the environment, are considered by all researchers (for instance the followers of the contingency theory originated in the late 1950s and early 1960s) as a sign of success and good management. But in the case of IJVs these internal 'upheavals' conjure up the spectre of failure as far as many, but not all, researchers are concerned. While adapting to external environments is applauded by some researchers (e.g. Killing, 1983; Doz, 1996), such instability is positively viewed as a healthy state of affairs in IJVs by others (Badaracco, 1991; and Yan and Zeng, 1999).

Having said all this, international joint ventures nevertheless appear to be particularly susceptible to failure on the management and other behavioural fronts, caused arguably by higher potential for cultural misunderstandings.

# Joint ventures and national culture

Earlier chapters in the book argued and demonstrated that national cultures are different from one another and approaches to work and its associated problems too differ from one nation to another. We also saw in Chapter 5 that the extent to which national culture, especially that of foreign countries, is relevant to a firm with overseas interests, depends on the form and depth of its internationalisation. For joint ventures, the relevance of culture is most pronounced at the initial stages of negotiations between the would-be alliance partners, and then later at the core values and strategic policies that they would develop jointly and the processes leading to their agreements on their characteristics, and, of course, the management of the venture's employees.

Business transactions, like so much of interactions between people, take place within the socio-political context where the actors involved live and work. In the case of international joint ventures this context spans more than one set of socio-political domain and is therefore eminently more complex.

National political and economic institutions of the partners' home country influence greatly the form that an IJV may take. In addition, the institutions of the country which hosts the venture influence the way in which it is set up and run. Moreover, the partnership is subject to rules and regulations of regional and global agreements and institutions to which host and home countries of the partners and their venture subscribe.

## Home-country

Freedom of movement of capital across borders and off-shore share ownership is a major influencing factor regarding the decision to enter in alliances with foreign firms operating outside one's own country.

In most liberal-trade nations portfolio investment and other forms of share-ownership in firms operating abroad are not hindered by the state, but in protectionist economies the flow of capital from the domestic market to foreign lands are either severely restricted or not permissible at all. For example, the Indian government until recently did not allow, and still continues to control somewhat, the movement of capital overseas to acquire foreign assets. As a result of such policies, the involvement of firms from India and other fellow protectionist countries in IJVs tend to be in the form of local partners of an incoming foreign investor.

Sometimes, because of home-country taxation policies, companies might prefer to engage in joint ventures, especially with minority equity ownership, rather than set up wholly-owned subsidiaries abroad. As Beamish (1993) points out, tax advantages in the home country result because in some countries the minority ownership is treated as an investment whereas wholly-owned subsidiaries and majority-owned joint ventures are not.

## Host-country

National culture and other institutions of the country in which an IJV is situated play a significant part in the actual form that the organisation and management style of the joint venture will take. In other words, the host country forms the immediate external environment of the IJV with which it has to interact and to whose pressures and expectations it has to respond. Companies undertaking expansion through IJVs need to understand the significant elements of local country culture, especially in terms of initial negotiations and partner selection and then later in terms of internal organisation and management.

Following the discussions in Chapters 2 and 3, major institutions which serve as the channels of influence of a host country on an IJV generally fall within six broad categories: legal system, political culture, industrial relations culture, level of economic advancement, membership of global and regional agreements, and the national culture as a whole (see Figure 8.1). These influences could of course be argued to apply to most foreign and domestic companies. But the foreign partners of an IJV, having scaled the entry hurdles, could be subject to further rules and regulations specifically targeted at such investors. The IJV's managerial prerogative might, for instance, be restricted not only with regard to strategic aspects of the IJV, but also the internal organisational aspects. Sometimes foreign partners in IJVs voluntarily give up some of their managerial prerogative, especially in the HRM area, because of local complications (see for example Namazie, 2000, on IJVs in Iran).

In most countries influences of national institutions on a venture's activities are incorporated in the rules and regulations governing businesses in general, some more explicitly than others.

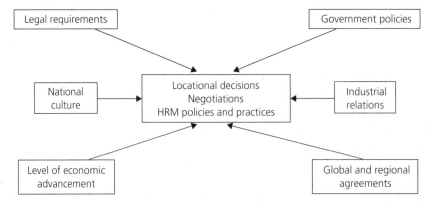

**Figure 8.1** Host country institutions influencing IJVs

# Effects of national culture on international joint venture operation

International joint ventures bring together two or more sets of employees whose national culture gives them fundamentally different views on what constitutes a desirable management style or appropriate organisational hierarchy (Norburn and Schoenberg, 1994). Schoenberg et al.'s (1995) research demonstrates the complexities involved.

Schoenberg and his colleagues studied four major Anglo-French joint ventures from the chemicals and engineering sectors which formed between 1986 and 1989. The researchers sought to establish the major organisational difficulties and opportunities that the partners experienced during the formation and management of the partnership, and the management practices that could overcome and/or make the most of these differences.

They compared the two nations on two of Hofstede's (1980) dimensions, 'power distance' and 'uncertainty avoidance'. They argued that the former would determine the views of each nationality on such issues as the preferred degree of centralisation and the appropriate levels for decision making whilst the latter would guide the preferences for the number of levels within the organisation and the rigidity of the organisational systems.

In Hofstede's study the French scored higher on both power distance and uncertainty avoidance indices than did the British. These differences of scores, Schoenberg and colleagues argued, were reflected in the management styles of the managers in the joint ventures studied.

The natural French management style was widely perceived as being more autocratic, with decision-making authority clearly concentrated at top management levels. In contrast, British executives were accustomed to leave more discretion to middle management levels, with strategic information more widely shared. The two national management styles failed to allocate decision-making discretion at the same organisational level.

British managers would assume that the purpose of a meeting was to arrive at a consensus view and then act upon that view. To French managers the purpose of a meeting was simply to clarify the arguments they would later put forward to their bosses for consideration.

Remuneration system and status of employees were another point of difference. For the French, hierarchical position and payment were dependent upon the educational qualifications of the incumbent. For the British they were both based on the content of the job itself. These two different approaches to remuneration had caused some serious problems. Following the French approach would mean that for similar jobs in the French parent company significant differences existed between the salary of an *ingenieur* and a *technicien*. In comparison, remuneration in the British partner tended to be based more exclusively upon the job actually done, which would mean an *engineer* and a *technician* would get the same salary if they did the same job, regardless of their qualifications.

In the two of the alliances where technical problems had to be solved by bi-national teams, the underlying scientific approaches could be seen to diverge. The French favoured the use of precise theoretical calculations to make sure in advance that a system would work, and would enjoy engineering sophisticated and very general solutions. The British were satisfied with a simpler system that was empirically proved to work.

These kinds of cultural clashes show the extent to which we all take our home-grown assumptions for granted and expect others to know them and to behave accordingly.

## National culture and misunderstandings in IJVs

Theoretical arguments in IJV literature suggest that cultural differences are the root-cause of many of the problems and misunderstandings in international joint ventures. Stephens and Greer (1995, p. 108), for example, argue that cross-national alliances almost certainly lead to conflicts when deeply-held cultural assumptions initiate or compound differences in organisational processes, technology, and other factors. Cultural values often lie at the heart of these challenges, making it difficult to resolve the problems.

Examples of the effects of cultural differences on international joint venture performance have been documented in many empirical studies. Peterson and Shimada (1978) and Simiar (1980) found that cultural differences frequently led to failure on the part of parent company managers to 'understand' one another. The resultant breakdown of communications generally had significant negative consequences, sometimes leading to collapse of the venture. Similarly, Stephens and Greer's (1995) study, referred to above, shows that cultural values affect managerial style, interpersonal trust and teamwork. Different patterns of values, beliefs, behaviour, and management practices are likely to be one of the main sources of conflicts. Elashmawi (1998) also reported cultural issues from his study of global joint ventures among American, Asian and European companies. For example, Americans are task-oriented while Japanese are considered process-oriented (see also Chapter 4 in the present book for other cultural differences between these two nations).

## National stereotypes and problems in IJVs

An important point to note here is that at times stereotypes regarding certain cultures rather than those cultures per se seem to cause problems among the multicultural workforce of an IJV (Lichtenberger, 1992; Salk, 1996). Salk for instance observed in her extensive qualitative study that all team members were marked by stereotyping and the creation of in-groups and out-groups. Members defined primary social identities and boundaries in terms of the corporate and national origins of members; in-group/out-group stereotyping was accompanied by attributions to cultural differences that members were reluctant to discuss openly or negotiate about with one another (Salk, 1996, p. 50). She then gives an interesting example to illustrate this point:

'I attended a meeting of Italian and British managers in which the Italians behaved in a quiet and withdrawn way; immediately after this meeting, British participants described the Italians' "loud and disruptive" behavior in meetings as a problem in that IJV.' (Salk, 1996, p. 51)

Similarly, Lichtenberger and Naulleau (1993, p. 302) make the following observations regarding French and German executives in the Franco-German joint ventures they studied:

'Being asked to characterize their French colleagues, German executives confirmed already known stereotypes of "French management". French managers [are] described as status- and position-oriented. Authority is being demonstrated through power and distinction. Management in France is considered rather as a "state of mind" than as a set of techniques. Managerial status is not part of a graded continuum, but rather a change of legal status as well as subtle changes in outlook and self-perception. . . . German managers are being perceived by French colleagues as functional, pragmatic and consensus-oriented on a strategic level, as time-efficient (use of time is linear) and systematic on the operational level and as very closed in their way of argumentation in external relations.'

However, it is worth noting that Schoenberg et al.'s (1995) study, referred to earlier, found the actual behaviours of managers and management styles in four Anglo-French joint ventures appeared to confirm the stereotypes attributed respectively to the two nations and their organisations.

Another major problem regarding the question of national culture and multi-parent companies is the extent to which in certain cases the actors involved appear to be unaware of cultural differences and hence not able to address the root-causes of some of the tensions and misunderstandings which may have been due to such differences. As Lichtenberger and Naulleau (1993, p. 300) point out, 'cultural blindness is both perceptual and conceptual: we neither see nor want to see differences' and that, according to research evidence, 'frequently similarity is being assumed even when differences exist'. Burger and Bass (1979) also found that managers described their foreign colleagues as more similar to themselves than they actually were.

## Perception of cultural and psychic distance between nations

A brief discussion on cultural and psychic distance between various cultures is relevant here.

Some researchers writing on internationalisation of firms have argued that multinational firms expand to other countries if there are cultural affinities between their home and host countries—the so-called cultural distance and psychic distance theories of internationalisation. Psychic distance, defined as factors preventing or disturbing the flows of information between firms and markets, is argued to be of utmost importance to international operations. Examples of such factors coming under the above definition are: differences in language, culture, political systems, level of education and level of industrial development. Companies are assumed to venture out into nations which are close to their home country in terms of psychic distance and accumulate experience there, before moving into economies further afield (see for example Beckermann, 1956; Johanson and Weidersheim-Paul, 1975; Hallén and Weidersheim-Paul, 1979).

One can apply this proposition to international joint ventures and argue that the larger the cultural and psychic distance between the partners the more likely that they will experience problems and misunderstandings. However, the fact that many western and south-east Asian multinational firms have set up business in all corners of the world, most of them culturally and psychically poles apart from their cultural origins, demonstrates a degree of weakness in the psychic/cultural distance proposition.

In addition, perception of cultural affinity (small cultural distance) might in fact obscure the real cultural distance between the people involved and as a result exacerbate misunderstandings between them precisely because they had not been prepared for real differences. O'Grady and Lane's (1996) investigation into Canadian retailers operating in the United States appears to confirm this view. The authors found that although the Canadian companies in their sample began their internationalisation by entering the United States, a country culturally closest to their home-country, when one looks beyond the sequence of entry to performance one encounters a paradox. Instead of similar cultures being easy to enter and to do business in, the researchers argue, it may be very difficult to enter these markets because decision makers may not be prepared for differences.

A case study of three American manufacturing firms operating in Britain, conducted by Tayeb and Dott (2000) provides another example.

The British and American cultures are on the surface very similar in many respects, not least because of common historical, political and economic bonds. Most British people, from politicians to artists, academics, journalists and the 'ordinary' men and women in the street like to think that they are far closer to their cousins across the Atlantic Ocean than to their fellow Europeans next door. An objective observer can see the tangible traces of Americanism in almost every aspect of modern British life, from the mass communication media, to economic and foreign policies. But, notwithstanding the shared common cultural heritage, these two nations are not really that close 'under the skin', even though they may be perceived as such.

The three-company case study explored the implications of cultural differences and similarities between the two nations for the management of the participating firms. It found that, among other things, significant differences do exist between the UK and the US which have direct implications for the work environment. The Americans' can-do attitude, emphasis on entrepreneurship and innovation, positive attitudes to change and future orientation, legalist approach to contracts, informality yet a preference for written rules and procedures, dislike of trade unions, preference for HRM over unionisation, certain industrial relations practices (such as hire and fire policies, patterns of negotiations with unions and working arrangements), and pension funds issues, manifested themselves in their work-related behaviours, actions and attitudes in the three American MNCs' subsidiaries investigated in the study. On the British side, their dislike of change, strong traditional values, past orientation, flexibility yet a preference to work according to the rules, certain industrial relations practices and policies (such as the divisive them-and-us attitude, negotiation patterns, and shift-work arrangements) were present in these subsidiaries. These differences had created a certain degree of tension and frustration and at times had resulted in visible cultural clashes.

The above examples show that the actual and perceived cultural affinity between the partners and employees of an IJV may still not be enough to prevent cultural misunderstandings and clashes in the venture.

## Organisational culture and IJVs

In addition to national cultural differences, differences in corporate cultures of the partners involved also play a part in the joint venture's human resource management. Corporate cultures embody ways of doing things, such as power structures and control systems, management and leadership styles, and attitudes to investment and risks. Variations in organisational cultures across the parent companies and within the venture might constitute a major impediment to effective implementation of the IJV's HRM policies. The partnership between GEC and Siemens in the 1990s, for instance, was reported to be marked by contrasts between British firm's decentralised and short-term approach and the centralised longer-term style of the German partner (*Financial Times*, 3 July 1990).

One of the international joint ventures among Faulkner's (1995) sample provides another example. This joint venture, EVC, was set up by its British and Italian parent companies, ICI and Enichem. EVC faced two strong but very different cultures. ICI had a strong internal culture based on teamwork and debate, whilst Enichem was much more functionally driven. The production director at Enichem got on with production and was somewhat loath to express opinion related to other areas. In ICI, the concept of Board Member was more broadly interpreted. These different cultures could not fuse easily in EVC, and the chief executive officer had some trouble over clashing cultures as a result.

## Company language in IJVs

The question of adoption of a common language as a means of facilitating communication among employees has been addressed to some extent in the studies which examined the matter within the context of parent–subsidiary relationships, usually concerning expatriates and local employees. Lester (1994) for instance reports that Siemens, Electrolux and Olivetti, are among several major multinational companies that have nominated one official language as the basis of communication within the company. In some cases this is the parent company's home country language, in others another language.

In this connection, Marschan-Piekkari et al. (1999), writing within the MNC context, argue that the adoption of a common language has many advantages from a management perspective:

'It facilitates formal reporting between units in the various foreign locations, thus minimizing the potential for miscommunication and allowing for ease of access to company documents such as technical and product manuals; operating procedures; and record-keeping . . . It enhances informal communication and information flow between subsidiaries . . . It assists in fostering a sense of belonging to a global "family", which has been suggested as an important element in the multinational's use of soft control mechanisms such as corporate culture [Ferner et al., 1995].' (Marschan-Piekkari et al., 1999, p. 379)

In a multinational company with subsidiaries scattered around the world, the use of such a language, as is shown in the above quote, may be largely confined to documents and other written company-wide formal rules and procedures, occasional meetings held by taskforces and teams composed of representatives from different sites, and communication between subsidiaries' senior managers and their colleagues at the HQ. In addition, the decision regarding the choice of common language may ultimately rest with the parent company, which is the dominant figure of the whole enterprise, even if the subsidiaries feel frustrated. In an investigation conducted by the present author (Tayeb and Thory, 2000) into HRM policies and practices of multinational companies in Scotland, the frustration of a senior Scottish manager of a French company is quite clear:

'We are not a multinational company, we are a French national company who happens to have a factory in Scotland. We are very French, . . . French is the company's language and if you go to France you speak French, and you like to think that when the French come over here they speak a bit of English, well they don't. Even if they can.'

However, in joint ventures where sometimes a large number of employees from the partners join forces into a third company, the use of common language goes well beyond the above-mentioned cases and becomes an absolute necessity in the detailed day to day communication among the rank and file as well as senior managers and their colleagues at the HQ of the partners. And frustrations such as those felt by the Scottish manager quoted above can be very destructive. Moreover, in joint ventures where the partners are equal, the choice of the common language can become a more complicated affair than would be the case in MNCs. It is nevertheless important, as Schoenberg et al. (1995) point out, to create parity in the joint venture in terms of nationality and language. The founding partners could provide equal opportunity to all the nationalities involved to staff the joint venture. Languages of the partners might be used as the official languages of the venture.

## Human resource management in joint ventures

We saw in Chapter 2 that different nations deal differently with bread and butter HRM issues, such as recruitment, selection, training and development, performance appraisal, motivational policies, and industrial relations. These differences have of course implications for IJVs as well. Other employee management issues, such as employees' expectations from their workplace, can also be of relevance to IJVs. In some Asian countries for instance employees have an emotional relationship with their company, and look up to it for help when experiencing difficulties in their private life, and the organisation is usually expected, and does step in, to offer help—a loan to purchase a house, guidance on marital problems, even an active role to arrange a marriage for the employee. This is a far cry from the strictly contractual relationship between the employee and his or her workplace in European and Northern American nations—a day's work for a day's pay, nothing more nothing less.

Any joint venture with parents from nations holding widely differing views and preferences regarding these aspects of employee management is a potential hot bed of conflict and tension. An added complication is that the notion of HRM itself, its various models, its role and scope in the company are heavily culture-specific (see Chapter 2 for further details).

## Dealing with difficulties associated with HRM in international joint ventures

International human resource strategies are organisation-specific to some extent. For instance, there is a distinct difference between the HRM policies of multidomestic firms and globally integrated corporations (see also Chapter 6).

In this connection, Lorange (1996) proposes four types of cooperative ventures in his conceptual framework: (1) cooperative ventures with permanent, complementary roles by the parents; (2) a string of negotiated cooperative agreements; (3) project-based cooperative networks; and (4) jointly-owned ventures based on an ongoing business concept. Each of these types, Lorange argues, faces a different set of HRM issues and challenges. In the first type such issues are mostly handled by the respective parent and in the fourth type they are largely tackled within the venture by its own managers.

Based on preliminary clinical studies conducted by Lorange and Roos (1992), Lorange (1996, pp. 91–2) further identifies five critical HRM issues which can be argued to be directly relevant to cross-border cooperative ventures:

- Assignment of human resources to cooperative ventures: who should be assigned where?
- Transferability of human resources: who 'controls' a particular manager?
- The trade-off in time spending between operating and strategic tasks among various managers involved in the cooperative venture.
- Human resource competency: avoidance of judgement biases.
- Management loyalty: to the cooperative venture or to the parent?

Lorange then superimposes these five sets of crucial issues on the four types of cross-border ventures referred to above. Each of the HRM issues is handled differently depending on the type of the venture involved. He argues that in a project-based cooperative venture, the HRM function will largely be carried out by each partner in a 'compartmentalised' manner, and largely on behalf of his or her own organisational entity. Similar types of separate HRM arrangements among partners may be made in renegotiated alliances such as in licensing-type cooperative agreements. The HRM function will probably also to some extent be dealt with independently by each parent in the cooperative venture with permanent complementary roles by the parents. In all these three cases coordination, communication and consultation play a significant role in ensuring the smooth running of the venture and its success. For jointly-owned ongoing cooperative venture businesses a strong and fully-fledged HRM function will have to be established within the joint venture itself.

Overall, Lorange argues:

'. . . the HRM function within all types of cooperative ventures will have to undertake two types of tasks: First, it will have to assign and motivate people in appropriate ways so that the value creation within the cooperative venture will proceed as well as possible. To create such an arrangement requires particular attention to job skills, compatibility of styles, communication compatibility and so on. Second, human resources will not only have to be allocated with a view toward the needs of the cooperative venture activity, but also with a view toward potential repatriation to a parent, to be used later in other contexts for strategic purposes. As such the cooperative venture must be seen as a vehicle to produce not only financial rewards, but also managerial capabilities, which can be used later in other strategic settings.' (Lorange, 1996, p. 102)

Notwithstanding the above discussion, there are issues and difficulties involved in the management of human resources in an international context that are more or less common to the companies concerned. In order to tackle these there are practices that can be safely and profitably adopted by a vast majority of international firms such as joint ventures. Actions aimed at increasing awareness of and sensitivity to corporate and national cultural differences of partners are examples of such practices. Faulkner (1995) in the research referred to earlier, found that the following attitudes were outstandingly associated with joint venture success:

- Commitment by top management
- Mutual trust
- Sensitivity to company culture

- Commitment at lower levels
- Sensitivity to national culture
- Information widely disseminated
- Good dispute resolution mechanisms
- Learning dissemination
- Reviewed learning

As the list shows, 'sensitivity to company culture' and 'sensitivity to national culture' are among the top five attitudes which have a strong association with alliance success.

Faulkner's study suggests that nine out of ten joint ventures surveyed claimed to have positive attitudes on both or all sides towards national and corporate cultural differences. However, the situation was not always totally trouble-free. For example, in ICI–Pharma, a joint venture of British and Japanese parentage, the relationship seems to have met with culture problems. There seems to be, at least on the ICI side, a fundamental difficulty in moving mentally out of the strong ICI culture, into a sensitive understanding of partners from other cultures. The ICI-Pharma joint venture has been in existence since 1972, yet ICI can still say: 'One of the things that still holds us back in Japan is our lack of under-standing of Japanese culture. Relationships are very important in Japan, and we are much less certain about what might spoil a relationship than we would be with a European or US company' (p. 19).

In another joint venture, the Courtaulds–Nippon Paint joint venture, attitude problems also seem to have placed a brake on the development of the relationship. The venture started off well because the people setting it up were sensitive to their cultural differences: '. . . then there were people changes, and the older people who knew Nippon very well retired, and the younger people came in and didn't understand the Japanese culture, and way of doing things' (p. 19).

This demonstrates the inherent difficulties involved in adopting and maintaining positive cooperative attitudes in international strategic alliances. This internal conflict only empha-sises the apparent importance of the attitude question in sustaining a positive alliance relationship (Faulkner, 1995).

## How might international joint ventures tackle the culture 'problem'?

The first step may be to consider the cultural mix of employees not as a *problem* but as an *asset* to be developed and built upon. There are various ways in which this might be done.

At the individual level, training of managers and other employees is of utmost impor-tance. Staff members involved in long-term intercultural cooperations should be specially trained and prepared for the difficulties and building cross-cultural working relationships. Employees should be encouraged to learn the language of their foreign colleagues. They could be sent on special courses and training programmes. It might be even more useful to send employees of partner cultures together on these courses. This would encourage the building of informal cross-cultural contacts and help to overcome employee inertia in recognising cultural dimensions. In addition, selected employees could be sent to work in the partner's company for a while as part of their training.

Creating and sustaining a measure of cross-cultural empathy is another action which can prepare staff for cross-cultural understanding and can in turn contribute to the success of a joint venture. Yager et al. (1994) found in their study in China that in the successful Chinese joint ventures there existed a genuine appreciation for the complexity involved and for the length of time required in China to bring a project up to fully functioning status. A key American corporate executive made a statement during the joint venture formation process that made an indelible impression: 'We may not see the fruits of this effort in my lifetime or in my son's lifetime, but hopefully people will be able to look back in my grandson's lifetime and say that this was a good decision.' The local general manager who was present exclaimed: 'He is talking like a Chinese!'

Yager et al.'s research further suggests the following as the 'secrets' of joint venture success in China, which can of course easily be adopted and adapted in IJVs located in other countries:

- Chinese partners are carefully chosen.
- Expatriates are experienced in China and knowledgeable about and sensitive to Chinese culture.
- Task behaviours are carefully specified and strict controls are maintained through work rules and observation (over-supervision to the point of micro-management).
- Incentives are provided that are genuinely tied to specific performance.
- Extensive training is provided not only on technical aspects of task performance, but also in work habits and work ethic.
- A productive work culture is created using every means possible: a well-designed facility, cleanliness, tangible benefits from organisational membership (such as good treatment by the managers and an attractive work place).
- There exists a capacity to absorb contingencies of all types, particularly the capacity to remain calm in the face of adversity.
- Managers have international experience and an interest in cross-cultural understanding, perhaps from a broader perspective than their immediate job.
- Patience and a tolerance for ambiguity are essential.
- Managers are at peace with their environs, and want to be where they are, rather than having to fulfil a required assignment or supervise a prescribed project.

The sensitive areas of differences in values, styles, practices, and stereotypes are often difficult to address objectively but are as important as any other consideration (Zander and Lerpold, 2003). Child and Faulkner (1998) offer a model of two fundamental policy choices at either side of a continuum. First the 'domination strategy' which involves the domination of one partner's culture rather than striving for a balance between cultural contributions from both partners. Second, the 'integration strategy', which attempts to integrate both partners' cultures with the aim of creating synergies from them. The purpose is to combine the best elements in the different cultures to bring about an effective management system and use of resources. The idea is that the whole is greater than the sum of its parts.

**Table 8.2**  Managing cultural differences in IJVs

Use of synergy: the combination of 'our way' and 'their way' can provide the best way to organise and work

Cross-cultural orientation and training programs such as brief lectures, group discussions, role-playing, video presentations, multimedia presentations and case studies

Compromise and implementation of corporate goals that satisfy the multicultural business needs of each partner

Relationships build upon trust, friendship, understanding cultural differences, understanding the values and behavioural expectations of each other along with consensus seeking

Through learning in acquisitions and joint ventures

Understanding, accessing, and adopting innovative practices that can mitigate the compounding effects of cultural differences

Adapted from: Yesil (2003, p. 17)

**Table 8.3**  Auditing HRM in the global environment

| Areas audited | Issues to consider |
| --- | --- |
| Partner selection | Is there a commitment to internal or external labour market, and at what levels? |
| | What is the resource allocation for training and development and where is it concentrated? |
| | Are compensation policies anchored in internal and external equity consideration? |
| | To what extent does top management promote or tolerate employee involvement? |
| | What is the firm's industrial relations posture and track record? |
| | How does it pursue workforce flexibility? |
| | What is its compliance history with respect to employment laws? |
| Start-up | How much influence is the partner attempting to exercise over the choice of joint venture general manager and key technical or professional staff? |
| | What mechanisms, if any, ensure that the selection criteria for these positions will be consistent with the parent's strategic purposes for venture participation? |
| | How structured is the parent's role in assessing venture training needs and deciding on programme content? |
| | Has sufficient control been retained over joint venture performance appraisal and compensation policies to reinforce the parent's strategic objectives? |
| Venture | Have adequate efforts been made to educate joint venture management assignees about the strategic intent underlying partnership? |
| | Are local staff with loyalties to the venture being developed not to block knowledge transfer? |
| | Is there reciprocity in training between the parents? |
| | How formalised is the responsibility for learning (e.g. writing into business plans)? |
| | Are there sufficient economic and career incentives for sustained learning within and across strategic business units? |
| | Where does ultimate accountability for learning reside—in the joint venture or the parents' headquarters? |
| | Are there regular, comprehensive reviews of the learning process? |
| | Will the existing mix of joint venture assignees expedite knowledge transfer to the parents which stand to gain the most from its utilisation? |

Adapted from: Florkowski and Schuler (1994)

These two strategies lead to three possibilities which offer different degrees of cultural fit and another of integration failure ultimately leading to alliance termination (Zander and Lerpold, 2003):

- The synergy possibility aims at integrating by trying to equally meld the partners' cultures.

- The domination possibility aims at cultural integration through the domination of one partner's culture.
- The segregation possibility aims at a balance between the influence in the alliance of each partner's culture but does not really strive to integrate them.
- The breakdown possibility occurs when one partner seeks cultural domination and the alliance fails to secure integration.

Table 8.2 summarises some of the major recommendations made by various researchers as to how to manage cultural differences in IJVs.

Finally, Florkowski and Schuler's (1994) idea of an HRM audit offers a useful mechanism to identify the specific needs of an international joint venture. As firms become more global in order to compete and even survive, all functions need to contribute to their maximum level. For the human resource function this means auditing its functional capacity and responsiveness as extensively as possible worldwide. Maximising the contribution of human resource management to the effectiveness of the company as a whole will require auditing to see how well human resources policies and practices are being done elsewhere.

International human resource management auditing can address concerns by critiquing the practices that govern partner selection, international joint venture start-ups and venture management. Table 8.3 shows the kind of issues and questions that could be examined in an HRM audit exercise. The list of items is by no means exhaustive and covers only a narrow range of HRM activities. Nevertheless, it provides a useful model.

### ▧ CHAPTER SUMMARY

The chapter discussed briefly the rationale for engagement in international strategic alliances in general and international joint ventures in particular. It then explored the ways in which the multi-parentage of joint ventures might influence their HRM policies and practices. It was argued that a major influencing factor is the national culture of the parents and that of the host country which provides the context within which IJVs operate.

The discussion was especially centred on the ways in which cultural misunderstanding could lead to problems and tensions which in turn could have implications for the performance of international joint ventures. It was also pointed out that in some cases cultural stereotypes and unjustified perceptions of other people's cultures rather than their actual cultures lead to misunderstandings.

Various suggestions as to how to deal with such problems were explored. The chapter ended by recommending the use of an HRM audit as a means of identifying the areas of potential problems within IJVs and deciding on appropriate remedies.

### ▧ REVISION QUESTIONS

1. What are the major causes of poor performance records among international joint ventures and to what extent might these records have been exaggerated or misinterpreted?

2. In what ways are IJVs similar to and different from multinational companies with regard to cultural issues?

3. What areas of HRM and broader employee management in IJVs are particularly prone to cultural misunderstanding and how can they be addressed?

4. How would Florkowski and Schuler's HRM audit help with resolving the kind of issues identified in your answer to question 3?

# Case study: Knowledge transfer in Intentia International

*By Helene Kubon and Monir Tayeb (with Nigel Shaw)*

This case examines the issue of knowledge transfer in international strategic alliances. The information given here is based on the first author's research conducted in four international alliances within Intentia International, a Swedish multinational company. Three alliances are located in Sweden and Norway with similar national and business cultures, and one in France, whose business and national cultures are different from those of the parent company's home country. The data were collected through interviews with senior directors, including a chief executive, and a questionnaire survey among the employees of the Paris- and Oslo-based units.

Intentia International is a Swedish Software company, and has within a short period of time grown into a worldwide company with over 3,200 professionals working in 40 different countries. Intentia International operates within 3 major geographic regions, namely Europe, the Americas and the Asia Specific, and has a customer base of 2,650 manufacturing and distribution companies worldwide.

Intentia's products and services are aimed at improving business processes in manufacturing and distribution companies. The company offers the Intentia Solution, made up of three parts: Movex, the ERP system (Enterprise Process Manager), and Implex. Movex is an integrated suite of collaborative applications for the design, management and control of business operations. Movex aims to make business processes more efficient in the areas of sales, marketing, logistics, production, finance and human resources. The ERP system helps the company in designing and configuring business processes, while Implex is Intentia's method of implementing Movex.

Intentia's professional services offerings consist of project management, business consulting, application engineering and system engineering. The industries they focus on are automotive, distribution, fashion, food and beverage, furniture, mechanical engineering, paper, service and rental, and steel.

## International expansion policies

Intentia employs a collaboration strategy when going international. Their policy is first to enter in strategic alliance with another company in order to find out whether the two companies can work effectively together or not. If the companies do cooperate effectively, an acquisition is likely to take place. These partner networks are supported through training, access to new technology, and both parties aim to benefit from knowledge transfer and knowledge implementation.

## Creation of knowledge within Intentia

The company has an Intentia University which offers high quality education and training to their own staff and their customers. It drives the ongoing skill development of their most important resource—the people who sell, serve and create partnership with the customers.

To avoid barriers to effective knowledge transfer, Intentia has a central Research and Development department where products and methods are developed. By doing so, the organisation as a whole benefits from new innovations and creativity as well as the transfer of know-how throughout the network. The Chief Executive in Oslo states that:

'It is crucial that the managers in all divisions understand that knowledge transfer among partners will enhance innovation and an innovative culture, hence knowledge transfer is a very important element of our competitive strategy.'

However, there is an important difference between consultant alliances and R&D alliances. In the consultant alliances the focus is on explicit knowledge, while the R&D alliances seek to explore new opportunities through the transference of tacit knowledge (see Chapter 7 on tacit and explicit knowledge).

The motives behind Intentia's consultant alliances are internationalisation and market knowledge, while the R&D alliances are mainly concerned with technology development and innovation. Therefore, the R&D alliances are more likely to become learning alliances, as they have a higher degree of tacit knowledge sharing, but the consultant alliances are not, since they focus on explicit knowledge.

## Management of knowledge transfer within Intentia

On the basis of the literature presented in the previous chapter and the research carried out within Intentia International the model shown in Figure 8.2 has been developed.

The model shows how firms A and B must have matching motives in order to enter an alliance and at the same time they must establish an appropriate level of trust and cultural

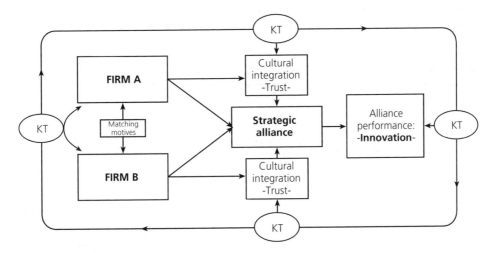

KT = Knowledge transfer

**Figure 8.2** Factors influencing alliance performance

integration. This, together with knowledge transfer on a continuous basis will affect the alliance performance in terms of innovation. If knowledge transfer is not managed effectively throughout all stages of the model, and on a continuous basis, the alliance performance is likely to become weakened.

The remainder of the case study will explain the model in relation to Intentia International in more depth.

The model shows that Intentia has continuous knowledge transfer before, during and after international alliance formation in order for the strategic alliance to work effectively.

There are some very important features within Intentia that should motivate employees to be open to such knowledge transfers, and increase their capacity to learn. These are summarised in Table 8.4.

In Intentia, 50 percent of all the contracts they work with involve international customers, knowledge transfer in the project teams is therefore crucial. Due to the increase in international projects, the knowledge transfer across borders has increased during the previous past two years.

Intentia's management recognise that their employees must learn to be able to internalise the knowledge transferred to them. That is why the company has set up the Intentia University, where the aim is to enhance knowledge transfer across borders. Here competence building takes place at the same time as contacts and relationships are established. Annual 'Kick offs' are held in order for employees to establish and maintain contacts with colleagues working in different countries. These are meetings where employees evaluate Intentia's performance in the previous year.

Within the centralised R&D function, knowledge transfer works very well, but not so well within Intentia's consultant operations. The problem seems to be that it takes a long time before sufficient competencies are established within the consultant alliances, because the consultants are often not willing to learn and gain new competencies.

Employee bonuses depend upon the performance of the company; if Intentia Group meet their overall objectives bonuses of 20 percent will be given to the employees. This policy was introduced in January 2003. The aim is to encourage knowledge transfer on a global scale by linking the employees' individual goals and interests to that of the organisation's goals and objectives. This new policy was considered as necessary, as a senior manager in Copenhagen states:

'The knowledge transfer and communication are good, but without incentives to the individual worker it will never work—"tell me how you measure me, and I will tell you how I behave" is very much alive in this organisation.'

**Table 8.4** Mechanisms of knowledge transfer in Intentia

| Tools used to transfer knowledge | Type of knowledge |
| --- | --- |
| International project teams | Explicit and tacit knowledge |
| Intentia University | Explicit knowledge |
| Annual Kick offs | Explicit knowledge |
| Centralised functions, i.e. Intentia R&D | Explicit and tacit knowledge |
| Salary System | Explicit and arguably tacit knowledge |
| Experience Groups | Tacit knowledge |
| Intranet – "The Wire" | Explicit knowledge |

## Managing different cultures

The model presented in Figure 8.2 shows that cultural integration and trust building are necessary for the successful management of Intentia's relationship with its international strategic alliance partners in general and knowledge transfer to and from the partners in particular.

Intentia has an informal corporate culture. There are, however, differences throughout the world, and of course between the company's alliance partners. These cultural differences do pose as a barrier and thus lead to tensions especially when Intentia employees work in international project teams. As the Sales Director in Bergen (Norway) puts it:

'When working in international project teams, we experience cultural barriers. These cultural barriers may seem small, but can often result in tensions between the different team members.'

The following are the cultural barriers which have been experienced by employees of Intentia:

* Language
* Body language
* Work behaviour: consultants/developers
* Differing norms and values in networks
* Differing motivational factors
* Educational background
* Level of openness
* Hierarchy vs network organisations
* Formal vs informal communication
* Formal vs informal titles

In order to create learning alliances, as Intentia aims and strives for, commitment and trust must be established within the partnership, through among other things, integration of the activities of various alliances and units (Morrison and Mezentseff, 1997). It is however important to note that integration between different cultures is easier if they are similar to one another (small cultural and psychic distance). Such cultural similarities could be especially helpful in case of transfer of tacit knowledge across units.

In Intentia it is easier to build commitment and trust within Scandinavian alliances, compared to French partners. This is mainly due to the fact that Scandinavian countries have similar national cultures, which are also reflected in the similarities between corporate cultures. As a result most of Intentia's R&D alliances are with Scandinavian partners, where the focus is on tacit knowledge transfer.

Intentia realises it is difficult to ignore cultural differences and have managed to gain the right level of integration and differentiation in order to build commitment and trust within its international alliances. Intentia's way is to introduce a Swedish 'flavour' in the alliances, but still including local characteristics.

## Innovation as a result of knowledge transfer

The final part of the model presented in Figure 8.2 shows that knowledge transfer within Intentia's international strategic alliances will improve its performance through increased creativity and innovation.

Intentia knows that it is a competence organisation, and always needs to be innovative in order to remain competitive. It is constantly faced with market opportunities and challenges, given the nature of its customer base. New partnerships are established to fuel innovation, and the overall cooperation must be good and communication effective. But it does sometimes have problems with regard to the effectiveness of knowledge transfer within its alliances, especially consultant alliances which are generally involved with creation and transfer of explicit knowledge and are less motivated in any case.

It is clear that Intentia need to focus more on the transfer of tacit knowledge throughout the whole network, and not only within the R&D function. The consultants would then be able to adopt to new policies quicker, and their willingness to learn should increase.

## ■ CASE STUDY QUESTIONS

**1.** How is knowledge created and transferred within Intentia alliance partnerships?

**2.** What are the major impediments to effective knowledge creation and transfer in the company?

**3.** What factors help or hinder the company's efforts to maintain cultural integration?

## ■ RECOMMENDED FURTHER READING

Akdeve, E. and Song, X. (2002). *Managing Joint Venture: Control, HRM, and Performance*. Göteborg: Graduate Business School.

Datta, D. K. and Rasheed, A. M. A. (1993). 'Planning international joint ventures: the role of human resource management', in R Culpan (ed.), *Multinational Strategic Alliances*. New York: International Business Press. pp. 251–72.

## ■ REFERENCES

Badaracco, J. L. (1991). *The Knowledge Link: How Firms Compete Through Strategic Alliances*. Boston, MA: Harvard Business School Press.

Beamish, P. W. (1993). 'The characteristics of joint ventures in the People's Republic of China', *Journal of International Marketing*, vol. 1, no. 2, pp. 29–48.

—— Killing, J. P., Le Craw, D. J., and Morrison, A. (1994). *International Management: Text and Cases*. Homewood, Ill.: Irwin.

Beckermann, W. (1956). 'Distance and the pattern of intra-European trade', *Review of Economics and Statistics*, vol. 28, pp. 31–40.

Bleeke, J. and Ernst, D. (1995). 'Is your strategic alliance really a sale?', *Harvard Business Review*, January–February, pp. 97–105.

Burger, P. and Bass, B. M. (1979). *Assessment of Managers: An International Comparison*. New York: Free Press.

Child, J. and Faulkner, D. (1998). *Strategies of Cooperation: Managing Alliances, Networks and Joint Ventures*. Oxford University Press.

Contractor, F. J. and Lorange, P. (1988). *Co-operative Strategies in International Business*. Lexington: Lexington Books.

Datta, D. K. (1988). 'International joint ventures: a framework for analysis', *Journal of General Management*, vol. 14, no. 2, pp. 78–91.

Doz, Y. L. (1996). 'The evolution of cooperation in strategic alliances: initial conditions or learning processes?', *Strategic Management Journal*, vol. 17, Summer, pp. 55–85.

Elashmawi, F. (1998). 'Overcoming multicultural clashes in global joint ventures', *European Business Review*, vol. 98, no. 4, pp. 211–16.

Faulkner, D. O. (1995). 'The management of international strategic alliances', paper presented to the Annual Conference of AIB (UK), Bradford, April.

Ferner, A., Edwards, P., and Sisson, K. (1995). 'Coming unstuck? In search of the "corporate glue" in an international professional service firm', *Human Resource Management*, vol. 34, no. 3, pp. 343–61.

Florkowski, G. W. and Schuler, R. S. (1994). 'Auditing HRM in the global environment', *International Journal of Human Resource Management*, vol. 5, pp. 827–52.

Geringer, J. M. (1988). *Joint Venture Partner Selection: Strategies for Developed Countries*. Westport, Conn: Quorum Books.

—— (1991). 'Strategic determinants of partner selection in international joint ventures', *Journal of International Business Studies* , vol. 22, no.1, pp. 41–62.

Glaister, K. W. (1990). 'International joint ventures', *Business Studies*, vol. 2, no. 3, pp. 17–21.

—— and Buckley, P. J. (1996). 'Strategic motives for international alliance formation', *Journal of International Business Studies*, vol. 33, no. 3, pp. 301–32.

Gugler, P. (1992). 'Building transnational alliances to create competitive advantage', *Long Range Planning*, vol. 25, pp. 90–9.

Hallén, L. and Weidersheim-Paul, F. (1979). 'Psychic distance and buyer-seller interaction', *Organisasjon, Marked og Samfund*, vol. 16, no. 3, pp. 308–24, reprinted in English in P. Buckley and P. Ghauri, 1999, (eds), *The internationalisation of the Firm: A reader*, Second edition, London: International Thompson.

Harrigan, K. R. (1986). *Managing for Joint Venture Success*. Boston: Lexington Books.

—— (1988). 'Joint ventures and competitive strategy', *Strategic Management Journal*, vol. 9, no. 2, pp.141–58.

Harrington, W. (1988). 'Focused joint ventures in transforming economies', *Academy of Management Executive*, vol. 6, pp. 67–75.

Hébert, L. and Beamish, P. W. (1997). 'Characteristics of Canada-based international joint ventures', in P. W. Beamish and J. P. Killing (eds), *Cooperative Strategies: North American Perspective*. San Francisco: New Lexington Press.

Hofstede, G. (1980). *Culture's Consequences*. California: Sage Publications.

Johanson, J. and Weidersheim-Paul, F. (1975). 'The internationalization of the firm: four Swedish cases', *Journal of Management Studies*, October, pp. 305–22.

Killing, J. P. (1982). 'How to make a global joint venture work', *Harvard Business Review*, May–June, pp. 120–7.

—— (1983). *Strategies for Joint Venture Success*. New York: Praeger.

Kogut, B. and Singh, K. (1988). 'The effect of national culture on the choice of entry mode', *Journal of International Business Studies*, vol.19, pp. 411–30.

Lester, T. (1994). 'Pulling down the language barrier', *International Management*, July–August, pp. 42–4.

Lichtenberger, B. (1992). *Interkulturelle Mitarbeiterführung: Überlegungen und Konsequenzen für das Internationale Personalmanagement*. Stuttgart: M&P. Cited in Lichtenberger and Naulleau (1993).

—— and Naulleau, G. (1993). 'French–German joint ventures: cultural conflicts and synergies', *International Business Review*, vol. 2, no. 3, pp. 297–307.

Lorange, P. (1996). 'A strategic human resource perspective applied to multinational cooperative ventures', *International Studies of Management and Organization*, vol. 26, no. 1, pp. 87–103.

—— and Roos, J. (1992). *Strategic Alliances—Formation, Implementation and Evolution*. Cambridge, MA: Blackwell.

Marschan-Piekkari, R., Welch, D., and Welch, L. (1999). 'Adopting a common corporate language: IHRM implications', *International Journal of Human Resource Management*, vol. 10, no. 3, pp. 377–90.

Morrison, M. and Mezentseff, L. (1997). 'Learning alliances: a new dimension of strategic alliances', *Management Decision*, vol. 35, no. 5, pp. 351–7.

Namazie, P. (2000). 'A preliminary review of factors affecting international joint ventures in Iran, paper to be presented at the 27th Annual Conference of Academy of International Business (UK Chapter), Strathclyde University, April.

Niederkofler, M. (1991). 'The evolution of strategic alliances: opportunities for management influence', *Journal of Business Venturing*, vol. 6, pp. 237–57.

Norburn, D. and Schoenberg, R. (1994). 'European cross-border acquisition: how was it for you?', *Long Range Planning*, vol. 27, pp. 25–34.

O'Grady, S. and Lane, H. W. (1996). 'The psychic distance paradox', *Journal of International Business Studies*, vol. 27, no. 2, pp. 309–33.

Peterson, R. B. and Shimada, J. Y. (1978). 'Sources of management problems in Japanese-American joint ventures', *Academy of Management Review*, October, pp. 796–804.

Porter, M. E. and Fuller, M. B. (1986). 'Coalitions and global strategy', in M. E. Porter (ed.) *Competition in Global Industries*. Boston: Harvard Business School Press. pp. 315–44.

Salk, S. (1996). 'Partners and other strangers: cultural boundaries and cross-cultural encounters in international joint venture teams', *International Studies of Management and Organization*, vol. 26, no. 4, pp. 48–72.

Schoenberg, R., Denuelle, N., and Norburn, D. (1995). 'National conflict within Anglo–French joint ventures', *European Business Journal*, vol. 7, no. 1, pp. 8–16.

Simiar, F. (1980). 'Major causes of joint venture failures in the Middle East: the case of war', *Management International Review*, vol. 23, pp. 58–68.

Stephens, G. K. and Greer, C. R. (1995). 'Doing business in Mexico: understanding cultural differences', *Organization Dynamics*, vol. 24, no. 1, pp. 39–56.

Tallman, S., Sutcliffe, A. G., and Antonian, B. A. (1997). 'Strategic and organizational issues in international joint ventures in Moscow', in P. W. Beamish, and J. P. Killing (eds), *Cooperative Strategies: European Perspective*. San Francisco: New Lexington Press. Chapter 8.

Tayeb, M. H. (ed.) (2001). *International Business Partnerships: Issues and Concerns*. Basingstoke: Palgrave (Macmillan).

—— and Dott, E. (2000). 'Two nations divided by a common culture: three American companies in Scotland', in M. D. Hughes and J. H. Taggart (eds), *International Business: European Dimension*. Basingstoke: Macmillan. Chapter 5.

—— and Thory, K. (2000). 'Human resource management within the context of parent–subsidiary relationships: a Scottish experience', paper presented at the 27th Annual Conference of Academy of International Business (UK Chapter), Strathclyde University, April.

Yager, W. F., Thad Barnowe, J., and Nengquan, W. (1994). 'Human resource management in China: joint venture experiences in Guangdong Province', paper presented to the 4th Conference on International Human Resource Management, Gold Coast, Queensland, Australia, July.

Yan, A. and Zeng, M. (1999). 'International joint venture instability: a critique of previous research, a reconceptualization, and directions for future research', *Journal of International Business Studies*, vol. 30, no. 2, pp. 397–414.

Yesil, S. (2003). *Top management Teams within International Joint Ventures in Turkey: Exploring the Implications of Culture and Demography on Process and Performance*. Unpublished PhD thesis, University of Nottingham.

Zander, L. and Lerpold, L. (2003). 'Managing international alliance and acquisition integration', in M. H. Tayeb (ed.) 2003, *International Management: Theories and Practices*. London: Pearson Education. Chapter 7.

# 9 Foreign Assignment

## Learning outcomes

When you finish reading this chapter you should:
- know why multinational companies (MNCs) send some of their staff on foreign assignment
- be familiar with main theoretical models and practical issues involved in such assignments
- be able to examine expatriation from both parent company's and foreign subsidiary's perspectives
- know about implications of foreign assignment for expatriated staff and their families while in foreign countries and once they are back home
- have some knowledge of those expatriates who are not an MNC's assignees and have therefore no allegiance to a 'parent' company
- know, through the closing case study, how the issue of expatriation is handled in a foreign subsidiary of a French multinational company.

## Introduction

This chapter will expand the theme of foreign assignment and expatriation touched upon in Chapter 6 since expatriates form a major part of multinational companies' HRM strategies, policies and practices.

The traditional role of expatriates who would convey HQ's policies to the subsidiaries and show the locals how to do things are increasingly complemented by, or even in some companies replaced with, much more subtle integrating roles. In addition there are now other types of expatriates as well, such as freelance expatriates, who do not work for any single MNC as a permanent or long-term member of staff. The chapter will discuss these and related issues, such as preparation of expatriates and their families for foreign assignments and the problems associated with return to their home country, such as career planning and 'reverse' culture shock. But the chapter begins by exploring the major reasons behind MNCs' decisions to dispatch some of their staff to foreign subsidiaries.

# Rationale for foreign assignment

The growing internationalisation of business and the ever increasing number of multinational companies and international joint ventures have resulted in an increase in the dispatch of mainly managerial and technical staff on foreign assignment, for periods ranging from a few months to a few years. The growing cost of foreign assignments shows the strategic importance that companies attach to this aspect of their operations. Selmer (2001) estimates that most companies spend between US$300,000 and US$1,000,000 annually on an individual on foreign assignment.

But who are the expatriates and why are they sent to foreign subsidiaries by their company?

Cohen (1977, p. 5) defines an expatriate as a 'voluntary temporary migrant, mostly from the affluent countries, who resides abroad for one of the following reasons—business, mission, teaching, research and culture or leisure'. Harry (2003, p. 284) uses the term expatriate to refer to professional or managerial staff employed outside their home country either on secondment from a parent organisation or directly by the host organisation. Following Harry, the expatriates considered in this chapter are those who are employed in some capacity and are not on research, cultural or leisure activities. They are located in the foreign country for a period of at least a year rather than being short-term visitors.

Increasingly researchers argue that foreign assignment is a means to enable the workforce to gain fluency in the ways of the world, since this fluency is nowadays a competitive necessity. As Black et al. (1999, p. xi) point out:

'If multinational firms are to prosper now and in the future, they must develop people who can success-fully function in a global context—formulating and implementing strategies, inventing and utilizing technologies, and creating and coordinating information. International assignments are the single most powerful means for developing future global leaders.'

Many companies dispatch expatriate managers and other senior staff to their subsidiaries in order to maintain their integration into a coherent whole (see also Chapter 6) and to maintain effective communication between the HQ and the foreign operation. Also, as Pucik (1998) points out, most international assignments are still 'demand driven', filling positions where local know-how is insufficient or where the authority of the centre needs to be upheld in a more direct fashion. In other words, international managers are teachers, transferring new capabilities and maintaining order.

In many companies expatriates sent from the HQ to the subsidiaries tend also to have a culture-building role. According to an HR manager of Compaq Computers interviewed by the present author:

'The company uses relocations as a way of getting us to know other cultures and be sensitive to their ways of doing things. I am myself from the Republic of Ireland on a three-year relocation here [a Scottish subsidiary]. The parent company's objective is to create a global outlook, facilitate the exchange of ideas and learning from others.'

In addition, when a subsidiary is set up from scratch or acquired through a merger or take-over, it is likely that the parent company would send some people to run crucial functions and advise the local managers on technical and managerial issues. Once the subsidiary is up and running and has gained sufficient experience, the number of expatriates is reduced.

Researchers have advanced other theories as to why multinational companies send HQ staff to their subsidiaries. Black et al. (1992) for instance argue that expatriates generally fulfil three broad strategic roles: control and coordination of operations, transfer of skills and knowledge, and managerial development.

Harry (2003, pp. 285–7) offers the following as reasons for multinational companies' decisions to send expatriates to foreign subsidiaries:

| | |
|---|---|
| • Expatriates as a means of control: | Many international organisations attempt to control their foreign operations by putting trusted expatriate staff in key jobs especially in the early stages of a venture. |
| • Difficulty of finding suitable host country nationals: | Finding suitable host country nationals is often more difficult than finding secondees within a Head Office, or other parent organisation location, who can be sent out as expatriates. |
| • Carriers of organisational culture: | Some organisations prefer to have a cadre of expatriates, not necessarily from the parent country, to act as 'cultural standard bearers' for the employing organisation. |
| • Expatriates as a symbol of commitment: | Many people in developing countries believe that the developed world fears them catching up and so will not transfer up-to-date technology and skills and apply patent and intellectual property rights to hold back their material progress. Sometimes organisations try to convince the host country that they are providing up-to-date technology and means of managing work by sending teams of expatriates to manage a facility, to provide technical training and be present on the ground to show that the parent is interested in developing the relationship with its customers. |

However it is important to note that the precise form that expatriates' roles will take in any given company depends on its overall international strategy, rather similar to internationalisation of HRM in general, as was argued in Chapter 1. Edstrom and Galbraith (1977) argue for example that companies which integrate their operations globally, assign expatriates for reasons of coordination, while those which follow a multidomestic strategy dispatch staff to their subsidiaries for control reasons.

## Resource-based theory of foreign assignment

Bonache and Fernández (1999), building on a resource-based view of multinational companies, point out that internationalisation allows firms to earn income from their existing

**Table 9.1** A resource-based typology of subsidiaries

| | |
|---|---|
| Implementor: | High on application of existing resources<br>Low on creation of new resources |
| Autonomous unit: | Low on application of existing resources<br>Low on creation of new resources |
| Learning unit: | Low on application of existing resources<br>High on creation of new resources |
| Globally integrated unit: | High on application of existing resources<br>High on creation of new resources |

*Source*: based on arguments advanced by Bonache and Fernández (1999)

resources and to create new expertise which can generate future income. The authors then propose a resource-based model of expatriation, depending on the extent (low or high) to which subsidiaries offer opportunities to the parent company to earn income from its existing resources and to offer opportunities to learn new expertise. The model classifies subsidiaries into four categories: implementor, autonomous unit, learning unit and globally integrated unit. Each of these categories contribute a different mix of opportunities to the parent company, as shown in Table 9.1.

Implementor subsidiaries apply the resources developed in the headquarters or other units of organisation to a specific geographic area.

Autonomous units are much less dependent on the human and organisational resources existing in the rest of the company's international network. Here the subsidiary is a vehicle to transfer capital or products rather than knowledge. The environment in which the units work is so idiosyncratic that they have to develop knowledge internally and the knowledge thus created cannot be transferred to other units because it is highly context-specific.

Learning units acquire and develop new resources that may later be exported to other parts of the organisation.

Globally integrated units develop new expertise but also use the resources generated in other subsidiaries or in the headquarters. These units best represent the modern subsidiary from a resource-based view.

Bonache and Fernández then go on to argue that while many expatriations involve more than one role, the relative importance of each varies by type of subsidiary. In other words, the type of subsidiary partly determines the expatriate's strategic role.

Implementor subsidiaries exploit knowledge, mostly of a tacit kind, from other units (see Chapter 7 on tacit knowledge). Given that tacit knowledge cannot be codified in manuals and can only be observed through its application, when a company decides to transfer tacit knowledge between different units it must assign employees to foreign operations (Pucik, 1992). Therefore skills and knowledge transfer is expected to be a critical reason for using expatriates in implementor subsidiaries.

A significant presence of knowledge transfer expatriates is also to be expected in the globally integrated units since there is a considerable input of knowledge into these subsidiaries. Coordination is also another reason to assign expatriates in this type of units.

In autonomous subsidiaries, there is no relevant transfer of knowledge from the HQ to the subsidiary or vice versa. Therefore there is little basis for using expatriates to transfer know-how.

As was noted earlier, because of the context-specific nature of the knowledge needed for this type of subsidiaries, expatriate's expertise may not suit them and their environment.

Learning units transfer their knowledge to other units. The dominant pattern of international transfer will be one of managers from these units to another country (Black et al., 1992).

However, as Bonache and Fernández note, in spite of the above considerations there may be circumstances that force the parent company to send expatriates to all types of subsidiaries in order to maintain control over their activities. Political risk, where an event is likely to occur that will change the profitability prospects of a specific investment, and cultural risk, when there is a large cultural distance between headquarters and subsidiary, are examples of such circumstances.

## Ethnocentric versus polycentric views of expatriation

The ethnocentric approach to expatriation is widely used among international companies as a basic human resource management strategy (Suutari and Brewster, 1999). It advocates the use of people from the home country in key positions in foreign subsidiaries (Heenan and Perlmutter, 1979). This approach is based partly on the belief that it is often difficult to find sufficient numbers of high potential local staff and partly because of the perception that home country staff give the parent company more control over the foreign operations (Brewster, 1991).

The underlying assumption of such an approach is a fundamentally universalistic view; that is, a good manager in one country will be a good manager in all countries. As Suutari and Brewster point out, this view has wide currency mainly because technical competence is seen as a crucial factor by all the actors involved: the multinational companies, the expatriates themselves and the host country staff. Despite the importance of technical competence for expatriated employees, it is also clear from the literature that applying those skills in a different cultural environment is not problem free (Suutari and Brewster, 1999). As we shall see below, much of the literature on expatriates takes almost as a given the impact of culture shock and the requirement for the expatriates to adjust to what is expected by the local host culture.

The expatriates' difficulties in working in a different culture are further compounded if they wish to manage the foreign subsidiaries and pass on the HQ's preferred management practices (see also Chapters 5 and 6).

The most immediate and major challenges for expatriates are:

- At the macro level: the host country's language, culture, political system, and ways of doing things in general.
- At the micro level: organisational culture, preferred and workable management policies and practices, informal relationships between employees.
- At the boundary spanning and interface level: relationships with customers, suppliers and various institutions and organisations with which the subsidiary needs to interact all the time.

We saw in earlier chapters that there are huge differences between various countries on all these aspects and much else besides and therefore different ways are required to deal with them. Parent company staff who might be quite outstanding as technical experts and managers at home are very unlikely to be equally outstanding when dealing with employees and organisations in different cultures—unless, that is, they are specifically trained for such roles.

Indeed it is important to note that, as Chapter 5 argued, subsidiaries are not always passive recipients of parent company policies and practices and this applies to expatriation as well. Some subsidiaries, mainly because of their experience and self-confidence, would on occasion accept expatriates from the HQ only on their own terms. The Compaq Computers' subsidiary in Scotland, researched by the present author, needed a senior technical employee to come over from the HQ for a few months. They interviewed the potential candidates at the parent company's office and selected the one they were happy to work with.

In addition, expatriation is not always one-way traffic from parent to subsidiary. In some cases expatriates are sent from the subsidiary to HQ, on the latter's request, to train the staff on locally-developed technical and managerial practices which have contributed to the subsidiary's high performance (see also Chapter 7 on knowledge transfer). A senior manager in the same subsidiary mentioned above told the present author that:

'The expatriation is more from here to Houston than the other way around. The expertise which we offer the HQ are in the areas of logistics management, finance, planning organisation, and engineering.'

# What price expatriation?

## Foreign assignment from parent company perspective

As was mentioned earlier, although expatriates are among the most costly employees of any business organisation (Selmer, 2001), they act as parent company's 'eyes and ears' and help integrate the geographically dispersed subsidiaries in the company as a whole. However, the cost of expatriation is increasingly forcing multinational companies to rethink their foreign assignment policies (Brewster and Scullion, 1997). There are various ways they can do this, for example by training local senior managers to replace the expatriates, by reducing or completely eliminating special foreign assignment benefits and perks, and by reducing the length of foreign assignment to a few months rather than a few years (Selmer, 2001).

Also, multinationals increasingly experience reluctance on the part of home country employees to accept foreign assignments. This is because foreign assignment, especially if it is for a medium to long term, say over one year, disrupts these employees' lives. The disruption is particularly unwanted if they have working or even non-working spouses and school-age children (see for instance Punnet, 1997). They all have to learn a foreign language and adapt to a new country and new ways of doing things. The working spouses may not find a suitable job or any job at all in the host country—imagine a senior female manager whose husband is sent to a country where women are not expected to hold such positions in organisations. The result is that she will not have the opportunity to continue with her professional life in the host country, and will have to either forego her career or stay behind. In addition, the period of foreign assignment more often than not disrupts the career progression of the assignees back at the HQ and when they get back home. They might even find that their foreign experience has been far from helpful in their promotion (Forster and Johnson, 1996; Tung, 1998).

## Foreign assignment from subsidiary perspective

There are some disadvantages and problems associated with having expatriates from the HQ and subsidiaries might take appropriate actions to deal with them as they see fit.

Traditionally multinationals have tended to fill senior positions in subsidiaries with home country staff, but research evidence shows that nowadays this is less the case, especially if the subsidiary is in an industrially advanced country. The present author's extensive research in HRM policies of Scottish subsidiaries of a large number of foreign companies shows that the managing director of all but a few were local people. The expatriates were largely occupying senior technical or marketing positions and their numbers were on average two or three in each subsidiary, and only occasionally over ten at a time. But the interviewees in all these subsidiaries mentioned that their parent company dispatches more expatriates and in higher positions to the subsidiaries in developing countries.

In addition, when a subsidiary is set up from scratch or through a take-over of an existing company, multinational companies tend to fill senior positions with their home-country staff and reduce the numbers gradually as the subsidiary 'grows up' and is immersed in the company's overall culture and ways of doing things. In most cases however, senior HRM positions tend to be given to local staff because of their familiarity with local circumstances. HRM, unlike for instance some technical functions, is a highly context-specific function and requires extensive expert tacit as well as explicit knowledge of the host country. Expatriates are usually far less qualified in this respect than are the local staff—regardless of the location and status of the subsidiary.

One of the disadvantages of having expatriates in senior positions is that local employees may not see themselves as ever being promoted to those high positions, no matter how competent they might be. This perceived 'glass ceiling' could of course deter local qualified people to apply for jobs in the foreign companies operating in their country. As a result a valuable resource will remain relatively untapped. However, as was mentioned above, the high cost of expatriation is forcing MNCs to adopt a localisation policy. The flip side, for lower positions, is that foreign companies tend to be considered as more attractive by local potential recruits, especially but not exclusively in developing countries. This is especially so if the multinational company is widely known and well respected and if it offers higher pay and benefits in comparison with the local firms.

Another disadvantage of having expatriates is the perceived inequality of treatment accorded to foreign HQ staff in comparison with the local staff in similar positions, especially in terms of pay and benefits and other perks. This can cause a great deal of tension within the subsidiary (see also the section on expatriates in host country below).

## aration for foreign assignment

Partly in order to avoid such tensions, and also for various other reasons, such as unfamiliarity with local culture and how their systems work, some but not all companies prepare their employees and their families well in advance of sending them to foreign subsidiaries.

### Selection

The first step in the preparation process is to select the 'right' kind of staff for foreign assignment—people who are quick to grasp and cope well with new and unfamiliar situations. Multinational companies normally select such staff not only for their technical and managerial expertise but also for their cross-cultural adaptability.

Dowling et al. (1999, p. 85) identify six major factors involved in expatriate selection, both in terms of the individual and the specifics of the situation concerned: (i) individual—technical ability, cross-cultural suitability, family requirements; (ii) situation—country-cultural requirements, language, MNC requirements.

Black et al. (1999, pp. 59–65) make the crucial point that before selecting candidates to send overseas, it is very important to assess the critical strategic functions of the international assignment (p. 59): Why are the expatriates being sent abroad and what is expected of them once they are there? For example, if the primary purposes of the assignment are to improve the control function between headquarters and the subsidiary and to increase the coordination function between the subsidiaries, then the candidate should have broad experience in the company, including a wide array of contacts throughout the company.

Black and his colleagues then propose a range of skills to be considered as part of the selection criteria, depending on the position the candidates will hold and the role they will play in the foreign subsidiary. The skills range includes professional skills, conflict resolution skills, leadership skills, communication skills, social skills, ethnocentricity (the extent to which candidates have an open mind about other cultures), flexibility and stability.

### Training

Training for foreign assignment necessarily involves cross-cultural training and enabling the assignees to adjust to unfamiliar cultures and 'foreign' ways of doing things. As Black and Mendenhall (1990, p. 258) and many others point out, expatriates' cultural training influences greatly their success abroad.

Based on the extant literature, Caligiuri et al. (2001, p. 358) define cross-cultural training as 'any intervention designed to increase the knowledge and skills of expatriates to help them operate effectively in the unfamiliar host culture'. They argue, again on the basis of the literature, that cross-cultural training:

- should enable expatriates to determine in advance the appropriate cultural behaviours and suitable ways of performing necessary tasks in the host country;
- should help expatriates cope with unforeseen events in the new cultures and reduce conflict due to unexpected situations and actions;
- should create realistic expectations for expatriates with respect to living and working in the host country.

Opinions among the academic community are divided as to how much and how far multinational companies give cultural training to the staff selected to work for a few years in their foreign subsidiaries. Selmer et al. (1998) for instance found that many international organisations do not provide systematic training for expatriate staff. Caligiuri et al. (2001) on the other hand point out that in the early 1980s only 32 per cent of MNCs offered cross-cultural training (Tung, 1981, 1982), but by 1998 the Global Relocation Trends Survey Report indicated that of 177 MNCs surveyed, 70 per cent had provided a one-day cross-cultural training for their expatriates before departure.

However it is doubtful if such short training sessions would be of much use if the expatriates were to go to a country totally different from their own, given what cross-cultural training is intended to achieve (see above). In the extensive research that the present author has conducted, the participating companies, with the exception of Japanese MNCs, had hardly prepared their staff for expatriation.

A Scottish subsidiary of NCR, an American MNC, investigated by the present author a few years ago (Tayeb, 1998), is fairly representative of all those surveyed by her. In this MNC expatriates do not receive any formal training for their foreign assignments before they leave their home country. But they do get help and support once they arrive in Dundee where the subsidiary is located. There is for instance a half-day programme put together not to train the newcomers, but to familiarise them with the living conditions there, such as cultural and social issues, and what they need to be aware of. The subsidiary also puts together an information pack, a little handbook, informing people how to drive there, what to do, where they can go to have fun, what the theatres are like, and so forth.

One of the expatriate managers, on the basis of his own experience, has taken additional initiatives in this respect:

'I was trying to find the best way to provide support both for the families and for the expatriates. So what I actually did was, I hired an expatriate's wife, so she works for me. She has already been through the experience and the problems of getting used to living here, transitioning from US life to here. It's her job and her responsibility to help other expatriates settle into life and usually it's the spouse. The spouse is usually at home etc., so she, for example when they first come here, she actually gets them in a car and gives them an orientation of the area, drives them round, shows them the area. She finds houses for them rather than throwing them to the estate agents, she finds the houses, she contacts the estate agents. She finds out what kind of housing they are looking for and then I tell her the limits and she goes out and finds the houses. She takes them round and shows them the houses, they decide, she helps them through the transition to local lifestyles. Plus a social network has been created of all the expatriates. The wives get together from time to time, they used to get together on a weekly basis, and so when a new ex-pat comes over they join the circle. It's a support circle and they get together, have lunch once a week, they had a sewing circle at one point, everyone would try sewing and embroidery. I think we were pretty creative, we created something called 'gourmet dinners'. We would pick a different country of the world and then we would take recipes and pass the recipes out and each family member would bring one and we'd have a pot-luck. So those are the kind of things we did and that was a real support network.'

The ways in which multinational firms manage their expatriates, in terms of pre-assignment preparation, and post-assignment support, are different from one another. And there appears to be a home-country imprint on differences between the companies in this regard, which may have implications for their performance as well.

Tung's (1984) survey of a sample of American and Japanese multinationals and their human resource management practices regarding their employees abroad found that, on the whole, Japanese companies had a better record compared to their American counterparts in terms of their employees' performance, among other things.

She found that such characteristics as employees' high level of commitment, managers' familiarity with and understanding of their subordinates' personal and family circumstances, extensive training programmes, including a spell of time spent abroad, a long-term perspective regarding employee performance and attitudes, all helped to create a better record of employee performance abroad compared to the American firms studied, which displayed almost the opposite of their Japanese counterparts on the above issues.

In subsequent surveys, Tung (1988) compared Japanese and American multinationals' expatriates management strategies and practices with those of a sample of European ones. Here she found that American multinationals fared worse compared to both their Japanese and European counterparts. The Americans had a much higher failure rate, which were found to have roots in their shorter time-perspective and less positive attitudes to and understanding of foreign cultures.

Some MNCs, especially major Japanese companies, provide mentoring for their staff while on foreign assignment. Each expatriate is assigned a mentor back at the HQ, whom he or she can turn to for guidance, moral support and help. Mentoring schemes are particularly useful in the earlier stage of the assignment when expatriates experience culture shock and other practical difficulties associated with working and living in unfamiliar surroundings.

# Expatriates in host country

## Loyalty and commitment

In addition to having to adjust to unfamiliar surroundings, expatriates are having to cope with a state of dual loyalty: to the HQ and to the subsidiary in which they work. At times, there could be some conflicts between the two, especially when there are fundamental disagreements over certain issues between the parent company and the foreign subsidiary. The expatriates have to cope with such conflicts and deal with them appropriately. In their interviews with expatriate managers, Black et al. (1999) found that the most common source of conflict for those expatriates who had high allegiance to both the parent company and subsidiary was conflicting expectations, demands or objectives between the parent and the foreign operation. Although it was clear what was expected of the expatriates, the expectations of the organisations were different.

In this connection Black et al. (1999, pp. 132–47) identify four types of expatriates, depending on the stand they take with respect to their loyalty.

1. Expatriates who 'go native' are those who have higher loyalty to the subsidiary than they do to the parent company and usually form a strong identification with and attachment to the larger cultural context in which they work, including its business practices and values.

    There are both advantages and disadvantages of going native. For example, it will be difficult for the parent company to get its corporate policies or programmes implemented properly in the foreign subsidiary. On the other hand, these expatriates understand host-country employees, customers and suppliers. As a result, they can adopt management styles which are compatible with the values and attitudes of the local employees; they can also adapt products and services to suit the local market.

2. Expatriates who 'leave their hearts at home' are those who have higher loyalty to the parent company than to the subsidiary and its wider business and cultural context.

    Here some of the advantages and disadvantages are the reverse of the above. These expatriates make it easier for the HQ to coordinate its activities with the foreign subsidiary. On the other hand, because of their tenuous identification with the host country, they may try to implement and enforce inappropriate programmes or even end up offending the local employees, customers and suppliers.

3. Expatriates who see themselves as 'dual citizens' are those who have high allegiance to both parent company and the local subsidiary. They feel a responsibility to try to serve the interests of both organisations.

    One of the advantages of such expatriates is that they can adjust well and quickly to the local culture and environment. At the same time they are responsive to directives from the HQ. However, they require serious thought and commitment from the company. They are also a rare breed and may be quite attractive to other firms who might head-hunt them.

4. Expatriates who see themselves as 'free agents' are those who have a low level of commitment to the parent firm *and* the subsidiary in which they work. These free agents are primarily committed to their own career and move from one firm to another and from one country to another. (See also the section on freelance expatriates below.)

    MNCs tend to view such free agents with a degree of ambivalence. On the one hand, these expatriates are relatively less expensive than those sent from home. And in addition they have already demonstrated that they can succeed in global settings and have specialised skills that may be lacking in the MNC's internal managerial or executive ranks. On the other hand, free-agent expatriates often leave with little notice, and replacing them is usually costly. Also, free agents sometimes serve their own short-term career objectives which may or may not be in the long-term interest of the local operation or the parent company.

## Envy and tension

Foreign assignment packages usually offer salary and benefits commensurate with the HQ scales, which might be much higher than in the host country, because of differences in cost of living in the two countries, and it may also include additional benefits such as company cars and housing, to compensate for the inconvenience that foreign assignment will cause to the expatriate and his or her family. All this can be seen by the local people as undue discrimination between local and HQ staff and could result in tension.

The study by the present author referred to earlier (Tayeb, 1998) provides an example of the tension caused by pay and benefit differentiation between home employees and the expatriates. The expatriates, for various reasons to do with deductions, maintenance of the expatriates' US lifestyle in Scotland, and other contractual obligations, would receive a relatively generous salary and housing benefits and were provided with company cars. Most local managers did not have company cars, only directors did. Local managers were therefore resentful, because they were working side by side the expatriates at the same level but they did not have any of these extra benefits. So there was definitely a lot of tension. This disappeared largely because many of the expatriates went back home and they were not as visible anymore. Also, the expatriates started communicating better with the workforce and informing them of the reasons they were there and their plans for the future. As one of the senior expatriates put it:

'Eventually that got healed over in that some of the folks started giving presentations and they would put out an announcement in the afternoon, you know, that on such and such an afternoon in the cafeteria they were going to have a presentation and explain what we are doing in this particular programme and anyone who is interested is invited. They actually would do the presentation a couple of times so they could meet shift changes and wouldn't have a disruption on the floor. They would start telling people what they were doing, and why they were doing it and what we hoped to achieve, you know. Yes we're number one in the total unit shipped each year and ATM [automated teller machine] self-service market, but our competitor is right behind us, there's just about that much space between us, and if we stumble and fall they're going to run right over the top of us. So this is the programme we got put in place and try to make work so that we could stay ahead of them. And then I think people began to understand a little bit better.'

The atmosphere became as a result much calmer and the expatriates and local employees at all levels got along better.


# Freelance expatriates

As noted earlier, expatriates experience a variety of professional and personal difficulties once they are in the host country, especially if they have not received adequate pre-departure training. As a result, foreign assignment has become increasingly unattractive to potential expatriates. One way of coping with this situation is to substitute local staff. But this is not always possible, mainly because of shortage or in some cases a lack of suitable host-country nationals, those who are sufficiently skilled in managerial and technical terms to take over the job of the parent-company's secondees. As a result, as Harry (2003, p. 288) points out, the lack of suitable host country nationals and of parent organisation secondees has led to a market for expatriates who are not part of a parent organisation but who sell their skills to the employer prepared to pay for their services. The employer of freelance expatriates is most often a local organisation with no link to an international body. Sometimes an international company which cannot find suitable secondees within its own ranks employs them. Many of the freelance expatriates have been with international organisations and found that their career progress had indeed been hampered by working as an expatriate or grew to enjoy the challenge and lifestyle which could not be offered by the parent organisation. Some transferred their employment and loyalty to the local operation and others became what Banai and Harry (2001) have called transnational managers, employed for their international skills not for their nationality or knowledge of their employer's organisation.

But what might be the specific reasons that make freelance expatriation attractive to both expatriates and employers? The following two paragraphs are extracts from Harry (2003, pp. 289) based on his extensive experience as an expatriate in a number of countries:

## Attractions to employers of freelance expatriates

Freelance expatriates can be hired and fired fairly easily so they have none of the problems of re-assimilation back into the parent at the end of the assignment. They have few claims on the employer other than for their pay and benefits. The employment of freelance expatriates is usually governed by a short term contract for a specific period. The laws of the host country apply to such contracts and these laws are usually of more benefit to the employer than to the employee. The employer does not give them the same level of training and development as is given to seconded expatriates. Any training is likely to be job specific as they are expected to be ready trained before they are taken to carry out a task. If the work changes and they are no longer capable of handling a job they will be replaced by another ready trained expatriate or by a host country national.

Like the host country nationals, the freelance expatriates' loyalty and commitment to their employer are not certain. This can be seen as an advantage for the employer as it feels no need to give support or commitment beyond that necessary to accomplish a particular task. The employer may also view the absence of loyalty and commitment as providing neutrality and impartiality.

Freelance expatriates tend to specialise in working in a particular region or industry. They have specific knowledge and capability not always available to other expatriates or to host-country nationals. They are often more willing to work in locations not attractive to other expatriates and seem to be more willing to take risks in their career—if the immediate reward is sufficient.

## Motivation of freelance expatriates

The motivation of freelance expatriates may be that they were among those who were seen as having 'gone native' and moved their loyalty to the host society. Or they may be motivated by the money and lifestyle which are higher than they could enjoy back home. Or they might enjoy the challenge and interest of the expatriate way of life. Or it might be that they are not capable of getting a suitable job back home!

## Freelance expatriates' loyalty and commitment

Research in the Middle East (Al-Meer, 1989; Tayeb, 2000) shows that the loyalty and commitment of some expatriates, especially those who work freelance and have no attachment to any particular company, can be tenuous.

One of the major characteristics of the countries in this region is the large number of foreign employees working in various organisations. These are usually Indian, Pakistani, Malaysian, and Filippino people, citizens of other Arab countries and those who come from the West. This high concentration of foreigners has of course been caused by the shortage of local skilled manpower in the region. This condition has prevailed since the discovery of oil and the estab-lishment of the oil industries in the 1930s. The oil-fired boom that followed the Yom Kippur war of 1973 turned these countries into large importers of labour. The rich countries of the Arabian peninsula still have small, unskilled native workforces, despite the continuous efforts of the governments and the oil companies to recruit and train local manpower.

Saudi Arabia provides a good example in this respect. According to Al-Meer (1989), since the oil price rises of the 1970s Saudi Arabia has embarked on five-year development plans involving a number of large-scale projects and huge expenditures. Because Saudi Arabia lacked necessary manpower to embark on these massive projects on its own, Americans, Europeans, Asians and others have come to the Kingdom to work and transfer technology in return for high salaries and other direct and indirect benefits. By 1983, more than 2 million expatriates (about 30 percent of the population and 56 percent of the labour force) had poured in from at least 50 countries.

This shortage of skilled manpower has caused at least two problems. First, competition for skilled and managerial manpower is severe and it is therefore difficult to retain these employees. The second problem concerns the difficulties of understanding and motivating a multinational staff, given their different values, attitudes, behaviour, and lifestyles.

The volatility and diversity of the imported labour market has also serious consequences for employee commitment to organisations. Al-Meer (1989) compared the commitment of local, Western and non-Western foreign workers in Saudi Arabia. His findings indicated that Asians expressed a higher level of organisational commitment than did Westerners and Saudis. Further, it was found that there was no significant difference between Westerners and Saudis in this regard.

Al-Meer attributes the Asians' higher level of organisational commitment to their higher wages in Saudi Arabia compared to what they can get at home. Also, because they are Muslims they want to work in Saudi Arabia. This gives them a chance to visit Muslim holy places which they and their families cannot otherwise afford to see. Moreover, expatriates who wish to work in Saudi Arabia must enter into a formal contract with a Saudi organisation, which arranges for their entry visa. This prevents these employees from moving between organisations. These underlying reasons for Al-Meer's sample of Asian workers staying with their work organisations do not necessarily translate into dedication and hard work.

The relatively low level of organisational commitment expressed by Westerners as compared with Asians has been attributed to the fact that Westerners have come to Saudi Arabia to transfer knowledge and expertise, in return for relatively high salaries and benefits. Since their values and religions are different from Saudis' values and religion, their presence in Saudi Arabia is temporary. As long as they are paid well, they will continue working for their organisations; otherwise, they will seek opportunities elsewhere or go back to their home countries.

The damage that this low and shaky employee commitment can inflict upon their work organisations is obvious, especially when it is compared with the high level of employee loyalty and commitment that companies in south-east Asia, especially Japan, enjoy.

## Expatriates back home

Returning home, or repatriation, may seem at the first instance as easy as when one gets back home from a holiday—you slot back in your own home country and your workplace. But of course it is not like that. During the 2–3 or more years that an expatriate has been abroad, not only he or she has changed, because of new experiences, but also have the community and the workplace that he or she left behind a few years ago. Friends and relatives have moved on, some colleagues may have left the company and others have joined, and the local community has also undergone transformations. Sometimes all these changes may be to an extent that the returning expatriate might find himself or herself in an unfamiliar environment, and even experience reverse culture shock (Black, 1992; Forster, 1994). The expatriates might find that their experience abroad far from being appreciated, may have in fact held back their promotion and find themselves at a disadvantage compared with those colleagues who did not go on a foreign assignment. In fact some expatriates spend time doing 'special projects' before being fitted into a job which ignores their development while they were an expatriate:

'So many employers seem to miss the opportunity of a repatriate adding to the stock of knowledge of the organisation. Even if the expatriate assignment was well planned and handled it seems rare for the repatriation to be more than an ad hoc attempt to slot the returnees back in and virtually tell them to forget about their holiday and get on with some real work.' (Harry, 2003, p. 298)

As Stroh et al. (2000) argue, for some expatriates the process of adjustment to their company back home may be so difficult that the only solution they see is to seek employment elsewhere. Black et al. (1999) estimate that turnover rates among repatriates at some firms range from 20 per cent to 50 per cent. Selmer (1998) puts the blame squarely on the company. His research led him to believe that organisational policies and practices made it very difficult for the expatriate to adjust back into the home country operation.

A policy which can help repatriated staff to slot back in would be a mentoring scheme. Feldman and Bolino (1999) show how an effective mentor is particularly valuable. Schemes such as this are important, because, personal disappointments and tragedies aside, the costs to companies of losing repatriates are significant both financially and strategically (Stroh et al., 2000).

In financial terms, research evidence collected in the US shows that an American company on average spends more than $1 million to send a manager abroad, provide support, and bring him or her back home (Black, 1988; Tung, 1988; Black et al., 1999).

Strategically, as Stroh et al. (2000, p. 682) point out, repatriates 'understand both the operations of corporate headquarters and of overseas operations. They can also transfer important technology or information from foreign subsidiaries back to the home country, or provide critical co-ordination and control functions from the home office out to local operations.' To lose such valuable employees is a huge cost that no company should want to inflict on itself.

## ■ CHAPTER SUMMARY

This chapter started off by discussing the rationale behind the expatriation of some HQ staff to foreign subsidiaries, and the roles they play in ensuring the implementation of the MNC's various strategies and policies. The issues related to foreign assignment were then explored through parent and subsidiary perspectives and major advantages and disadvantages from the viewpoint of both sides were highlighted.

The chapter then emphasised the importance of staff preparation for foreign assignment and drew attention to the consequences of inadequate policies in this regard.

Issues such as loyalty, commitment, envy and tension within the subsidiary become of concern to all the people involved once expatriates arrive in the host country and get settled in their new workplace. Real-life examples were given to illustrate these issues and how they might be dealt with.

The chapter then went on to describe the relatively new 'breed' of expatriates, freelance expatriates, and outlined the motives behind, and advantages and disadvantages of, freelance expatriation from both the expatriate's and the employer's point of view. A brief discussion of repatriation and the predicament of returning staff ended the chapter.

### ■ REVISION QUESTIONS

1. What are the major expatriation models and to what extent do they explain what in fact happens in MNCs?
2. If you were to work for a period of 2–3 years in a foreign unit of your company, what would you expect your company to do for you and your family by way of pre-departure preparation? Why?
3. What makes a freelance expatriate position attractive to an employer and an employee? What could make such a position unattractive for both firms and individuals?
4. Some researchers talk about 'reverse culture shock' experienced by foreign assignees on their return home at the end of a spell of expatriation. What do you think reverse culture shock means and how can it be avoided or reduced?

## Case study: Tubular Industries Scotland Ltd

Tubular Industries Scotland Ltd (TISL) is a subsidiary of Valeric, a French multinational company that has hundreds of small companies worldwide. TISL has several sites in the UK including two in Lanarkshire (Coatbridge and Bellshill), which between them employ around 300 people, and a small sales office in Aberdeen, with about 30 staff.

British Steel previously owned TISL; Valeric bought the company in 1994. The manufacturing sites had been making considerable losses up to that time and the new ownership saved them from the possible threat of closure.

TISL's main products are piping which is bought by some of the world's most prestigious oil companies including Shell, Elf and Total. The piping is manufactured in Lanarkshire specifically for the North Sea.

On the manufacturing sites there is a Scottish General Manager, a French Manufacturing Manager, a Pipe Shop Manager and a Coupling Shop Manager. Below them are foremen, shift-foremen (responsible for quality) and shopfloor staff.

### The management of TISL

When TISL was bought by Valeric the Scottish sites were in an advantageous position because the company had previously been a supplier to Valeric. The senior management of British Steel had communicated with the French company on a number of occasions and as some managers stayed on with TISL this ensured a solid starting point for building relations during and after the transition period. Valeric appointed a Scotsman as the General Manager for the Lanarkshire sites and he reports to the Head of Manufacturing in France. During the first 12 months the French Manufacturing Manager visited the Scottish site every 2 weeks. Nowadays he visits once a month and the General Manager makes regular trips to France.

There are three key French roles on the Scottish sites, including the Manufacturing Manager who oversees both sites and the Imperial Works manufacturing manager (main site). Each one is an engineer, all are here to install the main manufacturing initiatives operating in France. 'The objective is not to invade the Scottish sites with lots of French employees, but to transfer manufacturing practices that are in operation in France', one of the Frenchmen says. Indeed the General Manager was not forced to employ the French expatriates and he sees their presence as adding considerable knowledge and expertise to the factories. All have settled in well at the Scottish sites and are well liked by everyone. These harmonious relations were aided by the first Frenchman who arrived on the site. He had a good sense of humour which the Scots appreciated and that broke the ice and helped the locals to accept the presence of consecutive French expatriates.

The French are very keen to learn how the business runs and require meticulous figures and information from Scotland every month, e.g. sales, profits, losses. Many employees were 'shocked' at the level of detail that they required. Valeric rigorously audits and benchmarks all of their subsidiaries. This caused the Scottish sites to be a little secretive in the first instance. However, the situation has changed for the better and the relationship has become more like a cooperative alliance—France [parent company] has a wealth of manufacturing ideas and insights, for example quality programme, improving cycle times, which Scotland [subsidiary] has access to. The Scottish sites are now more open but it would take only one action by the expatriates which they do not agree with for the barriers to go up again.

The French have a very practical view towards their businesses—if someone else is doing something better then they make that information available to all subsidiaries. It is a learning opportunity for everybody and financially benefits the organisation as a whole. They have transferred manufacturing practices to many other sites.

The Scottish sites were already operating cell manufacturing (CM) before the French ownership; they now operate the more sophisticated French CM practices which include self-managed teams. In addition to the benchmarking activities which helped the French sites to implement CM, their success was aided by the level and availability of technical expertise from French engineers and their in-depth preparations before implementation.

There are some manufacturing practices that Scotland has refused to implement, e.g. the French method of pipe heating. They have 20 years of experience and are proud of their practices and their heating methods are considered by customers and other subsidiaries to be of high quality.

## Expatriation policies

Expatriation is used as a means to transfer knowledge and skills as quickly as possible to subsidiary sites. The main purpose of expatriation is not globalisation/internationalisation, and spreading of cultural values. 'We are naturally able to have cultural exchanges. But culture per se is not a target. We just have to cope with the difference in cultures and get the best of those. It's not a target, it's just a tool', says a French expatriate.

One Frenchman commented on the advantages of coming to Scotland : 'to understand and explain the cultural gaps to French colleagues, to help in and contribute to decision making on such issues as unions.' Every time they encounter a problem they can systematically differentiate the proportion of the problem that is attributable to cultural factors. He felt he had also benefited from Scottish experience because now he understands 'what you can get from a responsive environment'. He can understand what he needs to do to be more responsive. He feels that when you start something in Scotland everyone does it and follows it: 'this is a tremendous help in efficiency'. He says this responsiveness is demonstrated in many ways: 'the way people have lunch and how much time they dedicate to it; the way people educate their children. Everything is built on short-term, quick response. In France you take your time to think—sometimes too long.' Interestingly, 10 years ago the organisation had a shortage of good French salespeople because they were not able to be constantly responding to situations, moving forward.

The Scottish sites have never been forced to take on French expatriates—at the cost of £300,000 per person; they have 3 at the moment. The knowledge transfer is good, the expatriates are very skilled and the sites benefit from their expertise.

The corporate policy is to develop people with potential, get the managers in young and fast-track them, change their jobs to get a broad experience. The company selects on intelligence, attitude and loyalty. When someone is sent on foreign assignment, he is guaranteed that on his return he will have the same pay and benefits and position that he had while abroad.

Expatriates do not get any specific pre-departure training, but benefits are good when they move over to Scotland. There is no preparation for the locals on receipt of the expatriates either. The expatriates report to French management for salary and career progression, and the Scottish management for practical issues.

Not many Scottish employees are sent out to other sites. For example only one person has gone to the Far East, another to France; the latter was someone who was going to be made redundant and they found a position for him in France. Opportunities to get language training are available but employees, after five years of French ownership, do not see any potential career opportunities to move to France. The movement overseas from Scotland does not occur at very senior managerial levels, in any case. Technical people have more opportunities of moving around.

### ■ CASE STUDY QUESTIONS

**1.** What are the main reasons for a seemingly harmonious relationship between Scottish managers and employees on the one hand and the French expatriates on the other?

**2.** What do the expatriates see their roles as? And how have they been received by the local management?

**3.** How does the knowledge transfer between the subsidiary and parent company work? And how do the parties involved benefit from the process?

**4.** What are the main expatriation policies of the French parent company? Would they be workable in your country if there was a subsidiary of this company there? Why?

■ **RECOMMENDED FURTHER READING**

Mendenhall, M. and Oddou, G. (1995). 'Expatriation and cultural adaptation', in T. Jackson (ed.), *Cross-Cultural Management*. Oxford: Butterworth Heinemann.
Richards, D. (1996). 'Strangers in a strange land', *International Journal of Human Resource Management*, vol. 7, no. 2, pp. 553–71.
Tung, R. L. (1987). *The New Expatriates: Managing Human Resources Abroad*. Cambridge, Mass.: Ballinger.
—— (1999). 'Expatriates and their families abroad', in W. A. Oechsler and J. Engelhard (eds.), *International Management: Effects of Global Challenges, Corporate Strategies and Labor Markets*. Wiesbaden: Gabler Verlag, pp. 468–77.

■ **REFERENCES**

Al-Meer, A. H. A. (1989). 'Organizational commitment: a comparison of Westerners, Asians, and Saudis', *International Studies of Management and Organization*, vol. 19, no. 2, pp. 74–84.
Banai, M. and Harry, W. (2001). Unpublished research paper on Transnational Managers.
Black, J. S. (1988). 'Workrole transition: a study of American expatriate managers in Japan', *Journal of International Business Studies*, vol. 19, pp. 277–94.
—— (1992). 'Coming home: the relationship of expatriate expectations and repatriation adjustment and job performance', *Human Relations*, vol. 45, pp. 177–92.
—— Gregersen, H. B., and Mendenhall, M. E. (1992). *Global Assignment*. New York: Jossey Bass.
—— and Mendenhall, M. E. (1990). 'Cross-cultural training effectiveness: a review and theoretical framework', *Academy of Management Review*, vol. 15, pp. 113–36.
—— and Stroh, L. K. (1999). *Globalizing People Through International Assignment*. Reading, Mass: Addison-Wesley.
Bonache, J. and Fernández, Z. (1999). 'Strategic staffing in multinational companies: a resource-based approach', in C. Brewster and H. Harris, *International HRM: Contemporary issues in Europe*. London: Routledge. Chapter 9.
Brewster, C. (1991). *The Management of Expatriates*. London: Kogan Page.
—— and Scullion, H. (1997). 'A review and agenda for expatriate HRM', *Human Resource Management Journal*, vol. 73, no. 3, pp. 32–41.
Caligiuri, P., Phililips, J., Lazarova, M., Tarique, I., and Bürgi, P. (2001). 'The theory of met expectations applied to expatriate adjustment: the role of cross-cultural training', *International Journal of Human Resource Management*, vol. 12, no. 3, pp. 357–72.
Cohen, E. (1977). 'Expatriate communities', *Current sociology*, vol. 24, no. 3, pp. 5–129.
Dowling, P. J., Welch, D. E., and Schuler, R. S. (1999). *International Human Resource Management: Managing People in a Multinational Context*. Cincinnati, OH: South-Western College Publishing. Third edition.
Edstrom, A. and Galbraith, J. (1977). 'Transfer of managers as a coordination and control strategy in multinational organizations', *Administrative Science Quarterly*, vol. 22, pp. 248–63.
Feldman, D. C. and Bolino, M. C. (1999). 'The impact of on-site mentoring on expatriate socialization: a structural equation modelling approach', *International Journal of Human Resource Management*, vol. 10, pp. 54–71

Forster, N. (1994). 'The forgotten employees? The experiences of expatriate staff returning to the UK', *International Journal of Human Resource Management*, vol. 5, no. 2, pp. 405–25.

—— and Johnson, M. (1996). 'Expatriate management policies in UK companies new to the international scene', *International Journal of Human Resource Management*, vol. 7, no. 1, pp. 177–205.

Harry, W. (2003). 'Expatriates', in Tayeb, M. H. (ed.) 2003, *International Management: Theories and Practices*. London: Pearson Education. Chapter 13.

Heenan, D. A. and Perlmutter, H. (1979). *Multinational Organization Development*. Reading, Mass: Addison-Wesley.

Pucik, V. (1992). 'Globalization and human resource management', in V. Pucik, N. M. Tichy, and C. K. Barnett, *Globalizing Management*. Chichester: Wiley.

—— (1998). 'Creating leaders that are world-class', *Financial Times*, February, Survey page 4.

Punnet, B. J. (1997). 'Towards effective management of expatriate spouses', *Journal of World Business*, vol. 32, no. 3, pp. 243–57.

Selmer, J. (1998). 'Expatriation: corporate policy, personal intentions and international adjustment', *International Journal of Human Resource Management*, vol., 6, no. 9, pp. 996–1007.

—— (2001). 'Expatriate selection: back to basic?, *International Journal of Human Resource Management*, vol 12, no. 8, pp. 1219–33.

Stroh, L. K., Gregersen, H. B., and Black, J. S. (2000). 'Triumphs and tragedies: expectations and commitments upon repatmation', *International Journal of Human Resource Management*, vol. 11, no. 4, pp. 681–97.

Suutari, V. and Brewster, C. (1999). 'International assignments across European borders: no problems?', in C. Brewster and H. Harris, *International HRM: Contemporary issues in Europe*. London: Routledge. Chapter 10.

Tayeb, M. H. (1998). 'Transfer of HRM policies and practices across cultures: an American company in Scotland', *International Journal of Human Resource Management*, vol. 9, no. 2, pp. 332–58.

—— (2000). 'The non-tigers of Asia: the oil-rich Arab Middle East', Unpublished manuscript.

Tung, R. L. (1981). 'Selecting and training of personnel for overseas assignments', *Columbia Journal of World Business*, vol. 1, pp. 68–78.

Tung, R. L. (1982). 'Selection and training procedures of U.S., European and Japanese multinationals', *California International Review*, vol. 25, pp. 57–71.

—— (1984). *Key to Japan's Economic Strength: Human Power*. Lexington, MA: D C Heath.

—— (1988). *The New Expatriates*. Cambridge, Mass.: Ballinger.

—— (1998). 'American expatriates abroad: from neophytes to cosmopolitans', *Columbia Journal of World Business*, vol. 33, no. 2, pp. 125–45.

# Part III
# HRM and Globalisation

# 10 HRM in the Global Village: Cultural Impediments and Practical Complications

## Learning outcomes

When you finish reading this chapter you should:
- be familiar with the essence of globalisation debate with regard to HRM policies and practices
- know what factors might enhance globalisation of such policies and practices
- know what factors might enhance localisation of such policies and practices
- be able to assess the extent to which multinational companies (MNCs) can have company-wide HRM strategies, policies and practices
- have some idea, through an extensive case study, how in practice all these issues are dealt with by managers working in a major MNC.

## Introduction

The preceding nine chapters discussed major theories and practices of HRM from the perspective of multinational companies, including international joint ventures. MNCs are by definition the only major type of organisations which need to manage employees of diverse backgrounds located in diverse political economic and socio-cultural and national settings. The chapters also discussed the external and internal challenges that MNCs face on both strategic and day-to-day issues, and the ways in which they could, and indeed do, deal with these challenges.

The present chapter pulls together the threads running through all the chapters and concludes with a longish case study which incorporates all the major practical issues discussed in the book.

# HRM in the global village

One can examine this issue from two angles by trying to answer two familiar and inter-related questions:

## 1. *Internationalisation of HRM*

Will HRM ever become a ubiquitous off-the-shelf 'product' that can be purchased and applied in any organisation anywhere, with some added local flavouring and spices?

## 2. *International HRM*

Will MNCs ever be able to have unified company-wide HRM strategies, policies and practices?

Depending on one's point of view, the answer to each of the above could be 'yes', 'no' or 'yes and no'.

The discussions and arguments presented so for in this book suggest that there are no clear-cut answers. Let's have another look at the mitigating factors.

# Internationalisation of HRM

Notions such as 'internationalisation', 'globalisation' and 'universalism' within the context of management in general and HRM in particular, imply that, thanks to the relentless process of globalisation, companies face similar problems in the market place. In order to be successful they must adopt similar solutions to these common problems. In other words, the argument goes, globalisation has reduced differences between people and their needs and preferences as customers, suppliers, clients, and so forth. They all seem to be wanting similar products (e.g. personal computers) and services (e.g. Internet-based airline ticketing). The companies which serve these people or are served by them also face challenges which are increasingly becoming similar across the globe. And these similar challenges will be best met through tried and tested solutions—otherwise known as 'best practices' (see for instance Huselid, 1995; Wood and Albanese, 1995; Delery and Doty, 1996; Pfeffer, 1998; Wood and de Menzes, 1998; Ichniowski and Shaw, 1999). We are, after all, living in a global 'village'. But are we?

Many researchers have challenged the notion of universal best practices, especially with regard to HRM and other employee management issues (Tayeb, 1988; Baird and Meshoulam, 1988; Florkowski and Nath, 1993; Bird and Beechler, 1995; Brewster, 1995; Purcell, 1999; Dowling et al., 1999; Tayeb, 2000).

To start with, there are perhaps as many differences between the nations who inhabit our planet which separate them from one another as the similarities which bring them closer— just compare China, Angola, Brazil, Australia, France, Russia, Bangladesh, Saudi Arabia, Serbia, Canada, to name but a few.

As we saw earlier in the book, the concept of HRM itself, like all social constructs, takes its character and quality, if not its very existence, from the socio-cultural and political economic context which gave birth to it. Some of the employee management functions which were 'borrowed' from personnel management and were subsequently incorporated in HRM, such as performance appraisal, pay and benefits, are also influenced by the characteristics of the broader context in which companies operate. The successful internationalisation of HRM, in its pure form, therefore presupposes similarities of contextual factors between nations. This presupposition, we know, is neither plausible nor necessarily desirable. The HR managers of designer fabrics and textile workshops in Sri Lanka cannot even begin to imagine to have or hope to have in their country the same cultural characteristics and market related conditions as the United States, the birthplace of HRM, or any other country which has pioneered innovative employee management practices, for example Japanese company-based trade unionism.

In addition to the above broad contextual factors, there are internal organisational factors and concerns which influence the character and quality of HRM in a company, factors and concerns that in many cases are unique to an organisation.

Let us explore these propositions further.

## Contextual factors

Major contextual factors which have significant bearing on the character of HRM and its internationalisation could be grouped into three categories: national cultural factors, political economic factors and business imperatives factors.

| | |
|---|---|
| National cultural factors | work-related values and attitudes: individualism and collectivism, attitude to power and authority, tolerance for ambiguity and attitude to risk, interpersonal trust, preference for certain leadership behaviours, etc. |
| Political economic factors | domestic and foreign economic and trade policies, the role of the state, industrial relations and employment laws, pressure groups, state of the economy, membership of global and regional organisations, etc. |
| Business imperatives factors | market conditions: competition, interest rates, customers, clients, etc. |

Examples and case studies throughout the book in general and specific discussions of a sample of major economies in Chapter 4 demonstrated that (a) there are a great many differences among various nations with respect to the above factors, and (b) all these factors directly and indirectly influence significantly the ways in which companies manage their business affairs in general and their employees in particular. Chapter 7 examined the extent to which cross-national transfer of HRM strategies, policies and practices can also be affected by these contextual factors. Chapter 8 showed how misunderstanding and tension are generated in international joint ventures where employees from different cultural backgrounds work together. They bring with them different world views, assumptions, preferences and value systems. These may in turn result in conflicting preferences for management styles and HRM policies and practices.

Given the differences that exist between nations, one could envisage at least two possibilities in any given country: (1) a combination of these sets of factors are incompatible with unmodified imported HRM models, policies and practices; (2) some of the factors are incompatible but others are not. A good example of the latter is where cultural values and attitudes do not support the assumptions and value systems that underpin HRM, but business imperatives might require the implementation of proven best HRM practices so as to enable companies to compete successfully in domestic and international markets.

However, one cannot categorically suggest that contextual differences and internal issues will forever prevent HRM principles from being successfully applied by many companies in many countries. The experience throughout the history of human existence shows that we can all learn from each other and emulate those practices which we consider to be beneficial to us and serve our interests, regardless of their provenance. But the experience also shows that in many cases we may have to modify those practices to suit our own particular societies and needs.

In addition, it is important to note that the three sets of factors mentioned above are not written in tablets of stone, so to speak. They all change over time, some might change more slowly that others, but they all change nonetheless. As was mentioned in one of the previous chapters, who could have imagined that one day the Soviet Union 'empire' would fall and all its constituent republics and its puppet regimes in central and eastern Europe would reject the communist political economic model? Before the collapse of the system, HRM and many other management techniques and skills such as marketing were either unheard of in those countries or were not of much use. This was so because the quality and quantity of products and services depended not on market conditions but on the requirements set out by central planners; promotion and pay depended not on how well employees performed their jobs, but on how well they followed the communist party line. All that has changed now. Since the 1989 revolutions, many companies in the former communist countries in Europe and the ex-Soviet Union republics have been steadily familiarising themselves with the techniques and skills, including HRM, needed to function in a market-based economy. (Kubes and Benkovic, 1994; Koubek and Brewster, 1995; Mako, 1997; Suutari and Riusala, 1998; Illes, 2000).

## Internal organisational factors

Business organisations, like nations, have their own way of doing things, their own distinctive character, which evolves over time. Many factors along the way help to shape this distinctive character: founding fathers' philosophy and preferences, problems faced and workable solutions found for them, educational background and skill profile of the workforce, the so-called contingency factors: size, technology, product (or service), industry, ownership (public or private), age (recently-established or an old company), and so forth.

Same as with the contextual factors, internal organisational factors are not fixed forever. They too change over time: a new managing director comes in and brings a whole new set of priorities and preferences to the company; employees get trained in some new skills and practices and realise that not only has this upgraded their skill and knowledge, but also increased their chances of promotion to better paid jobs within the company or elsewhere; the R&D department comes up with a brand new innovative idea and/or product which soon propels the company from an obscure local employer to a world-class cutting edge path finder. All this may make some HRM policies and practices, previously considered

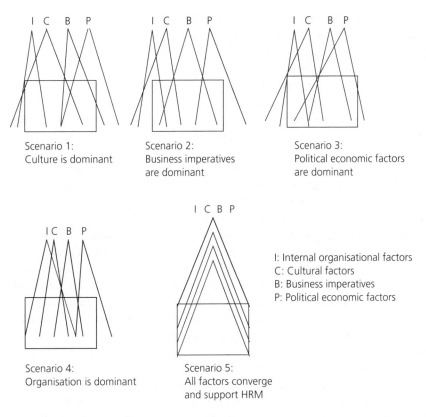

**Figure 10.1** A dynamic model of internationalisation of HRM

reasonable, redundant. Innovative 'best practices' with proven track records elsewhere might become more attractive now.

The foregoing discussion shows that the situation is dynamic and changes in both contextual and internal organisational factors and can at times provide favourable conditions for adoption of HRM and other best practices in any given country at any given time. Figure 10.1 above illustrates this argument and presents a dynamic model of internationalisation of HRM.

The first four exhibits in the figure show the dominance of one set of major factors which may help or hinder universal adoption of HRM as a best practice. The fifth exhibit is perhaps an unattainable state, where there are no impediments to the internationalisation of HRM and its successful transfer across borders without any modification or adaptation.

# International HRM—MNCs' perspective

As was discussed in previous chapters, an MNC's HRM policies and practices are influenced not only by the parent company's preferred strategies and philosophies but also the subsidiaries' own preferences. The headquarters of course has a great deal of power in this respect and exerts control over the subsidiaries. But the relationship between the HQ and subsidiaries is complex and dynamic and the subsidiaries have varying degrees of autonomy in how they carry out their functions. Also, in certain circumstances subsidiaries are able to influence the HQ's policies and practices and their fellow subsidiaries within the company.

Chapter 5 noted that in deciding how much or how little freedom to give to the subsidiaries, the parent companies can generally consider and choose from several strategic options, the most significant of which are: 'ethnocentric strategy', 'polycentric strategy', and 'global strategy'. It was also argued that the HQs can adopt a 'hybrid strategy', that is depending on the subsidiary concerned, or even a particular set of HRM practices and issues involved, they might change their strategies. In other words, in the same MNC, there might exist a polycentric strategy with regard to some subsidiaries, an ethnocentric one with regards to some others and so forth.

From the subsidiaries' perspective, there are certain factors which could in many cases make it difficult, if not impossible, for them to implement the HQ-generated HRM strategies, policies and practices without modification and adaptation. These factors are 'host-country culture', in terms of attitudes and values, 'host-country institutions', 'market conditions', and 'dependence on local resources'. In addition, there are subsidiaries which because of their proven track records, have earned an 'autonomy mandate' from the HQ to run their own affairs more or less autonomously. Also, some are able to generate new and innovative practices that can be exported to the HQ and other subsidiaries, the so-called 'reverse diffusion'.

Many of these factors are in essence the mirror image of what was outlined in the previous section under contextual and internal organisational factors. And all or some of them would give a certain amount of authority and clout to the subsidiaries which they can use to justify modification or even rejection of HQ-driven HRM strategies and policies as they see fit.

We saw in Chapter 6 that MNCs need to respond to differences in their individual subsidiaries' contexts and circumstances by differentiating their policies and practices when and where appropriate. At the same time they need to maintain the cohesion and integration of their strategies and operations, through various mechanisms such as expatriation, inpatriation and training (see also Chapter 9).

The above discussion highlights the fact that multinational companies more often than not function under opposing pressures. The sources of these pressures can be grouped into three categories: the socio-cultural and political economic characteristics of the location in which subsidiaries are situated, the subsidiaries' preferences, and the parent company's HRM strategies. It is important to note that the amount of influence that each of these can exert on a company's HRM changes over time and space. In other words, the relationship between the parent company and its subsidiaries is fluid and dynamic. Figure 10.2 illustrates this dynamic model.

As the hypothetical scenarios in the figure show, the quality and character of HRM policies and practices in each of the subsidiaries depend on which of the parties involved prevails at any point in time. If for instance a subsidiary is newly established and does not have a sufficient number of skilled employees and experienced local managers, the parent company can exert power and control as to how it should be run.

Conversely, if the subsidiary is long-established and has been able to show that it is in a better position to handle its affairs and respond to the local conditions, it will have more power and control over how it is run.

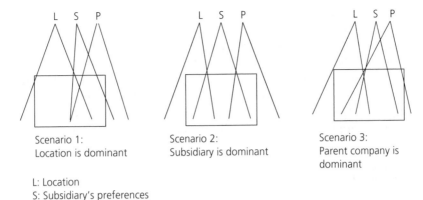

Scenario 1:
Location is dominant

Scenario 2:
Subsidiary is dominant

Scenario 3:
Parent company is
dominant

L: Location
S: Subsidiary's preferences
P: Parent company's HRM strategies

**Figure 10.2** A dynamic model of HRM in multinational companies

*Source*: Tayeb (1998), reproduced with permission.

In some cases the host countries may culturally, politically and in terms of economic conditions be very similar to the parent company's home, in which case there will be a degree of convergence between HQ and subsidiaries' HRM policies and practices. In other cases the host countries may be widely different on all those aspects from the country in which the parent company operates. The HQ might find it more practicable and in the long-run more beneficial if the subsidiaries are allowed to set out their own HRM policies and practices. Developing countries are a case in point here.

The vast majority of multinational companies originate in advanced industrial countries. The HQ-generated HRM strategies, policies and practices are therefore more likely to be more appropriate for developed countries than those which are still in the process of economic development and industrialisation. Many managers and employees may have lower levels of education and skill in these countries compared to their counterparts in the home country. In some developing countries, such as Iran, Pakistan, Malaysia, and Saudi Arabia, religion plays a significant role in people's private and public lives, albeit in varying degrees of intensity. In these countries strict Islamic laws are in operation, many of which directly affect HRM and other employee-management policies and practices (Endot, 1995; Tayeb, 1997; Khaliji, 2001; Tayeb, 2001).

What the model in Figure 10.2 shows is that MNCs may not always be able to devise and implement company-wide global HRM strategies and policies. Because the subsidiaries' individual circumstances and the specific locations in which they operate will make such a universal approach unworkable. Notions such as 'modifications', 'adaptations' and 'local variations' rather than 'global', 'international' and 'universal' more accurately characterise HRM in multinational companies.

## HRM as practised in a global company

The extensive case study which concludes this chapter, like all other case studies in this book, is based on interviews with practising managers in charge of and concerned with HRM and other employee management issues in their company. Using direct quotes and indirect citations, the case study intends to illustrate strategic and operative HR issues that are faced and dealt with in a multinational company with subsidiaries around the world. The case takes us back over the main issues covered in the previous chapters but also specifically examines the present chapter's main topic, i.e. HRM in the global village. It demonstrates how local issues and concerns are taken into account when subsidiaries try to implement the HQ-driven policies and strategies, how integration accompanies differentiation, and how opposing pressures from business imperatives and local cultures are reconciled.

### ■ REVISION QUESTIONS

**1.** How meaningful is it to talk about global HRM strategic, policies and practices?

**2.** What major challenges does globalisation pose to MNCs?

**3.** How is the tension between forces of globalisation and localisation normally played out and resolved in practice?

## Case study: Organon Laboratories Ltd, Scotland

Organon is one of the five units of the pharmaceutical business division of Akzo Nobel, a Dutch multinational company located in Arnhem. Organon's headquarters are in Oss, and it has 55 subsidiaries around the world, including two in the United Kingdom: Motherwell [New House] in Scotland (research, development and processing) and Cambridge in England (administration, marketing and the like). Akzo Nobel employs 70,000 worldwide and Organon 10,000. The subsidiary in Motherwell has just over 290 employees.

The Scottish subsidiary was set up in 1948 and its main products are human prescription pharmaceuticals (mainly endocrinology and gynaecology) and its market is prescription drug outlets. It is among the top four suppliers of oral contraceptives, and the second largest in infertility products. Its major competitors are GlaxoSmithKline (including Beecham) and Astra Zeneca.

## Global HR strategy

The mission statement for the company is issued through Akzo Nobel. However, being the principal player in the pharmaceutical division, Organon likes to retain its independence. Therefore references to Akzo Nobel are muted, for example the way employees answer the telephone is 'Organon Laboratories'. This is the case from the Managing Director downwards. If you go to other sub-divisions their identity is more closely linked to Akzo. Scotland site's independence does not cause any problem because it follows Akzo's principles.

Each of the two UK subsidiaries has an HR manager but there is a single UK Managing Director who is responsible for both and is based in Cambridge.

# General approach to HR policies and practices

Scotland's personnel policies are very little influenced by HQ. The HR manager has inherited the policies and practices which have evolved since 1948. The personnel team over the years have been allowed to formulate hours of work, contracts of employment and payment policies that would satisfy the company for its UK operation. They have had guidance from compensation experts in Organon in Oss through telephone conversations and a few visits over the past 20 years. The experts have not however tried to influence contractual matters. The Motherwell site has sought guidance and cooperation on, for example, contractual agreements and restricted covenants in order to ensure they are not significantly out of line with HQ practices. They do not get reels of paper saying 'you will follow this procedure'. There has been a good rapport with the directors who have been principal custodians of company policy in the UK over the years, i.e. Process Director and Research Director in Motherwell (New House) and Managing Director in Cambridge. They were relatively in agreement on employment matters, the parent company would give authorisation for senior salaries (covers about 20 senior managers). They would discuss with the HQ, usually by telephone, and decide what changes need to be made. Thereafter, each director would be responsible for salaries in their division.

# Specific HR functions

## Selection and recruitment

The personnel department is basically a servant to the organisation. It coordinates the efforts to put forward quality candidates to line management. It is the prime responsibility of the line management to identify and select the candidates for interview. There are some restrictions regarding the numbers to be interviewed (for cost reasons) and where they can be brought in from. The world is their recruitment arena especially at the senior management level, but they always think twice about bringing in candidates from outside the UK. They have in the past brought in someone from Canada, US and recently had a phone interview with someone from Australia.

Recruitment tools are very similar to those used by the HQ. The labour markets may be different, in terms of the applicants' experience and skill, but the recruitment procedures are similar. In Holland, there is a large number of applicants for various posts because Akzo Nobel is a very well known Dutch company. In Motherwell, the subsidiary has a harder time to recruit candidates with the quality and in the numbers they require because of the location.

Potential candidates are identified through advertisements in quality science journals and also through head-hunting, primarily within the UK; the interviewees are normally university graduates or people already in industry.

Applicants' curriculum vitae go to the personnel and to departmental heads, who then indicate who they would like to interview, usually five or six people. The company have a strong interview process; they do not use psychometrics or assessment centres. Each short-listed applicant is required to make a 20-minute presentation, followed by a 5–10 minute discussion on a topic of their interest. Normally between 4–12 people attend the presentation and then question the individual candidates and assess the quality of their science, how they present themselves and answer the questions, etc. They would then meet with the relevant section head and different members of the department, after which they decide if they could make an offer.

In following the above recruitment and selection procedures, the subsidiary has a great deal of freedom and is seldom restricted.

In Oss the recruitment procedures consist of structured interview, reporting of the findings of the interview, presentation, evaluation of the presentation and so forth. The procedures are more rigid and structured in comparison with Scotland, because the HQ 'is a big organisation and they need to ensure things are in place'.

An expatriate compares the selection procedures between the HQ and Scotland:

'What we do in Oss is about the same as here, but it's more structured. They invite candidates over for interview. There would be two interviews and there would be a robust discussion of both sides— what the candidate has to offer and what the company has to offer (e.g. career development, promotion).

That is something that I noticed here which struck me quite a lot; people were invited for interview and that's it and then people were offered jobs. I really feel you can't make that judgement, I think that's not fair to the individual.'

With regard to contracts of employment, the site has different hours of work and salary conditions compared with the HQ. They have endeavoured over the years to match, point by point, the conditions in Holland. However there is a problem in that many of the terms and conditions of employment in Holland are influenced by unions. In the UK they are not tied down to collective labour agreements. They tend to try to retain independence and freedom of thought and action and respond to the prevailing local conditions.

## Training and development

All new recruits go through a one-day induction course. They meet with the personnel and are taken through a video on personnel procedures, such as flex-time, attendance, etc.

New House has never been a mirror image of the practices and procedures in Holland, although it is perhaps moving closer to that situation, especially with regard to the career development process that operates in the parent organisation.

The headquarters have a more structured approach to training, due to the available resources and also their attitude to training. New House has not done a lot of management training.

If New House wants to run a training course it uses an external provider, for example for team training. It sometimes runs team training courses utilising a manager from Oss who comes over. It has used the Organon 'Introduction' programme for scientists where individuals are sent to Holland in the first year to become familiar with the company and its overall strategy and direction.

The HQ provides assistance in identifying development requirements which it feels is necessary. Organon's research is under increasing pressure to deliver. It wants to make the research process much smarter and to shorten the time scales between interesting finds to products.

New House puts aside about £500 per person every year for training in the research department.

## Performance appraisal

A performance management system is now in place which has been driven by the HQ in Holland. It is a system designed to bring out the best in people, and is meant to be transparent in its intentions with regard to salaries and career development in order to move towards the goal of being a centre of excellence.

Individual employees are assessed on research output (e.g. collaborations, publications) and quantity output (e.g. how many compounds they test within a certain period of time). They are then measured on a five-point scale from outstanding (5) to poor performance (1). The section head carries out the appraisal and looks at the overall appraisal in conjunction with their own development plan. It is then forwarded to the department head to ensure consistency and then to the research director.

The site's managers have had to conduct a critical review of the appraisal system (e.g. documentation, review process). For many years the company has had an appraisal system of sorts. The site has (in an interviewee's opinion) paid lip service to it. It has been an inconvenience for some and not a lot of time has been spent on it. Within the performance management system 'we say the appraisal system should be on-going. The idea that people will have a grading and they will know their objectives and special targets should become ingrained.' The two Dutch members of the senior management team bring an HQ perspective into this.

New House has given appraisal training to appraisers and appraisees over a few weeks. The significant different step they are undertaking here, in comparison with the HQ, is the bonus opportunity for achievement of targets. This will be interesting for the HQ because New House has a bonus system, but it is only in development and is not so prominent in basic research. They are also interested in how the subsidiary will manage to grade people and whether they can change their long-standing system. A senior manager thinks the HQ may want to change their bonus system after the system in the Scottish site is up and running.

## Pay and benefits

The company directors have been the custodians of principal links to salary structures. Pay and benefits are determined by the previous year's pay bill.

There are eight pay grades, each of which has a generic job description which defines its responsibilities in terms of teamworking, research output and innovation. 'As you go up the grades the job to be done becomes more complicated.' Individuals are set job objectives against their job description and on top of that there are targets which form the basis of bonus payment. The grades were agreed with the directors in Oss a long time ago. Scottish managers do not have any problem with the system and believe that this is not incompatible with the pattern in the UK anyway.

## Promotion and career development

The main criteria that the HQ have for promotion are the employee's overall ability and potential and his or her demonstrable ability to do a job at a higher level. The Scottish site is aiming to follow this within 2–3 years. The HQ have not been worried about the delay in this subsidiary's implementation of the policy, mainly because they have been producing good science.

In comparison with Scotland, there are more promotion opportunities in the Dutch sites because there are more positions—you can grow into in research, development, patenting and registration. New House is small and there are not many opportunities in that respect. As a result to get promoted within the company people may have to move to the Netherlands which not many seem to be that keen on.

## Teamwork

Almost all people work in teams, over 90 per cent of employees in fact. It is not possible to work without being in teams. A Scottish site manager makes an interesting observation with regard to teamworking here and in Holland:

'Oss is a more established site, teams are better established there. Here we still have a lot to learn and implement in terms of attitude change and communications. These are the two key issues on this site, in my opinion.

In Oss, people see themselves as more of a part of a team. Here, people see themselves as individuals who are also part of a team. Maybe this is partly because we are growing very fast and we happen to have a group of people who for 50 per cent have come from university and have not had any experience of working in multi-disciplinary teams. They have to grab the idea that if there is a problem the team has a problem, not the individual in the team. In Oss teamworking is better established because they are in a different situation. The staff have been there for a while, whereas 50 per cent of the staff here were recruited in the last 2 years. I am not sure if this is a cultural difference.'

There are no team-based pay policies on either Scottish or Dutch sites. The company have individual-based reward and bonus. They are trying to encourage and set up a team-based appraisal system: 'If you don't interact with others, it will be noted.' They look at the output of the team and the leader's and individual team member's performance. The assumption is that often an individual's output is dependent on others so if they do not achieve their targets it may be partly due to not working with others. One of the managers thinks that 90 per cent of staff need to communicate with others to achieve their individual goals.

The factory manager once suggested cascading team briefings, which they established and continued for a while but it was used politically. One or two members monopolised the meetings and then fed back controversial stuff so the site scrapped it. Information on various issues is now given by directors to departmental heads who in turn pass it down.

## Industrial relations

In Holland most employees belong to work councils and national unions play less of a key role. The unions are consulted by the management from time to time when required.

In the UK employees tend to belong to national unions. The Scottish subsidiary had some problems with the unions when implementing the performance management system. The unions were strongly opposed to the way the system was communicated in the first instance. But they now recognise its merits. The union representatives on the site do not have as much power as in some other companies in the region.

Employees tend to voice their concerns by going to section heads. There are also grievance procedures which are quite old and are in every person's contract but are rarely used.

There is far less of a 'them-and-us' industrial culture in the Netherlands than here. Akzo is a big company in the Netherlands, it is well accepted that you belong to a union. 'People watch the company closely as it's on the stock exchange. It gives you a feeling of being very strong and you know you can rely on the union if there is a problem.'

## Expatriation

In general Organon do not like expatriation, it is too expensive. They send employees on foreign assignment only when they feel they need someone they can trust in a host site. They prefer to recruit local people when and where appropriate.

There are a small number of Dutch expatriates in New House two of whom are in senior management positions. In general many do not want to come here because of personal reasons, such as schooling for kids. Those who do come have young families and the main reason they come is career development and promotion; they also want to see Scotland. While here, the expatriates sometimes provide formal training for the local employees in addition to performing their managerial and technical tasks. Some expatriates come over as part of an exchange programme the purpose of which is to give the individual experience to work on another site and to pick up 'new' techniques. Expatriate assignments normally last three to five years.

Pre-departure preparation usually consists of one or more one-week visits to Scotland to look around. Once here on assignment there is a two-day training programme for expatriates and their spouses. In the programme all kinds of things are discussed—culture, people and practical matters such as housing and schools.

### Cultural clash

The expatriates initially experience culture clash—one Dutch interviewee said he felt 'horrible' and after one week he wanted to return to the Netherlands. However, as they get to know the local culture they settle down well. Here are some of the observations the Dutch interviewees made regarding the ways in which the host culture differs from their own, especially at work.

'There are huge differences. Where do I start? The first most important thing is the different style of management. Here in this country, and maybe the whole of Britain, you are very aware of the authority and you don't question them, at least you don't question them in public. So whenever you meet one-to-one with a person you can come to some sort of deal or consensus. Then in a later discussion where the authority or boss is present, you hear completely different things because people are not that open when the boss is present. I see this not only within this company but also outside. I have two children and they go to school and I see the same thing. You don't question the teachers, if the teachers are present they are right. Maybe you have one-to-one meetings with them but whenever you are in a group . . . and in my experience it's not a very efficient way of having meetings because people in meetings are not as open as we are in Holland. In Holland we have this style of being very direct, you have clashes all the time, but it doesn't matter because you know the next day it will be all right.'

He observes that people here are reluctant to change and suggests this, together with attitude to authority, is hindering teamworking, among the older employees at least:

'The young people like to work in teams, they see the benefits. It's the older ones who are less keen to work in teams. They do their work at the bench and then pass it to their boss. I think the performance management system will help people to work in teams because it is one of the system's objectives.'

He apologises for being so critical, he loves being here on the whole. 'In the Netherlands it can be rough too. Pace of life is different.'

Another expatriate draws the attention to other aspects of the local culture that he perceives as being different from his home country:

'The culture is clearly different. Coming from the Netherlands, you start calling people by their first name, even the directors, here it's more distant. . . . Another clear difference is that people are less direct which can be quite irritating for other people. [Back home] at least you say your own opinion immediately and you don't mind if other people disagree with you because later on you have the discussion and you arrive at an agreement. But here it takes more time to know what exactly people mean. So people can be positive when you come up with a proposal although perhaps they realise it's not realistic and it takes you a long time for you to realise that they like the idea and they appreciate your efforts but they do not support the proposal for other reasons.'

A Scottish manager with long experience of working with Dutch colleagues gives his perspective on the two cultures:

'Dutch culture is a consensus culture—lots of discussion and they are very direct so it's not uncommon to have a direct at the point of rudeness exchange of views, from the Anglo-Saxon's perspective. They will argue over it across the table. This contrasts with the UK where the natural thing is to go around it and not to address it directly. . . .
    . . . I think that the Dutch culture also focuses on detail, for example a detailed planning system where maybe we would tend to fly by the seat of our pants, they would tend to plan it. You can over plan something but I think it's useful to bring these things into focus.'

He feels that a lot of time is lost with the Dutch mulling over projects and weighing up the pros and cons. He believes that the Dutch national behaviours come from the nation's history of trading and business which make people pay attention to detail.

## Expatriate's dilemma

A Scottish senior manager has run various Organon subsidiaries in a number of countries in Asia. This is how he describes some of his experiences in some of those subsidiaries:

'If you are an expatriate manager out in the sticks somewhere, you have the HQ who want things done a certain way and just see things through western HQ eyes. And then you have the local people who are stuck in their own culture. Now you are in an unfortunate position if you are sensitive; you see both ends and then you have to struggle to please both ends. The local people certainly cannot understand why the HQ want this done in a certain way and vice versa; the other people think the locals are all idiots and go around in grass skirts.'

He believes sensitivity means willingness to look, listen and learn:

'Coming in and saying: "I am here to teach you everything" does not work. Coming in and saying: "So, how do you do things? Well, that's different. Why do you do things that way and let's compare it to how I do things." This approach works well. There's usually a very good reason for why they do the things they do, for example the weather is too hot or because relationships are like this.'

In China the factory installed a shower because a lot of employees did not have a shower at home, or if they did they were in tin boxes and they did not have hot water during the winter. So this was a huge perk and each employee would have their 10-minute shower slot. 'You had to make allowances for that, all of them had to be allowed to come away from their work for 10 minutes.'

In Pakistan and Bangladesh the company built prayer rooms in the factory. In Indonesia they allowed Muslims to go to the mosque and pray on Fridays, if they wanted to—some went to the mosque, others did not. A Dutch colleague at first wanted them to take unpaid time off to do this, but eventually he came round to accepting this cultural practice.

## An expatriate's experience in China

The same senior manager cited above ran an Organon factory in China for a few years until 1998. The site was a joint venture with Organon and another company and employed 100 employees, mostly manual workers. It was established to get into the Chinese market.

His observations on some cultural issues and the ways in which he handled them are instructive.

'China is very different. In some sense you try to make things as much like a standard Organon company as possible. That's really regimented by the buildings, equipment and the products you are making. That forces a pattern on you and in some ways enforces a company culture. By implication Organon imposes a pharmaceutical way of working. That factory makes contraceptives. Everyone has to behave in terms of international standards, in the cleaning rooms the work is different from how they normally work but like anyone else, they can be taught to do it differently. Within that relatively rigid framework you then adapt to local conditions which I think is the right thing to do.'

He noticed that the way supervisors treated the workers was very different out there. He had assumed that they would get on well but that was not the case:

'They had appallingly bad personal relationships once you got behind the curtain and saw what was going on. You got supervisors who screamed and shouted at young girls and if they did something wrong they would stick them in the corner, facing the wall as if they were at school. You would not believe it. This was only a few years ago.'

He changed the situation through training:

'You would have your sterile environment workers, you would make one of them supervisor, and then you would find one who shone out and make her the boss girl and trained her up. We got rid of the supervisors who put the workers in the corner.'

He highlights the effect of personal relationships and networks on workplace behaviour:

'The other big thing you have to take into account in China is that things don't always go on merit, China works on *guanxi* which is about relationships. Certainly in more senior positions you have to make sure the person is connected in the right way before you give them the job otherwise they will fail completely. Some people you see stuck, not getting anywhere and the reason is that they don't gel with the people. . . . Your working group is your tribe, if you like. If you are accepted into your tribe that is fine, you work well with everybody and everything works swimmingly for you. If you got someone from outside, it would be different. I used to be amazed at the attitude. Someone you or I would normally accept from the outside, they just don't want to know. Unless they have been introduced by someone else or vouched for in some way. The whole country works like that.'

He further observes that the management style in Asia is more paternalistic and as a manager in charge one is expected to look after the workers. 'You can shout and scream and kick them around more than you would be allowed to here but on the other hand when something happens to them, if their family is in trouble or they need an operation, you take care of that.' He even had to get one member of staff out of jail for accidentally knocking someone over—this was in Indonesia. He and colleagues had to network and pay a fee to get him out.

In China the company had to provide a lot more for staff and had to treat staff like a family, organising for example a big outing once a year, which the workers liked. It was a bonding experience.

■ **CASE STUDY QUESTIONS**

**1.** In what ways are HRM practices in Organon's subsidiary in Motherwell different from or similar to those of the HQ in Oss?

**2.** What are the reasons for these differences and similarities?

**3.** Holland and Britain are two European countries with a great deal of socio-political similarities. Why do the Dutch expatriates still experience culture clash in Scotland?

**4.** What does the Scottish manager's extensive experience in Asia tell us about the forces of globalisation and localisation as played out within Organon and its subsidiaries?

**5.** How did he deal with these opposing forces?

■ **RECOMMENDED FURTHER READING**

Brewster, C. (1999). 'Different paradigms in strategic HRM: questions raised by comparative research', in P. Wright, L. Dyer, J. Boudreau, and G. Milkovich (eds.), *Research in Personnel and HRM*. Greenwich, CT: JAI Press.

Delery, J. E. and Doty, J. E. (1996). 'Modes of theorizing in strategic human resource management: tests of universalistic, contingency, and configurational performance predictions', *Academy of Management Journal*, vol. 39, no. 4, pp. 802–35.

Dunning, J. (1993). *Multinational Enterprises and the Global Economy*. New York: Addison-Wesley.

Marchington, M. and Grugulis, I. (2000). '"Best Practice" human resource management: perfect opportunity or dangerous illusion?', *International Journal of Human Resource Management*, vol. 11, no. 6, pp. 1104–24.

## ▓ REFERENCES

Baird, L. and Meshoulam, I. (1988). 'Managing two fits of strategic human resource management', *Academy of Management Review*, vol. 13, pp. 116–28.

Bird, A. and Beechler, S. (1995). 'Links between business strategy and human resource management', *Journal of International Business Studies*, vol. 26, no. 1, pp. 23–24.

Brewster, C. (1995). 'Towards a "European" model of human resource management', *Journal of International Business Studies*, vol. 26, no. 1, pp. 1–21.

Delery, J. E. and Doty, J. E. (1996). 'Modes of theorizing in strategic human resource management: tests of universalistic, contingency, and configurational performance predictions', *Academy of Management Journal*, vol. 39, no. 4, pp. 802–35.

Dowling, P. J., Welch, D. E., and Schuler, R. S. (1999). *International Human Resource Management: Managing People in a Multinational Context*. Cincinnati, OH: South West. Third edition.

Endot, S. (1995). *The Islamisation Process in Malaysia*. Unpublished PhD thesis, University of Bradford.

Florkowski, G. and Nath, R. (1993). 'MNC responses to the legal environment of international human resource management', *International Journal of Human Resource Management*, vol. 4, no. 2, pp. 305–24.

Huselid, M. (1995). 'The impact of human resource management practices on turnover, productivity and corporate financial performance', *Academy of Management Journal*, vol. 38, pp. 635–672.

Ichniowski, C. and Shaw, K. (1999). 'The effects of human resource management systems on economic performance: an international comparison of US and Japanese plants', *Management Science*, vol. 45, no. 5, pp. 704–21.

Illes, K. (2000). 'Changing management style in central and eastern Europe: the case of Hungary', in M. H. Tayeb (ed.), *International Business: Theories, Policies and Practices*. London: Pearson Education. pp. 476–86.

Khaliji, S. E. (2001). 'Human resource management in Pakistan', in P. S. Budhwar and Y. Debrah (eds.), *HRM in Developing Countries*. London: Routledge. Chapter 7.

Koubek, J. and Brewster, C. (1995). 'HRM in turbulent times, HRM in the Czech Republic', *International Journal of Human Resource Management*, vol. 6, no. 2, pp. 223–47.

Kubes, M. and Benkovic, P. (1994). 'Realities, paradoxes and perspectives of HRM in Eastern Europe: the case of Czechoslovakia', in P. Kirkbride (ed.), *Human Resource Management in Europe: Perspectives for the 1990's*. London: Routledge. pp. 178–97.

Mako, C. (1997). *Transferring Managerial Competence and Organisation from Western to Eastern Europe. Glasgow/Hungary—Final Report*. Phare ACE programme proposal P95-2625-F.

Pfeffer, J. (1998). *The Human Equation: Building Profits by Putting People First*. Boston, MA: Harvard Business School Press.

Purcell, J. (1999). 'The Search for best practice and best fit in human resource management: chimera or cul-de-sac?', *Human Resource Management Journal*, vol. 9, no. 3, pp. 26–41.

Suutari, V. and Riusala, K. (1998). 'Managing business operations in central and eastern Europe: problems faced by western expatriate managers', proceedings of the Academy of Business and Administrative Sciences, International Conference on Emerging Economies, Budapest, July.

Tayeb, M. H. (1988). *Organizations and National Culture: A Comparative Analysis*. London: Sage Publications.

—— (1997). 'Islamic revival in Asia and human resource management', *Employee Relations*, vol. 19, no. 4, pp. 352–64.

Tayeb, M. H. (2000). *The Management of International Enterprises: A Socio-Political View*. Basingstoke: Macmillan.

—— (2001). 'Human resource management in Iran', in P. S. Budhwar and Y. Debrah (eds.), *HRM in Developing Countries*. London: Routledge. Chapter 8.

Wood, S. and Albanese, M. T. (1995). 'Can we speak of a high commitment management on the shop floor?', *The Journal of Management Studies*, vol. 32, no. 2, pp. 215–48.

Wood, S. and De Menzes, L. (1998). 'High commitment management in the UK: evidence from the workplace industrial relations survey, and employers' manpower and skills practices survey', *Human Relations*, vol. 51, no. 4, pp. 485–515.

# ■ INDEX